Learn C
in Two Weeks

with RUN/C
and CBREEZE

LEARN C IN TWO WEEKS

with RUN/C and CBREEZE

Robert J. Traister

PRENTICE-HALL, INC.

Englewood Cliffs, New Jersey 07632

Library of Congress Cataloging-in-Publication Data

Traister, Robert J.
    Learn C in two weeks with RUN/C and CBREEZE.

    Includes index.
      1. C (Computer program language) 2. RUN/C
(Computer program) 3. CBREEZE (Computer program)
4. Microcomputers—Programming. I. Title.
QA76.73.C15T696 1987   005.26   86-12173
ISBN 0-13-527078-2

Editorial/production supervision and
   interior design: Kathryn Gollin Marshak
Cover design: Whitman Studio, Inc.
Manufacturing buyer: Gordon Osbourne

© 1987 by Prentice-Hall, Inc.
A division of Simon & Schuster
Englewood Cliffs, New Jersey 07632

All rights reserved. No part of this book may be
reproduced, in any form or by any means,
without permission in writing from the publisher.

Printed in the United States of America

10 9 8 7 6 5 4 3 2 1

ISBN   0-13-527078-2   025

PRENTICE-HALL INTERNATIONAL (UK) LIMITED, *London*
PRENTICE-HALL OF AUSTRALIA PTY. LIMITED, *Sydney*
PRENTICE-HALL CANADA INC., *Toronto*
PRENTICE-HALL HISPANOAMERICANA, S.A., *Mexico*
PRENTICE-HALL OF INDIA PRIVATE LIMITED, *New Delhi*
PRENTICE-HALL OF JAPAN, INC., *Tokyo*
PRENTICE-HALL OF SOUTHEAST ASIA PTE. LTD., *Singapore*
EDITORA PRENTICE-HALL DO BRASIL, LTDA., *Rio de Janeiro*

To Shirley, Johanna, and Elizabeth

Contents

	PREFACE	*ix*
1	*C LANGUAGE AND MICROCOMPUTERS*	*1*
2	*PREPARING TO LEARN C*	*8*
3	*BEGINNING C LANGUAGE*	*20*
4	*INPUT OPERATIONS*	*30*
5	*MATH OPERATIONS*	*38*
6	*C LANGUAGE STATEMENTS*	*48*
7	*LOOPS*	*61*
8	*CHARACTER CONVERSION*	*76*
9	*C LANGUAGE ARRAYS*	*82*
10	*STRING FUNCTIONS*	*88*
11	*POINTERS AND MEMORY ACCESS*	*96*

viii   Contents

12   STRUCTS AND UNIONS   *119*

13   INPUT/OUTPUT   *123*

14   WRITING YOUR OWN FUNCTIONS   *132*

15   PROGRAMMING MISTAKES   *144*

16   THE RUN/C INTERPRETER   *159*

17   CBREEZE   *179*

18   LEARN C IN TWO WEEKS   *208*

A   BASIC-TO-C EQUIVALENCIES   *214*

**B   BASIC STATEMENTS AND FUNCTIONS SUPPORTED
      BY CBREEZE**   *218*

     INDEX   *221*

Preface

If you are a BASIC programmer who is familiar with the entire BASIC language, you can learn C language within a two-week period! This is a direct statement that contains no hidden "catches." However, some expansion of this statement is necessary. First, any BASIC programmer can learn to write a few simple programs in C during the first day of study. This was not true a few years ago, when C language learning texts and aids were almost nonexistent. Those that were available were not aimed at the BASIC programmer, so many in this category spent weeks learning to write a first program from accumulated knowledge. The knowledge was often the result of inputting printed programs from high-level texts, experimenting with them for many hours by making changes, and generally, a lot of hair-pulling. Today, C is easier to learn due to a fair number of texts aimed at BASIC programmers. However, the opening statement in this preface does not mean that you can learn a "smattering" of C language in two weeks. Rather, it states that *the BASIC programmer who is willing to put in a full two weeks of intense study time and armed with the proper learning aids can be as proficient in C as he/she is in BASIC!*

This book alone is not enough. It provides a thorough introductory tutorial designed to help BASIC programmers over the BASIC-to-C hump, but you must also have a means of executing C programs, a C language compiler or interpreter. A few years ago, you would have had to spend about $500 for a C compiler. Most BASIC programmers who have a C compiler or interpreter can learn C by studying the numerous texts on the subject, but this is by no means an easy task or one that can be accomplished in two months, much less two weeks.

The third element in this "from BASIC to C in two weeks" scenario is an "edge." This is provided by two new products to the C language marketplace, the

RUN/C interpreter and the CBREEZE BASIC-to-C tutorial translator. Purchasing both will cost less than $225 and you will acquire a C language learning and application environment that will serve you for years to come. It is no longer necessary to spend a great deal of money to be able to program in C *and* it is no longer mandatory that you study for a year or more to grasp this exciting language, which is now the most used of all in software application development firms.

This text is in part an introductory C tutorial. If you have never seen a C language program before, you will gain a basic understanding of this language from the contents of the following pages. All discussions use BASIC as a reference source. Many BASIC programs are presented and then followed by their C language counterparts. A few years ago, such a text would have been unique, but today, there are many on the market.

However, this text involves far more than a tutorial. It also describes in detail the RUN/C interpreter and CBREEZE. Both of these products were designed to allow BASIC programmers to make the switch from BASIC to C easily and in the shortest possible time. By combining information from the tutorial section of this book with the learning environment provided by RUN/C and CBREEZE, a study program is established that will allow the BASIC programmer to progress to a point where he/she can do anything in C that can presently be done in BASIC!

This will take many hours of intense study, but this study takes the form of memorization, not hours of trying to figure out how to begin to proceed. Your course from BASIC to C in two weeks will be time consuming, but it should not be fraught with frustration. C language is here to stay, and C language programmers are in demand all over the world. If you can program in C, you have the capability of doing more with your microcomputer than you ever dreamed possible. Your C programming ability will also open up a wealth of employment opportunities should you ever decide to enter the professional software world.

A few hundred dollars and two weeks' time is not an expensive price to pay for increasing your programming power manyfold. By purchasing this book, you have taken the first step on your journey from BASIC to C. The next steps are found within the pages that follow.

ACKNOWLEDGMENTS

I wish to thank Age of Reason Company and Lifeboat Associates for their assistance in compiling information for this book. Special thanks to Todd Katz of Age of Reason Company for granting an interview and providing background information.

Robert J. Traister

Learn C
in Two Weeks

with RUN/C
and CBREEZE

CHAPTER ONE

C Language and Microcomputers

It was only a few years ago that C language made its debut in the microcomputer field. At that time there was much skepticism as to whether this small, infinitely versatile language would ever gain popularity among the group called "average microcomputer users." The most usual environment for C during these earlier years was found in the professional software world, where developers were finding the transportability of C to be cost-effective in designing software that would run on many different types of microcomputers.

C has been dubbed a shorthand version of assembly language, and programmers who feel comfortable with the latter will probably have the least difficulty in making the transition to this new mode. But C is making new inroads; every year, more and more advanced microcomputer users are learning to program in C. For some, this new language has all but replaced what has become a microcomputer universal standard, BASIC.

The question is still asked: Will C ever gain popularity among average microcomputer users? In my opinion, the answer is: Quite possibly! Of course, the term "average user" is one that begs for heated argument. If a definition can be arrived at, it must change as rapidly as those average users themselves change. The average microcomputer users of today are far different from those of only a few years past.

However, by the standards of today, C is still relegated to being used by the "advanced" group. A great portion of this can be attributed to the fact that BASIC is currently the first language most microcomputer users are taught. BASIC is supported far more than any other language for microcomputers. This applies to documentation and training manuals more than to complementary software.

If you want to learn BASIC, you can be certain that there are more materials

2   C Language and Microcomputers   Chap. One

available for this purpose than you could utilize in a lifetime. Certainly, much of
the credit given BASIC is deserved. This language has made it possible for hundreds
of thousands of persons to use and program computers who otherwise might never
have made the effort. Through BASIC interpreters, source programs can quickly be
input, run, and debugged without the seemingly endless waiting required by most
compilers. Unlike the languages that preceded it, BASIC offers the most desired,
complex operations through aptly named statements and functions. It has been said
that BASIC is responsible for the microcomputer boom of this decade. Although
this may be an overstatement, it is not a preposterous suggestion.

One of the main criticisms of BASIC is its slow execution speed. This is really
a comment that applies more to BASIC interpreters. Interpreters are, by nature,
quite slow in comparison to compilers. The former must read a line of source code,
convert it to machine language, execute, and then go back for the next source code
line. On the other hand, compilers go through most of this process, except that the
entire body of source code is converted to a machine language program that is executable. The source code is needed only once (for compilation). Afterward, the machine
language product of this source code is linked and becomes an executable file.

Those who complain about the slow execution speed of a BASIC interpreter
can quickly correct this deficiency by switching to a BASIC compiler. Most compilers
use the same source code as an interpreter, but convert the source code files to
executable files. These programs will not execute as rapidly as those written in assembly
language, but for many applications, the speed offered by a BASIC compiler is very
adequate.

In my opinion, the major shortcoming of BASIC is the confusion that results
when large, complex programs are written. This is also known as *lack of structure*.
To a great extent, this relates directly to the large number of GOTOs and GOSUBs
that such programs inherently contain. This "bouncing around" to various parts of
the program quickly becomes confusing to people trying to decipher its operation,
and to the authoring programmer as well.

BASIC does not have to be this unstructured. Although it is not thought of
as a structured language (compared with those languages that do fall into this category), the way it is taught and used seems to omit what structure there is or could
be. For example, a fair percentage of GOTO statements found in many BASIC programs could be avoided entirely by making proper use of WHILE-WEND loops.
Although most instruction manuals devote whole chapters to FOR-NEXT loops,
almost nothing is said about WHILE-WEND loops, which are often better for many
applications.

Even when used by skilled programmers, BASIC simply becomes too unwieldy
for many complex programming problems. This is not to say that this language
cannot be used to write such programs—only that there are better languages for
such applications.

If we think of BASIC as our first-grade primer, C language might be thought
of as the next logical step toward becoming fluent in language communications. Unfortunately, a school primer prepares us to move on to other reading materials, whereas

C Language and Microcomputers   Chap. One   **3**

BASIC does not provide a great deal of obvious preparation for learning C. Some will argue that learning to program a computer using any language will better prepare one for learning other languages. Others will insist that BASIC teaches so many bad habits that the student who is first introduced to computers through C or another structured language will progress faster.

Such discussions are academic, as the great majority of microcomputer users who will eventually use C will already be quite comfortable with BASIC. Two or three years ago, this fact meant many long months or even years of frustrating study for the BASIC programmer who wanted to learn C. There were several reasons for this. First, there were very few texts available from which this audience could learn. The few texts that were available usually addressed the assembly language programmer. It must be remembered that C was originally written for the software professional, not for the microcomputer hobbyist.

Second, a few years ago there were only a few C compilers available which were designed to operate with microcomputers. Some of these were excellent, whereas others were very limited. The latter did not allow the student of C to compile many program examples that were provided in those early texts.

Today, the road to C language is less of an uphill trek. Some texts are now appearing which assume a readership composed mostly of BASIC language programmers. The purpose of these books is to teach C using BASIC as a reference source. Today, most popular compilers are not subsets of the original language, but supersets, containing all the original language had to offer plus special functions designed to address microcomputer needs and traits.

Two relatively new additions to the C marketplace may ultimately be responsible for finally making C truly accessible to all levels of microcomputer programmers. One of these is the *C interpreter*.

I have waited for years for C interpreters to appear, as I have always thought that such a software package would greatly decrease the transition time required for the BASIC programmer to become comfortable with C. From a tutorial standpoint, interpreters are preferable to compilers because they allow source programs to be run immediately upon completion. Any errors that crop up in an initial run can quickly be corrected and the program run again. This allows for quick experimentation to see what happens if a certain line of source code is input.

Many early C compilers took up to five minutes to compile a simple source program. Add another minute for linking, and you can see that a great deal of time elapsed after the completion of the original source program. If a programming error was made, it was necessary to make corrections to the source program and go through the compiling and linking stages all over again before a run could be attempted.

It is certain that students of a new language are going to make a large number of simple programming errors (i.e., syntax errors). It is also true that these students will gain much from constant experimentation with a new language just to see what happens when changes are made in a working program. Often, the programs that do not work initially, and which must be debugged many times over, provide more

4   C Language and Microcomputers   Chap. One

of a learning experience than do those that work correctly on the first try. With a compiler, experimentation is often subdued by the time element required to arrive at an executable program. Frustration sets in when you wait five minutes to finish a compiling process only to have the program crash for the twentieth time. Many C students who get stuck with less-than-ideal compilers simply shut down the computer in disgust, swearing never to attempt C programming again. Fortunately, many persevere and go on to feel quite comfortable with C, but much of this is due to having obtained a much better and faster compiler which cut previously long compile times to about a minute for programs of modest size.

Today, a C interpreter allows experimentation with C to be as fast and as efficient as the same experiments performed under a BASIC interpreter. This means that C programs can be input and run immediately. If an error crops up, simply change the offending line and run it again. Instead of a learning session that runs for several hours, you may now be able to effect the same debugging operations and arrive at a successful run in minutes!

True, a program run under an interpreter executes much more slowly than under a compiler, but learning a new language depends far more on flexibility than on execution speed. By decreasing the time it takes to *begin* executing a program after the source code is input, an interpreter is ideal for learning purposes. Certainly, a C compiler is essential once the language has been learned. The fast execution speed of C is completely negated by an interpreter, but during the learning process, many students will want to opt for a full-range interpreter.

Discussions in this book center around the RUN/C C interpreter from the Age of Reason Company, marketed by Lifeboat Associates in New York City. The latter company is quite famous for its marketing of the Lattice C compiler, arguably acknowledged as the best C compiler available for the MS-DOS type of microcomputer. RUN/C documentation and operation are aimed directly at the BASIC programmer who wishes to learn C language, although this excellent interpreter will also serve programmers with far more experience in C language by providing a quick programming environment to test their C applications before compiling the debugged versions.

The second addition to the microcomputer field that makes it far easier to learn C is a product called CBREEZE. CBREEZE is a BASIC-to-C *tutorial* translator, written and marketed by Robert J. Traister & Associates. I emphasize "tutorial" here to differentiate CBREEZE from several other BASIC-to-C translators. The standard BASIC-to-C translators are designed to accept BASIC source code and convert it to a special type of C source code which can then be compiled and run. The reason for this conversion is specifically to speed up BASIC programs. The source code that is output from these translators is filled with special functions that are contained in the translator's library files. Their source code is not accessible to the user. In short, whereas the output code from these translators can be compiled, it is quite foreign in appearance and offers next to nothing from a tutorial standpoint. This is not a criticism of such translators, since their singular purpose is to translate BASIC source code into a code that can be compiled under C. They are not intended for tutorial purposes.

C Language and Microcomputers   Chap. One   5

However, the CBREEZE translator is a different story altogether. It is designed for the singular purpose of translating BASIC source code into C source code that is accurate, easy to understand, and most important, follows the standard style and convention of the C programming language. In other words, the output C code from CBREEZE looks like the C source code that you find in C tutorial texts. This allows the BASIC programmer to study C language by seeing how his/her BASIC programs would appear if written in C. When used with a good text tutorial and a C interpreter or compiler, CBREEZE becomes an important key to fast comprehension of this new language. Even good text tutorials which are designed to teach BASIC programmers the fundamentals of C often fall short in the area of programming examples. Traditionally, BASIC program listings are shown and then followed by the same program equivalent written in C language. This is fine as long as the author chooses program examples that not only appeal to the reader but which he/she understands. However, an author cannot know ahead of time the special areas in which some readers will require more explanation. Therefore, adequate examples of BASIC and C equivalents in these areas may not be provided and the reader may have to struggle for many weeks or months to sort out the needed information by other means.

The CBREEZE translator allows the student of C to provide his/her own examples. A program that the student understands is input in BASIC for the purpose of seeing how it would be correctly written in C. In a few seconds, the C equivalent of this student-supplied example appears on the screen. With the RUN/C interpreter, CBREEZE, and any good C reference source, the BASIC programmer should be able to reach a good level of competence in C language within a two-week period of study. Compare this with many months for the same level of competence before these new products came on the market and you begin to get an idea of how much RUN/C and CBREEZE will mean to C language on microcomputers.

Today, there seems to be a concentrated effort to introduce C language to more and more microcomputer users. C has been called "the best language for microcomputers" by many. These same persons often disagree about the overall status of C in regard to minis and mainframes. Some prefer it, whereas others believe another language is the best overall.

From my point of view, I prefer C to all other present microcomputer languages. This applies to general, wide-range program applications. Certainly, other languages may be better for specific types of applications. I look back on my experiences in learning to program in C and tremble slightly at the recollections. I do not believe that I have ever experienced such frustrations before or since. The fact is that I now feel perfectly comfortable while programming in C. I prefer it a hundred times over to BASIC, a language I know quite well. While learning C, I used to write desired programs in BASIC and performed all debugging under this language. Once I had an operating program, I would translate it to C. Today I do almost all initial programming in C. If, for some reason, I need a BASIC language equivalency, I translate this C source program into BASIC. I find that the latter programs are usually more efficient due to the influence and especially the structure of C, which can be mimicked (somewhat) in BASIC.

To say that I hated C at the start might be an understatement. With my BASIC-only background, I simply could not understand or appreciate its various workings. Everything seemed to be terribly difficult at first. C seemed to offer so few of the conveniences I was accustomed to. However, after many months of becoming familiar with C, I found that I had not only learned a new language, but I understood better the functioning of my computer. Additionally, I gained a fuller understanding of BASIC and prepared myself to move on more easily to other structured languages. Knowing C has taken me above the realm of "appliance operator." This term is often applied to persons who use a computer in the same manner in which they use a kitchen stove or television receiver. Appliance operators simply turn on their computers and accept what is offered without finding out why the machine does this or that. These persons are not to be criticized, because this may be all that they need or desire from their machines. But if you want to probe the depths of your computer and understand why it does what it does, C language can help with these explorations, possibly better than all other present-day languages with the exception of assembler. It should be remembered that C is sometimes known as a shorthand version of assembly language, which is only a stone's throw away from machine language, the language your computer knows without any interpretation, compilation, or translation. In addition, C has the advantage of being portable. It can be run on many different types of microcomputers.

Today, learning C language is almost a joyous task compared to what it was a few years ago. Regardless of the language with which you are currently familiar, study materials and books are available that will give you a helping hand. The compilers are far better today and include a larger number of functions that address the needs of microcomputer operators. With the advent of C interpreters and the CBREEZE translator at reasonable prices, there is no reason why a person who wants to learn C should not be successful. This is not to suggest that it will be a simple transition. A lot of personal effort is still required and always will be, but the periods of frustration should be decreased and you should progress faster than you might have earlier.

No, C language is not for everybody. It is still sought after mostly by the more advanced microcomputer hobbyist and user. But even this may not be true a few years from now as more and more beginners are introduced to C. The capability of today's microcomputers just begs for more comprehensive applications. I feel that C source code will be used to program many of these. C language for microcomputers is here to stay for quite some time. Perhaps it will be replaced by an even better language, but for now, C will allow you to get the most from your microcomputer, both from the standpoint of useful programs and in knowing more about how your computer operates.

If you are more than a microcomputer hobbyist or a present hobbyist who wishes to train to enter into the world of professional programming, C is the language you will probably need to know. Check the want ads in any metropolitan newspaper under the category of computers, and you will see that many companies, large and small, are seeking C programmers with one or more years' experience. Although COBOL programmers are still in greatest demand, C ranks second in the general

C Language and Microcomputers   Chap. One   7

category of computer programmers. However, C ranks first in the needs of companies who are heavily into software applications development. Persons who know C are often in a better position to be considered for the higher-paying programmer positions. Knowing C is always an asset, regardless of the specific needs of any company. Today, the great majority of new software applications are written in C. Persons who know how to program in this language are thus in great demand.

Regardless of your future intentions, you are obviously interested in the possibility of learning C or you would not be reading these words. Hopefully, this book will aid you in this quest. Forthcoming chapters discuss the RUN/C C interpreter and the CBREEZE BASIC-to-C translator. Others provide a basic tutorial in C language aimed directly at the BASIC programmer. It is my feeling that the accomplished BASIC programmer, equipped with the CBREEZE translator, the RUN/C interpreter, and the tutorial information in this and other books, can learn to be proficient in C language within 14 days. If you just want to get your feet wet, the tutorial information in this text will be adequate, but to really program in C, you will need to have the capability of running your programs. This is where the interpreter comes in. It is quite inexpensive and very, very effective as a teaching environment. To become accomplished at C, you will need to reference many books on the subject to give your programming direction. However, the CBREEZE translator can take the place of many of these, almost allowing you to write your own tutorial through supplying it with BASIC program examples to be translated into their C language counterparts. The scope of capability of CBREEZE gives the BASIC programmer a more valuable reference source for C programs than any text tutorial can possibly deliver.

Fortunately, the combination of the RUN/C interpreter and the CBREEZE translator will cost far less than most C compilers. Even after you have learned C, both of these C programming tools will be used again and again to check out new programming ideas and to provide a constant source of reference.

Learning C language does not have to be one-tenth the drudgery it was a few years ago. Modern learning tools and thorough instructional texts will allow you to accomplish in two weeks what took many of us months or even years to attain. When you have finished your initial education in C language, you will be ready to strike out on your own and be able to accomplish what you desire in a programming environment that boasts an excellent future.

CHAPTER TWO

Preparing to Learn C

Before jumping into the C arena, it is best to establish a few rules that must be followed and which do not apply as strictly in BASIC as they do in C. Most problems encountered by beginning C students arise from the "looseness" that is allowed in BASIC. This is not true of most other languages.

KNOW YOUR VARIABLE TYPES

If there is one rule that must be adhered to at all times in C, it is: *Know the types of variables and constants with which you are working and when they are required.* BASIC programmers generally tend to think of variable types in two categories: numeric and string. Thus we too often see programs such as

```
10   FOR X=1 TO 20
20   PRINT X
30   NEXT X
```

The result of this program is to display the values 1 to 20 on the display screen. However, variable X is a single-precision floating-point type. Therefore, when X is assigned a value of 1, which is an integer, the computer stores it in X as 1.000000. On each pass of the loop, the computer must check to see if there is any fractional portion, since it is reading a floating-point number and *not* an integer. This takes extra processing time. In BASIC, a floating-point value that contains no decimal portion is displayed as an integer. Thus PRINT X will display the value 1 (integer)

Know Your Variable Types   9

when, in truth, X is equal to 1.000000. Since the foregoing program is to display
integer values, the correct and most efficient method of writing the same routine is

```
10  FOR X%=1 TO 20
20  PRINT X%
30  NEXT X%
```

Now when X% is assigned a value of 1, it will be stored in memory as integer 1.
This program displays the same output as the first program, but it executes far more
rapidly because of the use of the integer variable X% rather than floating-point
variable X. In C, the first program would have displayed

```
1.000000
2.000000
3.000000
4.000000
etc.
```

assuming a FOR loop that uses a FLOAT variable rather than an integer type.

In C, integer variables are used to represent integer values just as they are or
should be in BASIC. However, BASIC allows programmers to get away with murder
in that floating-point values can be used with statements and functions that should
receive integer values, such as

```
10  DIM A$(100)
20  X=1;
30  A$(X)="COMPUTER"
40  PRINT A$(X)
```

Obviously, the array element positions are numbered as integers, as in

```
A$(1)  A$(2)  A$(3)  A$(4)  . . .
```

There is no A$(1.000000) position, but that is the position argument supplied in
lines 30 and 40 in the program above. BASIC automatically converts array position
arguments which are in floating-point format to equivalent integers. Again, this requires more processing time and slows execution speed. *Warning: C language does
not do this. For C language arrays, an integer position argument is always required,
and to provide another type is an error.*

Now, suppose that there is a need to use variable X in the foregoing program
as a floating-point variable, presumably in some routine that will follow the code
shown. In other words, it is desirable that X be used to name an array position
and also to represent a floating-point value in another program portion. No problem.
BASIC offers the tools to arrive at a proper program, as in

10   Preparing to Learn C   Chap. Two

```
10  DIM A$(100)
20  X=1
30  A$(FIX(X))="COMPUTER"
40  PRINT A$(FIX(X))
```

In this example, the FIX function is used to convert the value in X to an integer *before* it is used as an array position argument. (*Note*: FIX is used here instead of INT because the former converts floats to integers by truncating or dropping the fractional portion of a number. This corresponds to the way floats are converted to integers in C.) This is the way it would be accomplished in C, but there is a problem. Although the preceding program is more technically correct than the example that preceded it, this new program is, unfortunately, not as efficient. It takes longer to execute than the first version (about 25 percent longer). The best method is demonstrated by the following BASIC program:

```
10  DIM A$(100)
20  X%=1
30  A$(X%)="COMPUTER"
40  PRINT A$(X%)
```

This program uses integer variable X% to name the array position, which results in an execution speed that is about 25 percent faster than the first example and 50 percent faster than the second. However, what about the possible need of using the value in X% as a floating-point number in a later routine? Simply use the CSNG function in BASIC to convert to a single-precision floating-point value when a float is needed, as in

```
Y = CSNG(X%)
```

An even simpler method is to use another variable for the floating-point operation and assign it the value of X%, as in

```
Y=X%
```

Here the variable Y is assigned an integer value, but since Y is a floating-point variable, the value of X% is represented in floating-point format. If this discussion is leading you to believe that numbers are handled in C in a completely different manner than in BASIC, you are incorrect. Numbers are handled in a very similar manner by both languages. This is true of most computer languages. It is only that BASIC provides built-in numbers conversion where necessary, whereas C does not.

In either BASIC or C, it is highly desirable to use integer variables wherever possible. Computers handle integer values far more efficiently than floating-point types. This relates directly to the speed at which a program is executed. Now, you might feel that speed is not that important in the applications you are writing at present, but eventually it will be. Get in the habit now of taking best advantage of your

Know Your Variable Types   **11**

computer's abilities by using integer variables to represent integer values. Never use a floating-point variable for any purpose other than to represent true floating-point values. Remember:

$$1 <> 1.000000$$

as far as your computer is concerned. It will *make* them equal in many BASIC applications, but this involves a conversion process. You will quickly learn that C is more particular about the various types of numbers handed to its statements and functions.

Here is another example of poor numbers usage in BASIC programming:

```
10  A$="COMPUTER"
20  X=1
30  Y=4
40  B$=MID$(A$,X,Y)
```

I hope the problem with this program is obvious by now. Why use floating-point variables to name the starting and ending character positions of A$ within the MID$ function? What line 40 actually looks like to the computer (initially) is

```
40  B$=MID$(A$,1.000000,4.000000)
```

There is no character position that cannot be described as an integer, so do not use floating-point values. This is a waste of power that can be put toward better program efficiency and a better understanding of how computers process numbers in any language.

When X and Y in the foregoing program are changed to X% and Y%, there is a 25 percent increase in speed. Such an increase has held rather constant when comparing it to other programs presented so far. However, these programs have been run under an interpreter. Most C language applications will be compiled, although the C interpreter is preferred for learning the language. A compiler will naturally increase the overall speed of a program compared to the use of an interpreter for the same language. *But* compilers bring about even more dramatic speed increases when comparing programs that use integer variables and those that use floats. For example, a simple loop that counts X% from 1 to 10000 will execute as much as *30 times* faster than the same program which uses floating-point variable X. This assumes that both programs are run under the same compiler. In other words, comparing the speed of two programs using an interpreter might result in only a 25 percent speed increase when floats are changed to integer variables, but the same two programs run under a BASIC compiler might indicate a 3000 percent difference in execution speed when comparing integer to floating-point operations. Such an increase is so significant that it must be taken advantage of, especially when working with compilers, which all C programmers will do eventually.

FLOATING-POINT VARIABLES

There are other situations where floating-point values are expected as opposed to integer values. Certain functions in both BASIC and C expect floating-point arguments and return floating-point values as a part of their operation.

BASIC functions such as LOG, EXP, SQR, and raise-to (^) convert integer arguments to double precision before processing begins. In these functions, the use of integer constants or variables will not speed up execution. Technically, it will slow up execution time due to the conversion that is necessary. However, it is far simpler to convert an integer value to a floating-point value than it is to do the reverse. Therefore, you will not realize any noticeable speed decrease when integers are supplied to functions that require floats when operating under most BASIC interpreters.

This is not so of C language. Using an integer argument with a function that requires a floating-point argument will usually lead to that function's returning erroneous values. LOG, SIN, SQR, TAN, and raise-to in BASIC correspond to *log*(), *sin*(), *sqrt*(), *tan*(), and *pow*() in C, and these functions expect to receive double-precision floating-point arguments. If you supply an integer variable or constant or a single-precision floating-point variable, the program will probably compile without an error message. However, your program will not run correctly, as bad values will be returned. The RUN/C interpreter used for testing many programs in this book does catch this error and halts execution with an appropriate prompt. This interpreter is excellent for beginning C programmers, but when the move is made to a compiler, do not expect such fine error-checking capabilities.

The point to be made is that C requires *you* to be aware of the types of arguments that each function expects *and* what types of returns are provided. C will not allow an avant-garde use of data types as does BASIC. Instead of thinking of data types as strings and numbers, you must realize that there are many different types of numbers. These can be broken down into two basic types, integers and *real* numbers, the latter also being known as floating-point numbers.

Of course, these two categories have their own subcategories. Floating-point, or real, numbers are often divided into two subcategories, single precision and double precision. Fortunately, BASIC directly supports both types. On most 16-bit machines, a single-precision real number is one that is not an integer and is written with seven or fewer digits or in exponential form using E. A double-precision real number is one that is not an integer and is written with eight or more digits or in exponential form using D. Rounding occurs at the sixth and fifteenth decimal places, respectively. In BASIC, single-precision variables are those represented as A, B, C, D, for example; double-precision variables would be represented as A#, B#, C#, D#. Integer variables would be A%, B%, C%, D%. Using the proper numeric variable type is usually unnecessary in most forms of BASIC (*Note*: Microsoft BASIC 3.0 was used as a model for this book) if all you are looking for is a program run that is free of error messages; however, this leads to misunderstanding on the part of the programmer. Such practices will lead to disaster when carried over to C and most other languages.

Floating-Point Variables
13

In C, there are two basic types of real numbers. Those which are of single precision are known as FLOAT types. Double-precision values are of type DOUBLE. C language integer subcategories are more numerous, but the two major types used in microcomputer programming are called INT and LONG. An INT is an integer value that is within the normal integer range of the computer. For most 16-bit machines, this will be the range −32768 to +32767. Whole numbers that lie outside either end of this range are called LONG or LONG INT. There are also other INT categories in C, including UNSIGNED, a data type that consists of *positive* integer values, usually in the range 0 to 65535. Another data type is SHORT or SHORT INT. SHORT data types are a holdover from the minicomputer. They are not used often in most microcomputer programming. Exactly what a SHORT is will depend on the type of compiler, interpreter, or computer you are using. In most instances, a SHORT is the same size as an INT. As a universal rule, a SHORT is never larger than an INT but may be the same size. This definition is a bit muddy because of the lack of a specific standard for such data types. Fortunately, it will not be necessary to use SHORTs in most implementations, as INTs will serve the same purpose.

The names LONG, SHORT, DOUBLE, FLOAT, INT, and UNSIGNED are *data types* in C. They are used to name variables. In C, if we want variables x, y, and z to be integer types, we do not follow each variable name with a percent (%) sign as we do in BASIC. In C, *all* variables that are to be used by the program must be declared at the *start* of the program. For example,

```
int a, b, c;
long d, e, f;
float h, i, j;
double k, l, m;
```

are *declarations* of variables. Here the variables a, b, and c are INT types and correspond to A%, B%, and C% in BASIC. The variables d, e, and f are LONG INT variables which may be used to represent any whole number within the computer's maximum range. FLOAT variables h, i, and j correspond to H, I, and J in BASIC. These are used to represent single-precision floating-point values, accurate to six decimal places. If more accuracy is needed, the variables k, l, and m would be used. These correspond to K#, L#, and M# in BASIC and are used to represent double-precision floating-point values.

Of special note to BASIC programmers is the fact that most types of C language variables are not set to zero when declared. In BASIC, all variables are set to zero or NULL until assigned some other value. The following BASIC program demonstrates this:

10 PRINT X

This single-line program is an instruction to print the value of variable X. Since this is the only line in the program and the variable has not been assigned any

14 Preparing to Learn C   Chap. Two

previous value, the result displayed will be zero (0). However, a C language variable that is declared but not assigned an initial value can be equal to almost anything. When programming in C, you must assign all variables before an attempt is made to use their values in a mathematical operation. If you want a variable to be equal to zero, this value must be assigned. If you do not do this, the variable will represent a random value. There are exceptions to this rule within certain storage classes.

It is traditional to use lowercase characters throughout C programs, except in special cases. Again, this is traditional, but uppercase characters may also be used to name variables. However, C makes a distinct differentiation between the variables *x* and *X*, for instance. These are two separate variables.

The same is true of C statements and functions. In BASIC, *PRINT* and *print* mean the same thing when entered as statements. In fact, most BASIC interpreters automatically convert all nonquoted program contents to uppercase. But in C, *PRINTF* and *printf* (equivalent to PRINT in BASIC) are two different functions. Lowercase *printf* is a standard C function, while *PRINTF* is not a part of the function set and is meaningless unless this is the name given to a special function that the user writes. However, some microcomputer implementations of the C programming language may act like BASIC in that they treat upper- and lowercase function names the same. This is especially true of MS-DOS implementations of C compilers, where the linker does not distinguish between upper- and lowercase library file names. This will not apply to variables. In any event, with very few exceptions, all C language functions, statements, data types, and so on, are expressed in lowercase, as are variables. Rarely will you see an uppercase character in most C programs.

CHARACTERS AND STRINGS

BASIC makes little obvious differentiation between single characters and strings. Both are usually represented as strings, as in

A$="H"

or

A$="HELLO"

Both of these assignments use string variables [identified by the trailing dollar sign ($)] and constants enclosed in double quotes ("). The CHR$ function returns the string equivalent of an ASCII character, as in

A$=CHR$(65)

This program line assigns A$ the character value of ASCII 65, which is the letter "A". Still, this letter is represented as a string quantity rather than as another data type.

Characters and Strings

15

What does the term "string" mean? This is derived from other computer languages, where individual characters and character strings are represented in a different manner. "String" means a string or series of characters all tied together as a single data unit. The term is an abbreviation for "character string." In many languages, the *character* is the main unit for the representation of standard and special text and numeric characters.

C follows this principle and uses CHAR to name a variable designed specifically to hold a character. But there is more to it than that. A CHAR variable is usually one that is capable of holding a single byte of data. An INT usually represents 2 bytes, whereas LONGs and FLOATs represent 4-byte quantities. DOUBLEs represent 8-byte quantities. This applies to most C implementations on 16-bit microcomputers.

A CHAR variable is one that may be equal to any integer value in the ASCII character set (range 0 to 255) or to the value of the character itself. On a bit basis, CHAR has a length of 8 bits. INT, SHORT, and UNSIGNED are 16 bits in length, while LONG and FLOAT contain 32 bits. Finally, DOUBLE variables represent 64-bit quantities. Again, the actual bit lengths of the various data types are machine-dependent, but the values given are standard for most C implementations on 16-bit microcomputers.

CHAR variables are defined in the following manner:

```
char c;
```

where *c* is to be assigned a character value in the range 0 to 255. We may assign *c* a value of "A" by one of the following two methods:

```
c = 'A';
c = 65;
```

Disregard the trailing semicolons for now. These appear at the end of every C function line and indicate the end of that particular statement. The main point here is that the character "A" may be assigned to a CHAR variable either as a constant or as its equivalent ASCII value (i.e., "A" = ASCII 65). Notice that in the first example the character itself is used and is surrounded by single quotes. In the second example, the ASCII value is used without any surrounding quotes.

However, in both cases *c* will be equal to ASCII 65. The line

```
c = 'A';
```

is exactly the same as writing

```
c = 65;
```

at least as far as computer storage is concerned.

One other important point lies in the fact that C converts all CHAR values to INT values before any processing takes place. This also means that INT variables may be used to hold CHAR values, as in

16   Preparing to Learn C   Chap. Two

```
int x;
x = 'A';
```

This is the same as assigning *x* a value of 65. Remember, an INT can hold any value a CHAR can and more. A CHAR variable is limited to ASCII 0 to 255 or integers 0 to 255. It cannot represent a number greater than 255 or a value of less than zero. If you want to display a single character on the screen in C, you might first assign that character to a CHAR variable or an INT variable. Often, INTs are used, because this may be more efficient. This is true because, as stated earlier, CHARs are converted to INTs before processing. This conversion takes time. Either a CHAR or an INT variable assigned a value from 0 to 255 or the character constants represented by these values can be displayed on the screen as the character or as the value itself.

All of this might lead you to wonder why there is a CHAR variable type at all. Why not just settle for INT if the two can be used interchangeably to represent characters? The reason lies in the fact that CHAR data types more often declare arrays that hold a number of characters. These characters often form *words* which are known as *character strings*. So, by a very roundabout method, I have returned to the original subject, which was the representation of string data.

We can roughly represent the way C stores character strings through a simple BASIC program and some imagination:

```
 10  REM ASSIGN ASCII VALUES TO INTEGER ARRAY
 20  DIM A%(5)
 30  A%(0)=72
 40  A%(1)=69
 50  A%(2)=76
 60  A%(3)=76
 70  A%(4)=79
 80  A%(5)=0
 90  REM ASSIGN ASCII CHARACTERS TO A$
100  X%=0
110  WHILE A%(X%)<>0
120  A$=A$+CHR$(A%(X%))
130  X%=X%+1
140  WEND
150  REM DISPLAY CHARACTER STRING
160  PRINT A$
```

This program assigns A$ a string value of "HELLO" and describes the mechanism your computer uses when it interprets the C language equivalent of the BASIC program line

A$="HELLO"

An array is established that is large enough to hold five characters *plus* a special terminating character represented by ASCII zero. The five integer values assigned

Characters and Strings

to the first five positions of integer array A% represent the ASCII codes for the characters H, E, L, L, and O. The last array position is filled by ASCII zero, which is a terminating character. It lets the computer know when the end of the character string has been reached. C has no other way of detecting the end of this string, and it is always necessary to include the terminator or null character when building a C language character string one character at a time. Fortunately, C also offers functions whereby an entire string of characters can be assigned to a CHAR array in one operation. Such functions automatically tack on the terminator.

Once the foregoing program has assigned the various values to the integer array, it assigns the entire string of characters to string variable A$. This is done using CHR$, but this is also where the comparison with C language breaks down. Technically, the assigned integer array is all that a string variable is in C. The variable that names the array is called a *pointer*, because it points to the start of the array (element 0). When an instruction is issued to print the contents of the array, the pointer tells the computer where to start reading memory. Each integer value is printed as the character it represents.

In this BASIC program example, A$ is used to hold the contents of the array. Each element of the array is read within the WHILE-WEND loop and CHR$ is used to convert the integer values into their character equivalents. This is similar to the way that CHAR arrays are read in C. Notice that the read continues to take place until WHILE detects the presence of the 0. This signals the end of the array and the string it holds. The read stops at the 0. In C, this zero character is a true character which is represented as \0. It is most often referred to as the NULL character. Without a NULL character at the end of the string, the computer will continue to read sequential bytes of memory. Most C functions that write character arrays automatically place the \0 at the end of the string, but in some operations, a character string may be built a character at a time by the programmer. It would be done in much the same manner as was demonstrated in the BASIC program example just discussed. When a character array is built a position at a time, it is mandatory that the last character in the array be the NULL character. This must be assigned to the last position by the programmer. Without it, the reading of that character array will not stop at the desired point but will continue until a NULL is found somewhere (at random) in memory.

The following C program portion is equivalent to the BASIC program just discussed:

```
char a[6];

a[0] = 'H';
a[1] = 'E';
a[2] = 'L';
a[3] = 'L';
a[4] = 'O';
a[5] = '\0';
```

18   Preparing to Learn C   Chap. Two

Variable *a*, which is declared a CHAR array, now contains the sequential elements that spell "HELLO". When an instruction is given to print *a*, this portion of memory is accessed and each character in the array is displayed on the screen until the \0 is reached.

This is doing it the hard way for demonstration purposes. The most practical way to assign the array contents is to use a standard C function such as *strcpy*, which stands for "string copy." The following program portion demonstrates this:

```
char a[6];

strcpy(a, "HELLO");
```

This function does exactly the same thing as the first C example. It actually calls the former routine that copies the character string into memory. However, it is important to know how C functions accomplish their purposes on a primitive level to gain the best understanding of C.

Maybe you noticed that the BASIC program example used an array that was DIMmed with a five-element argument, while the C examples used an array argument of 6. The two arguments name different quantities. In BASIC, the argument to an array dimension statement names the top *array position*, which in this example is 5. Assuming that the first element of this array is 0, there are six total elements (0 through 5). However, the array argument in C simply states the *total number* of elements that are to be set aside for the array. In both examples, we required six elements. We arrive at this by specifying the last element in the BASIC array as 5 and the total number of elements in the C array as 6. Both arrays are the same size. The only difference is in the way the dimensioning instructions are specified.

BASIC handles strings in much the same way as C, but this is hidden from the average programmer by the various BASIC statements and functions. BASIC does not allow access to each element of a string without the use of special functions such as MID$, LEFT$, RIGHT$, and so on. For instance, assume that A$ is equal to "HELLO". To access the second element in A$, it would be necessary to use MID$, as in

```
MID$(A$,2,1)
```

BASIC tends to treat string variables as whole quantities that cannot be broken down into more primitive elements, except through special functions such as MID$. However, C is not so restricted. If C CHAR array *a* is equal to H, E, L, L, O, \0, the second element is accessed by

```
a[1];
```

Remember, the first element in the array is *a*[0], so the second element is *a*[1], which in this example is equal to the letter 'E'. *a*[1] does not represent a string but a single character or the integer that is its ASCII code. Such access to the elements

Summary **19**

that make up a character string may at first glance appear strange to BASIC programmers. However, the utility provided by this easy access can go a long way toward reducing code size. Once you get used to the idea, I think you will find that string management in C is far more versatile and just plain easier than it is in BASIC.

SUMMARY

In this chapter we have merely touched on a few areas of C programming language to provide a semitechnical introduction to this environment. Fortunately, you will find that mathematical operations and variables in C closely match the same operations in BASIC. In this chapter we have spent some time discussing numeric variable types because many BASIC programmers take a relaxed approach to numbers management. This is due to the built-in conversions that BASIC offers. Hopefully, a better understanding of various numeric types in BASIC and their corresponding elements in C will aid in the transition from BASIC to C.

It is in the area of character manipulation and the variables used to access characters and strings that most BASIC programmers run into snags. In Chapter 8 we deal specifically with CHAR types and introduce you to the world of C language text handling.

Remember, C language requires that *all* variables be declared *before* they are used and at the beginning of the program. You must also remember that an unassigned variable (i.e., one that has been declared but to which no initial value has been assigned) is not necessarily equal to zero as it is in BASIC. It is important to know, at all times, the type of numeric variable required for a certain operation. Do not use integers where floats are required and do not use floats when integers are required or preferred. If you remember these simple rules, your journey from BASIC to C will be far more enjoyable.

CHAPTER THREE

Beginning C Language

This chapter serves as the introduction to practical C programming in this text. In Chapter 2 we discussed some of the rules and principles governing C, but these are only of academic benefit if not coupled with actual program examples. As is the case with BASIC, to put this language to practical use, it is not necessary to know *all* of the theoretical principles behind C. As you go further in this text, both theory and practical examples increase in complexity.

The easiest way for a BASIC programmer to begin to learn C is with a simple C program example such as

```
main()
{
        int x;

        x = 24;

        printf("%d\n", x);

}
```

This C program does the same thing as the following BASIC program:

```
10  X%=24
20  PRINT X%
```

Let's examine each element of the C program. First, *main*() is a function that is called at the beginning of every C program. It tells the computer that this is the

20

Beginning C Language   Chap. Three   **21**

point at which execution is to begin. All executable C programs contain the *main* ()
function.

The next line contains a brace (|). This is called the *opening brace* and indicates
the beginning of the program portion, which is grouped with the function that precedes
it [in this case *main* ()]. Note that a *closing brace* (|) is found at the bottom of this
program. This marks the end of the program portion that is executed under the
control of *main* ().

Below the opening brace is a *declaration line*. This tells the computer that
variable *x* is an *int* type or an integer variable just like X% in BASIC. Such a
variable can only represent integer values. In C, all variables must be declared as
to type. Unlike BASIC, C does not allow us to name new variables anywhere in a
program. Variable declarations must be declared at the beginning.

The next element in our sample C program might be called an *assignment
line*. This line assigns variable *x* the value 24. This is done in the same manner as
assignments in BASIC. Notice that the declaration line and the assignment line are
terminated by a semicolon (;). The semicolon is used to signal the end of most C
operations. In some ways, it is similar to the colon (:) in BASIC, which allows multiple
statements to be entered on one line. In C the semicolon is mandatory after all
functions. It effectively turns C functions into program statements that can then be
executed. Most of the elements we use in C programs are called *functions* and require
semicolons to turn them into statements, but there are some built-in statements that
do not need semicolons. These are discussed later.

The next line in our sample program uses the *printf* function to display the
value of the variable *x* on the monitor screen. It is the equivalent of the PRINT
statement in BASIC and is the primary function used for writing to the screen.
You probably do not realize just how complex the BASIC PRINT statement really
is. It does many, many things that are realized only upon close examination. The
same is true of C language's *printf*.

Let's examine the *printf* function in more detail:

```
printf("%d\n", x);
```

Note that it is terminated by a semicolon, which means that this is a function that
is used to make a program statement. Following *printf* is an open parenthesis. C
functions enclose their arguments in parentheses. Multiple arguments are separated
by commas. Therefore, this use of *printf* has two arguments. The first is

```
"%d\n"
```

while the second is simply

```
x
```

The first argument in this example is the *control string*. This is the argument
that tells *printf* what to expect in the way of arguments and the format in which

22   Beginning C Language   Chap. Three

these arguments are to be printed. The second argument in this example is the variable x.

```
printf("%d\n", x)
```

means "print the value of the variable x as an integer and follow this printing with a carriage return and line feed." The value of x will replace the %d in the control string. Here %d is a *conversion specification* and means that the value of x is expected to be an integer and will be displayed as such. The \n designation is called a *newline character*. This character is not actually written on the screen but causes a carriage return to take place. Without the newline character, the cursor would remain in the position just to the right of the printed value of x.

The C program line

```
printf("%d", x);
```

is equivalent to the BASIC line

```
10 PRINT X%;
```

In these examples, no carriage return and line feed are provided. BASIC automatically terminates the PRINT statement argument with a newline unless a semicolon follows. However, C requires that the newline be specified with the \n character designation. In the C example, the newline character has been omitted, so no carriage return/ line feed will be printed. In the BASIC example, a semicolon follows the last PRINT statement argument. This tells BASIC to omit the newline. Remember, the trailing semicolon in C converts a C function into a program statement. It has no relationship whatsoever to the trailing semicolon in the BASIC program line.

The newline (\n) is a bona fide character just like any character that might be typed at the keyboard. Technically, printing \n in C is the same as

```
10 PRINT CHR$(13)
```

in BASIC. Remember, the newline character is enclosed within quotation marks as a part of the control string when used with *printf*. It is to be treated like all other character constants.

The end result of our sample program will be the displaying of 24 on the monitor screen, this being the value of x. However, we have also learned that this program does something else to the screen that is not readily visible: namely, inserting a carriage return in response to the inclusion of the newline (\n) character. When the closing brace at the end of the program is detected, the program run terminates. This brace may be thought of as comparable to the END statement in BASIC.

Numeric Variables in C   **23**

Review

- The executable portions of C programs always begin with *main* ().
- Opening and closing braces encompass the statements that are to be executed under the control of *main* ().
- All variables must be declared as to type before they are assigned.
- *Printf* is a C function that writes information to the monitor.
- *\n* is the newline character, which performs a carriage return when printed.
- The trailing semicolon turns C functions into C program statements.

NUMERIC VARIABLES IN C

Integer variables are declared type *int* and are used to represent whole numbers ranging from −32768 to +32767 on most MS-DOS microcomputers. All variables that are to be used to represent integers in this range must be declared *int* at the opening of the C program. The C program line

```
int a, b, c;
```

states that variables *a*, *b*, and *c* may be used to represent integer values, as in

```
a = 10;

b = 15;

c = -12;
```

Another type of variable can be used to represent floating-point values, also called real numbers. This variable type is declared *float*. Such variables are used to represent single-precision floating-point values, as the following program portion demonstrates:

```
float x, y, z;


x = 14.3267;

y = -1.8894;

z = 0.887;
```

Float variables may also be assigned integer values, although these values will still be stored in floating-point form (i.e., 14 = 14.0000). (*Note*: All single-precision floating-

24   Beginning C Language   Chap. Three

point values are converted to double-precision form before being used in C programs.) *Floats* are single-precision real numbers with accuracy to six or seven decimal places on most MS-DOS machines.

Still another type of floating-point variable is called a *double* and represents a double-precision floating-point number. *Doubles* are real numbers with 15 to 16 decimal places of precision. The following program portion demonstrates the use of *double*:

```
double x, y, z;

x = 12.0034512897;

y = -0.001452989976443;

z = 438.89445;
```

It is important to know that *floats* are converted to *doubles* within a C program. This means that *floats* take longer to process because of this conversion. On the other hand, *doubles* offer higher precision and execute considerably faster. Therefore, *doubles* should be used to declare all floating-point variables where *execution speed* is important. Where *conservation of memory* is more important than execution speed, *floats* are preferred. *Doubles* usually offer the premium of faster execution and far better precision, so they are most often used in C programs when memory does not need to be drastically conserved. *Floats* are stored as 32-bit quantities, and *doubles* are stored in 64 bits.

Just as floating-point variables have more than one subcategory (i.e., *float* and *double*), the same is true of integer variables. In addition to *int*, there are *short* or *short int* and *long* or *long int*. On most microcomputers, *shorts* are no different from standard *ints*. The declaration has to do with the number of bytes of memory set aside for storing their values. This is machine-dependent but breaks down to 2 bytes for *ints* and *shorts*, 4 bytes for *floats* and *longs*, and 8 bytes for *doubles*.

The *long* declaration is used to name an integer variable whose value exceeds the range described. For example, +40,000 or −40,000 would be a *long* integer, since it is out of the normal range of standard *ints*. There is still another type of integer, an *unsigned* integer, which is always positive and can range from 0 to 65535. Fortunately, most C language programs deal with *int*, *long*, *float*, and *double* variables, with *int* and *double* being the types seen most often.

Review

- All C variables must be declared at the beginning of a program.
- There are two basic types of numeric variables, *ints* (integers) and *floats*.
- *Int* types may also be subclassed as *unsigned*, *short*, and *long*.
- *Float* types include *float* and *double* declarations.

Going Further 25

- Variables declared *double* execute faster than *float*s, but require more memory for storage.

GOING FURTHER

Now, let's use some of what has been learned to learn even more. The following program uses several numeric data types.

```
main()
{
        int a;
        float b;
        double c;
        long d;

        a = 1467;
        b = 22.8765;
        c = 0.0019765892;
        d = 1467982;

        printf("%d %f %lf %ld\n", a, b, c, d);

}
```

Again *printf* is used to display the values of all four variables, but notice the different conversion specifiers. The line

```
printf("%d %f %lf %ld\n", a, b, c, d);
```

is an instruction to print the values of *a*, *b*, *c*, and *d* side by side on the screen with one space separation. Notice that a space separates each conversion specification within the control string (in double quotes). Anything placed within the control string is printed as it appears, with the exception of control characters such as \n and conversion specifiers such as *%d* or *%f*. You will remember that the latter are replaced by the values of the variables they represent. In this example, the first specifier is *%d* and is replaced by the value of *a*, which is the first variable argument to *printf*. The next specifier is *%f*. This indicates a floating-point value which is represented by variable *b*. The next specifier is *%lf*, which stands for "long float" or *double*. Variable *c* was declared a *double*. Finally, *%ld* stands for "long int" and variable *d* was declared a *long*. This is a multiargument example of using *printf*. Notice that it is necessary to tell this function what types of arguments are to be printed. This is done using conversion specifiers such as *%d* for integers, *%f* for floats, *%ld* for longs, and *%lf* for doubles.

Let us modify the *printf* line to read

26   Beginning C Language   Chap. Three

```
printf("%d\n%f\n%lf\n%ld\n", a, b, c, d);
```

This seems quite confusing at first, but if you look closely, you will see that each conversion specifier is followed by the newline character (\n) instead of a space. How will this affect the screen write?

The answer is that instead of a horizontal printing format, the values will be displayed in a vertical format. Each time a value is displayed, it will be followed by a newline or carriage return. The next "written" character will be displayed on the line below the previous one. In BASIC this one line of C code would be equal to

```
10  PRINT A%
20  PRINT B
30  PRINT C
40  PRINT D#
```

(*Note*: There is no LONG data type in BASIC. It is represented here as single-precision floating-point variable C.) The C program line could be changed to

```
printf("%d %f\n%lf %ld\n", a, b, c, d);
```

Now the first two variable values will be displayed side by side while the next two will be side by side on the next line. This is equivalent to the following BASIC program:

```
10  PRINT A%;B
20  PRINT C;D#
```

Remember, the newline character is treated like any other printable character. In the C program, a space is inserted in the control string between each of the two sets of conversion specifiers. The space is contained as a part of the quoted control string, so it is printed on the screen as a space. This provides spacing between values displayed on the same line. *Any value that is contained within the control string that is not a conversion specifier is printed as it appears*. To demonstrate this, the following program segment uses *printf* to display a string constant:

```
printf("Computer\n");
```

Here there is a control string but no argument list. Since there is no conversion specification within the control string, no arguments are needed or expected. This line would print the string "Computer" on the screen and follow it with a newline character (carriage return). This line is exactly equivalent to the BASIC program line

```
10  PRINT "Computer"
```

Going Further   27

Now let's see how to print a quoted string followed by the value of a variable.
The first example is a BASIC program that does just this:

```
10  X%=22
20  PRINT"THE  VALUE  OF  X  IS";X%
```

This program will display

                        THE VALUE of X IS 22

The equivalent of this in C would be

```
main()
{

    int x;

    x = 22;

    printf ("THE VALUE OF X IS %d\n", x);

}
```

Here the quoted phrase is contained in the control string. In this same string is the
%d conversion specification and the *n* newline character that are necessary to emulate
the previous BASIC program exactly. Notice that a space precedes the conversion
specifier. This space is also printed, which provides the needed separation between
the last letter ("S") in the quoted phrase and the displayed value of *x*. This is not
necessary in BASIC, because all numeric quantities have a preceding and a trailing
space when displayed by the PRINT statement. This is not so in C. The monitor
display will exactly match the instructions provided in the control string. Therefore,
if a space separator is desired, it must be included in the control string.

This C program could be rewritten slightly to put the quantity of the variable
ahead of a quoted phrase, as in

```
main()
{

    int x;

    x = 22;

    printf("%d IS THE VALUE OF X\n", x);

}
```

This program will display

                        22 IS THE VALUE OF X

28   Beginning C Language   Chap. Three

We can also perform mathematical operations as a part of the argument to *printf* or any other C function that accepts numbers. The following is a good example:

```
main()
{

    printf("%d\n", 4 + 3);

}
```

This program will print the value of 7 on the monitor screen and is the equivalent of the BASIC program

10   PRINT 4+3

Most of the discussion to this point has involved numeric quantities. However, C is capable of handling character strings and single characters much more easily than BASIC is. The following program declares a character array and prints it on the monitor screen:

```
main()
{

    char a[80];
    strcpy(a, "hello");

    printf("%s\n", a);

}
```

Variable *a* is declared a *char* array with a maximum length of 80 characters, or 79 printable characters and a NULL terminating character (0) which signals the end of a string. The *strcpy* function is used to copy the string "hello" into the memory space reserved for *a*. In BASIC this would read, A$="hello".

The *printf* function is handed a *%s* conversion specifier, which tells it to expect a string of characters from the matching argument. Used as an argument, *a* points to the first character in the string, at array position *a*[0]. *Printf* continues to read sequential memory positions starting at *a*[0] until the NULL character is reached. The string is stored in *a* as

```
a[0] = 'h'
a[1] = 'e'
a[2] = 'l'
a[3] = 'l'
a[4] = 'o'
a[5] = '\0'
```

Summary   **29**

Naturally, arguments to *printf* may be mixed and matched, as in

```
main()
{

        char a[80];
        int x;
        double y;

        strcpy(a, "computer");

        x = 14;
        y = 32.16;

        printf("%s %d %lf\n", a, x, y);

}
```

This program will display

                        computer 14 32.16

SUMMARY

In this chapter we have dealt with the beginning stages of C program development.
Although the programs presented here were quite simple, they do provide a firm
basis on which to build more complex programs in C. The *printf* function was used
for each example, but many of the principles that apply to arguments to *printf* will
apply throughout C language in general. It should be obvious from each example
that it is mandatory to know what types of variables or constants are being used
for arguments. This will be a main theme throughout, as knowledge of data types
will be mandatory any time that you program in C.

We also introduced various aspects of C structure, including proper formatting
or presentation of C source code. You will have noticed that certain program lines
were indented and that spaces separate numeric operators such as "+" from values
or variables on either side. None of these formalities is necessary to arrive at a working
C program. As a matter of fact, C completely disregards spaces (more frequently
called *whitespace*) during the compiling or execution phase. The format conventions
in C are there to allow C source code to be more understandable. As you delve
further into C, you will find this formatting (which at present must seem to be a
real headache) to be invaluable in understanding the various blocks of a complete
C program.

Hopefully, you have also learned that C is not a completely foreign language.
Many similarities can be found between C and BASIC. You can use your current
knowledge of BASIC to learn the C programming language quickly and efficiently.

CHAPTER FOUR

Input Operations

In Chapter 3 we introduced beginning C programming and explained methods by which information could be written to the screen. This type of operation used the *standard output* or monitor to receive the results of the operation. In this chapter we discuss the *standard input*, better known as the *keyboard*, and how to retrieve information from this source.

The following BASIC program retrieves an integer from the keyboard and displays it on the screen:

```
10  INPUT X%
20  PRINT X%
```

The INPUT statement is used in the first line. When BASIC reads this statement, execution is halted temporarily until the <return> key is pressed. Any numeric value input before the <return> is assigned to integer variable X%. The PRINT statement then displays the value of X% on the monitor screen.

The C language equivalent of this BASIC program is

```c
main()
{
    int x;

    scanf("%d", &x);

    printf("%d\n", x);

}
```

30

Input Operations   Chap. Four   **31**

A new C function is found in this program and is the basic means of retrieving information from the keyboard. *Scanf* is the C function that is the closest equivalent to the BASIC INPUT statement. We can think of INPUT as being the opposite of PRINT in BASIC. The first statement retrieves information from the standard input; the second writes information to the standard output. The same comparison can be made of *scanf* and *printf* in C. One reads the standard input and the other writes to the standard output.

Scanf even requires the same types of arguments as *printf*. The control string is enclosed in double quotes and tells *scanf* what to expect in the way of input. The argument(s) to *scanf* is the variable to which keyboard input is to be assigned. However, all variables must be *pointers* when used with *scanf*. In Chapter 11 we discuss pointers in detail, but for now, think of a pointer as a special variable that points to a place in memory that your computer has set aside for storage. In the example above, *x* has been declared an integer variable. This means that a small area of memory has been set aside, specifically to store what might be assigned to *x*. In the *scanf* line, you will notice that *x* is preceded by an ampersand (&). This means that &*x* points to that special area of memory reserved for assignments to *x*. The &*x* designation gives the starting address of this area of memory, and *scanf* needs this address to write the information input at the keyboard. All arguments to scanf must be pointers.

Like INPUT, *scanf* causes execution to halt temporarily until a <return> is detected *or* the keyboard input no longer matches what its control string tells it to expect. For instance, you can type 14 and follow this by a carriage return. This is fine, and the value of 14 will be placed at the memory location pointed to by &*x*. But if you type 14.1, *scanf* will stop scanning as soon as the decimal point is received, because a decimal point is not part of an integer value. The value of 14 will still be read into the memory location reserved for variable *x*, but the decimal point and everything typed past this point are ignored. *Scanf* stops scanning the keyboard as soon as the input no longer matches what its control string tells it to expect (i.e., an integer).

Here is another way to use INPUT in BASIC:

```
10   INPUT A%,B#
20   PRINT A%;B#
```

This program retrieves two values from the keyboard, an integer and a double-precision floating-point number. In BASIC, the comma separator between the two variables used with INPUT means that the first value input at the keyboard must be separated from the second by a comma. When BASIC reads the comma typed at the keyboard, it suspends assignment to the first variable and begins collecting data for the second. After the data have been input and the <return> key pressed, execution continues to the next line, where the input values are displayed on the screen.

The C language version of the preceding program is

32 Input Operations Chap. Four

```
main()
{

        int a;
        double b;

        scanf("%d,%lf", &a, &b);

        printf("%d %lf\n", a, b);

}
```

Again, the *scanf* function is used to scan the keyboard for data. Notice that a comma is used to separate the first conversion specifier from the second. The comma is part of the control string and is the character that signifies the end of the scan for the value of the first character. When the comma is read, scanning begins for the next value. Finally, pressing <return> causes execution to continue at the next line.

There is a difference in *scanf* and INPUT, however, even though it may not be obvious at present. For one thing, *scanf* will stop scanning the keyboard whenever the input characters are not of the type expected.

To amplify on this, when the first key is hit, *scanf* begins "recording," so to speak. Each number you type will eventually be assigned to *a*. Now if you type "123.666," the value of 123 will be assigned to *a*. Since the conversion specifier signaled an integer, a whole number is expected. When *scanf* received the 1, it began recording and continued scanning through the input of 2 and 3. However, when it read the decimal point, it stopped scanning for this variable, because a decimal point is not a part of an integer. If the comma separator were not part of the control string, the next field or scan for the next character would take place immediately. But with the presence of the comma, no further characters are assigned to *a* and nothing is registered for *b* until *scanf* reads a comma from the keyboard. This is the signal to start recording for the next variable.

If the *scanf* line in the foregoing program read

```
        scanf("%d%lf", &a, &b);
```

then an input of

123.666

followed by <return> would result in *a* being equal to 123 and *b* being equal to .666000. It is not necessary to specify a separation character (such as a comma) between variable scan fields, although a space is often used. *Scanf* will read as long as legal input is coming in for the conversion specifier controlling the scan field, or until a separation character is read.

Now that we know how to retrieve numbers from the keyboard, how about

Input Operations   Chap. Four

strings or single alphabetic characters? The following BASIC program will set up this discussion:

```
10  INPUT A$
20  PRINT A$
```

This program reads a string input from the keyboard and displays it on the screen. The C language version might be written as

```
main()
{

    char a[80];

    scanf("%s", a);

    printf("%s\n", a);

}
```

Scanf is used in this program with a different conversion specification. As with *printf*, a *%s* conversion specifier in the *scanf* control string specifies a string of characters. The *scanf* function will read characters into the array until <return> is pressed. Any characters are legal, except for spaces. A space terminates the keyboard scan. In BASIC, commas are illegal as a part of string variables. This is not true in C, but *scanf* will always terminate a scan whenever it detects a space. This means that *scanf* can only be used to read a single word from the keyboard. It cannot assign "Down the road" as a single character string, because this phrase is composed of three words. Spaces separate each word, and *scanf* will stop scanning when it detects a space.

Notice that an ampersand (&) does not precede the *a* array variable. *Scanf* requires that all of its arguments be pointers, but *char* array names are pointers. The *a* designation is a pointer to the start of the character string. When variables that name or point to character strings are used as arguments to *scanf*, these are already pointers and it is an error to precede them with the ampersand.

A new BASIC program will initiate another discussion about input in C language programs:

```
10  INPUT A$,B$
20  PRINT A$;B$
```

This example uses INPUT to read two string values from the keyboard. Again, a comma is used to separate the two values. Unfortunately, there is no exact C language conversion of this program available using standard C functions. The closest would be

34   Input Operations   Chap. Four

```
main()
{
        char a[80], b[80];

        scanf("%s%s, a, b);

        printf("%s%s\n", a, b);

}
```

The only way to separate string values in *scanf* is with a space. This also applies if the first field is a string and the next is some other type of value. Once *scanf* begins scanning the keyboard for a string, it does not stop until a space is read. It then moves on to the next field. An exception to this would occur when a string specifier is the last field or the only field in *scanf*. Then the <return> key would also end the scan. Therefore, if you use *scanf* to retrieve a string value from the keyboard, you must remember to hit a space bar to signal the separation of fields.

This BASIC program inputs three different values from the keyboard:

```
10  INPUT A$,B%,C#
20  PRINT A$;B%;C#
```

The C language equivalent would be

```
main()
{

        int b;
        double c;
        char a[80];

        scanf("%s%d%lf", a, &b, &c);

        printf("%s %d %lf \n", a, b, c);

}
```

In this example, the conversion specifiers in *scanf* are not separated by break characters. Therefore, a space will signal the end of any field scan. Notice that the *char* array variable is not preceded by an ampersand, whereas the numeric variables are. After the last field has been scanned and a <return> is detected, the values of the three variables will be displayed by *printf*.

Notice the separation of the conversion specifications in the control field of the *printf* function line. This mimics the way BASIC displays the various data types. CBREEZE will translate BASIC PRINT statement lines in this manner, as it provides a literal interpretation of what it translates. In BASIC, string values are displayed without leading or trailing spaces, but numeric quantities are always preceded by a space and followed by a space. There are two spaces in the control string between

Input Operations   Chap. Four   **35**

%d and %lf. The first of these is the trailing space after the printing of the value of b. The second one is the leading space prior to printing the value of c.

You may have noticed a possible problem in using scanf to read string values from the keyboard. Suppose that you wish to read in a whole sentence and have it assigned to a single character array. You cannot do this using scanf, because it will stop scanning a particular field whenever a space is encountered.

Fortunately, there is a function designed especially to retrieve string values of any type from the keyboard. This function is called gets (pronounced "get-ess"), and it will continue to scan the keyboard until it reads a <return>. The return or newline character is not made a part of the string but is replaced by a NULL character (\0), indicating the string termination point. The following C program shows how gets may be used:

```
main()
{

    char a[80];

    gets(s);

    printf("%s\n", s);


}
```

In C, gets works just like INPUT in BASIC when its only argument is a string variable. This function will read any and every character typed at the keyboard, with the exception of the newline which is sent when the <return> key is hit. This action terminates the keyboard scan.

Therefore, scanf may be used whenever a single word is to be retrieved and gets is used to retrieve any type of string. You will find that gets is used far more often than scanf when string values are to be read at the keyboard. Scanf is used mainly for reading numeric values.

In C there are other input functions, each designed to fulfill a special need. All of these address the input of a single character from the keyboard. Most of these are implemented as macros. A macro is a special definition of a series of C statements or functions made prior to the executable partof a C program. It is similar to the DEF FN statement in BASIC and lets the programmer define special functions. During the compiling or executing process, the series of statements or functions that make up this definition are actually substituted in the program whenever the macro name is encountered. These macro definitions are often contained in a special "header file" which must be made a part of the program using the #include preprocessor directive. This is not necessary with RUN/C, but it is with most compilers. The macro definition is most often found in the header file named "stdio.h".

The first of these special input features to be discussed is getchar. This may be implemented as a macro or as a pure function, but either way, it retrieves a

36   Input Operations   Chap. Four

single character from the keyboard. Its name is an acronym for "get character." It
is used in the following way:

```
main()
{

    int x;

    x = getchar();

    printf("%c\n", x);

}
```

In this program, *getchar* is used to return a single character from the keyboard to
int variable *x*. Why is *x* declared an *int* when *getchar* returns a character? Remember
an earlier discussion which stated that C converts all *char* values to integers (their
ASCII equivalents). In most cases, it would be all right to declare *x* a *char* data
type instead of an *int*. However, *getchar* returns a value of −1 if for some reason
there is an error and it cannot read a value from the keyboard. You will remember
that *char* data types can represent only integer values corresponding to the ASCII
character set or decimal 0 to 255. A value of −1 does not fall within this range,
and all kinds of problems can develop if this type of assignment is attempted. Therefore,
x is declared an *int* type. Either way, the ASCII value of the character typed at
the keyboard is returned to *x*—or a value of −1 if there is an error.

In this example, the *printf* function uses a conversion specification of %*c*, which
means that the value in *x* is to be displayed as a character, not as a number. If
you type the letter 'A' in response to *getchar*, a value of 65 is returned to *x*. This
is the ASCII value of 'A'. This letter will also appear on the screen as you type it.
It will appear again when *printf* is executed.

Different C environments handle *getchar* is different ways. Most systems capture
the single character and ignore all the rest but halt execution until <return> is
pressed. Others (including RUN/C) continue execution as soon as a single key is
hit.

A similar function or macro is called *getch*. It, too, retrieves a single character,
but it does not echo the keyboard hit to the screen. Most implementations of *getch*
continue execution immediately after a keyboard strike. No <return> is required.
The following program is a copy of the preceding one, except that *getch* replaces
getchar:

```
main()
{

    int x;

    x = getch();
    printf("%c\n", x);

}
```

Summary   **37**

In this example, the letter typed at the keyboard will be seen only once on the screen, and only after it is written by *printf*. *Getch* does not echo the key strike to the screen as does *getchar*.

SUMMARY

The C language function set is quite rich in functions that perform input operations. Those discussed in this chapter receive information from the standard input (the keyboard) and write it into memory. However, there are other functions with similar names that perform similar operations. These, however, are able to accept data from any input device, such as a disk drive, a COM port, and so on. Fortunately, these functions work in the same manner as those discussed in this chapter. A later chapter is devoted to these other functions. Once you are familiar with the standard input functions, you are just a short study time away from mastering those that allow you to read information from many other devices as easily as it is read from the keyboard.

CHAPTER FIVE

Math Operations

Simple mathematical operations are often a beginning step in becoming comfortable with BASIC. There is no reason why this should not apply to C as well. Fortunately, C language math operations and program presentation are very similar to those found in BASIC. The main difference lies in the fact that the C programmer must know what types of numeric variables are required and what types of numeric values will be returned by the various operations.

As a starting example, observe the following BASIC program:

```
10  X%=20
20  Y%=X%-14
```

This program displays nothing on the monitor screen but makes simple assignments to integer variables. In line 20, Y% will be equal to 20 − 14, or 6. In C, this program would be written as

```
main()
{

    int x, y;

    x = 20;
    y = x - 14;

}
```

38

Math Operations   Chap. Five   **39**

First, x and y are declared *int*. This declaration automatically sets aside the required data space for each variable to represent an integer value. Next, x is assigned a value of 20. If you remove the trailing semicolon on this line, the assignment would look just like one made in BASIC. The same is true of the next line, which assigns y the value $x - 14$. The end result of this program is integer variable y being equal to 6.

We could just have easily used other mathematical operations, such as

```
y = x * 2;
y = x - 12;
y = x * x;
y = x / 4;
```

In each case, these simple mathematical operations make assignments just as they do in BASIC.

There are exceptions, however, especially when dealing with floating-point variables or constants or when the mathematical operation results in a value that does not fit the type of variable used to represent it. It is mandatory that a variable used to represent the result of a mathematical operation be of the data type that is the same as the mathematical return. For example,

```
y = 32000 * 2;
```

will cause problems if y is declared an *int*. Why? Because an *int* variable is used to represent values that range from -32768 to $+32767$. Although 32000 is an *int* value and 2 is an *int* value, 32000 * 2 is not. The result of this mathematical operation is 64000. This value would be an integer but would lie outside the range of a standard *int*. If y had been declared *unsigned* (range 0 to 65535) or *long*, there would be no problem. This illustrates that the result of common mathematical operations involving *standard* integers may not be a standard integer value.

Working with floating-point values is, outwardly, just as simple. The following C program illustrates a simple assignment routine using single-precision floating-point values and variables:

```
main()
{

    float x, y;

    x = 22.123;
    y = x * 2.5;

}
```

This is the equivalent of the following BASIC program:

```
10 X = 22.123
20 Y = X*2.5
```

40   Math Operations   Chap. Five

Both of these examples might be called do-nothing programs, since the results of their operations are known only to the computer—but bear with this train of discussion a bit longer. Soon we will put these operations to practical use.

How about the combination of floating-point numbers and integers? This can be done quite easily in BASIC and the same is true in C. Let's begin with a simple BASIC program:

```
10  Y=10.115
20  X%=Y
```

This program first assigns single-precision floating-point variable Y the value of 10.115. The next line assigns X% the value of Y—or does it? Actually, the second line assigns X% the integer equivalent of floating-point variable Y. This occurs because X% is an integer variable, capable of representing only integer values. When an integer variable is assigned a floating-point value, the fractional portion of the number is deleted.

In C, this program could be written as

```
main()
{

    int x;
    float y;

    y = 10.115;
    x = y;

}
```

The end result of both programs is a value of 10.115 for Y (*y*) and a value of 10 for X% (*x*). This was simple, but it gets a bit more difficult as we progress.

C LIKES INTS BEST

The heading of this section may be a bit glib, but the fact is that C likes to consider every numeric variable and constant as an integer unless specifically told otherwise. This might be confusing, but the following program examples will shed some light on the subject.

```
10  X=10/4
20  PRINT X
```

In BASIC, this program runs perfectly. The value of 2.5 is displayed on the monitor screen. The following program demonstrates how the same operation might be written in C by a beginning programmer:

C Likes Ints Best   **41**

```
main()
{

    float x;                              WRONG!

    x = 10 / 4;

    printf("%f\n", x);

}
```

This looks fine at first glance, but the value displayed on the screen will be 2.000000. Why? The answer can be found by going back to the heading of this section. "C likes *ints* best." Even though *x* was declared a float, the mathematical operation 10 / 4 involves two integers, 10 and 4. Therefore, *integer division* was performed and the integer product of 10 / 4 is 2. The fractional portion is truncated, which is a fancy way of saying that it is deleted or lopped off. Float variable *x* then received a value of 2, which is converted to 2.000000. Thus, when the value of *x* was displayed by *printf*, the integer result of integer division was returned as a converted floating-point value.

To write this program in a proper manner, we must specify standard floating-point division. This is done quite simply when constants are divided. The following program is the correct version of the one attempted above:

```
main()
{

    float x;

    x = 10.0 / 4.0;

    printf("%f\n", x);

}
```

Now the value of 2.500000 will be displayed on the screen. Floating-point division is specified in this example by converting the two integer constants involved to floating point. This is done by tacking on .0. Actually, it is not necessary to convert both constants, and

```
                          x = 10 / 4.0;
```

or

```
                          x = 10.0 / 4;
```

will bring about the desired floating-point division. However, converting both sides is good practice in the initial stages of learning C, because this conforms to an under-

42   Math Operations   Chap. Five

standable style. Floating-point constants must have a decimal point even when the fractional portion is 0.

This rule of representing constants does not apply to floating-point variables that are to be divided or when a floating-point variable is divided by an integer constant. For example,

```
main()
{
        float x, y;

        x = 22;
        y = x / 10;

        printf("%f\n", y);

}
```

will display the value 2.200000 on the screen. It is not necessary to convert 10 to 10.0 in this instance (although it is desirable from the standpoint of program comprehension), because x has already been declared a float and this invokes floating-point mathematical operations.

Now, suppose that you wish to divide two integer variables, which will result in a floating-point answer. The following program demonstrates how this is done in BASIC:

```
10   X%=4
20   Y%=3
30   Z=X%/Y%
40   PRINT Z
```

The displayed result will be 1.333333, which is correct. BASIC has no problems with returning a floating-point result from a mathematical operation performed on two integers, but a direct conversion will not work in C, as in

```
main()
{
        int x, y;
        float z;
                                    WRONG!
        x = 4;
        y = 3;
        z = x / y;
        print("%f\n", z);

}
```

This program will assign z the integer division equivalent of 4 / 3, for a resulting display of 1.000000.

UNIX Math Functions   **43**

For this program to work correctly, we must somehow let the C environment know that floating-point division is desired. The best way to accomplish this is to convert one of the integer values to a float. In BASIC, this could be done in the following manner:

```
10  X%=4
20  Y%=3
30  Z=X%/CSNG(Y%)
40  PRINT Z
```

The CSNG function is used to convert the integer value of Y% to a single-precision floating-point value. The C equivalent would be

```
main()
{
        int x, y;
        float z;

        x = 4;
        y = 3;
        z = x / (float) y;

        printf("%f\n", z);

}
```

The change here is the addition of (*float*), which is known as a *cast operator*. This effectively converts the integer value returned by *y* to a floating-point value. Now floating-point division will take place and the answer desired will be displayed on the screen. Cast operators are used anytime it is necessary to convert the value of a variable or a constant from its present data type to that of the cast. For example,

```
x = (float) 4;
```

assigns *x* the value of 4.000000, assuming that *x* is a floating-point variable. Cast operators may also name other data types, such as (*double*), (*long*), (*short*), (*char* *), and so on.

UNIX MATH FUNCTIONS

The C programming language was originally designed to be used in the environment of the UNIX operating system, not with MS-DOS, CPM, or any of the systems now available for microcomputers. UNIX contains a math library that offers the higher math functions, such as *sqrt*(), *exp*(), *log*(), and *pow*(). Many of the earlier C compilers were devoid of these functions. Only in recent years have most of them come equipped with these higher math capabilities.

44   Math Operations   Chap. Five

RUN/C and most modern C compilers will offer most of the UNIX math functions, so it is not necessary to purchase an expensive, adjunct software package that offers these higher math functions, which are often vital in many different programming applications. Although these functions do many of the same things that their equivalents in BASIC do, there are certain protocols for calling them. In this section we explore most of these.

The following table shows the UNIX or C language math functions on the left and their closest BASIC equivalents on the right:

UNIX/C	BASIC
sqrt( )	SQR
pow( )	∧ (raise to a power)
sin( )	SIN
cos( )	COS
tan( )	TAN
log( )	LOG
exp( )	EXP

Most of the BASIC math functions on this order will return double-precision values, with the exception of SIN, COS, and TAN. As is the case with most BASIC statements and functions, you can provide arguments of any numeric type.

In C, the equivalent functions always return a double-precision value and all of them expect a double-precision argument. If you supply another type of argument, such as an *int* or *float*, the functions will probably return an erroneous value.

It was mentioned previously that functions which return any value other than an integer must be declared at the beginning of the program that calls them. This applies especially to these higher math functions. If you do not declare them, integer values may be returned by some C environments, whereas others may return random values. This does not apply to RUN/C (at least through Version 1.32), as these functions are declared double internally. If you try to declare them again, an error message will result and program execution will be discontinued.

The following BASIC program will begin a practical exercise into these higher math functions:

```
10  X#=14.3
20  Y#=SQR(X#)
30  PRINT Y#
```

Here the square root of 14.3 is returned to double-precision variable Y# using the SQR function. This has been written in a form that can be translated correctly by CBREEZE, since this translator will not correct improper argument types, even though they may run under BASIC. The C language equivalent of this program is

UNIX Math Functions   45

```
main()
{
    double x, y, sqrt();

    x = 14.3;
    y = sqrt(x);

    printf("%lf\n", y);

}
```

Again, if you are going to run this program under RUN/C, you must delete the declaration of *sqrt*() as a double. Note that all variables (as well as the *sqrt* function) have been declared double at the beginning of the program. The argument to *sqrt*() is *x*, which is a double-precision variable. This satisfies the argument requirement to this function. When the value is written to the screen, the *%lf* conversion specification is used because *y* represents a double-precision value, the one returned by *sqrt*().

This program could have been greatly simplified, as in

```
main()
{
    double sqrt();

    printf("%lf\n", sqrt(14.3));

}
```

In every case, the function must be declared double, expects a double argument, and returns a double value. If the *printf* line had been written as

```
printf("%lf\n", sqrt(14));
```

an error message might be generated by some C environments. Others would compile the program as if everything were fine, but the value returned by *sqrt*() would be equal to zero or some random number. This is due to the fact that the value supplied (14) is not a double but an integer. When constants are used, the precision makes no difference. Just make sure that each is written in floating-point format with a decimal point.

What's wrong with the following program?

```
main()
{
    double x;

    x = 1.543;

    printf("%lf\n", sqrt(x / .55));

}
```

46   Math Operations   Chap. Five

If you are using RUN/C, there is nothing wrong with this program. But for almost every other environment, the fault lies in the fact that *sqrt*() has not been declared double.

Now let's convert the following BASIC program to C:

```
10   X%=12
20   Y#=AQR(X%)
30   PRINT Y#
```

Literally translated by CBREEZE, the C equivalent would be

```
main()
{

    int x;
    double y, sqrt();                    WRONG!

    x = 12;
    y = sqrt(x);

    printf("%lf\n", y);

}
```

This program simply will not run. RUN/C will print an error message, even after you remove *sqrt*() from the declaration line. Some compilers will create executable code without a complaint, but the square root of 12 will not be returned, because variable *x* is an integer. Remember, *sqrt*() and all of the higher math functions *must* have double arguments or they return garbage.

The following program shows the correct form for the one above:

```
main()
{
    int x;
    double y, sqrt();

    x = 12;
    y = sqrt((double) x);

    printf("%lf\n", y);

}
```

The (double) cast operator is used to convert the value in *x* to a double-precision data type. This satisfies the argument requirement to *sqrt*() and the function returns the proper value.

The next BASIC program will also require a higher-level math function when translated into C:

Summary   **47**

```
10  X#=10
20  Y#=2.5
30  PRINT X#^Y#
```

This program simply prints the value of X# raised to the power Y#. In C, it could be written as

```
main()
{

    double x, y, pow();

    x = 10;
    y = 2.5;

    printf("%lf\n", pow(x, y));

}
```

The *raise-to* function in BASIC corresponds to the *pow*() function in C. This function requires two arguments. The first is the root value and the second is the power to which this root is to be raised. *Both arguments to pow() must be double-precision values.* If one is double and the other is not, an erroneous value will be returned.

The other high-level math functions in C require the same care in argument selection. Remember, any BASIC programs that are translated by CBREEZE must adhere to this argument convention. CBREEZE will not change argument types. It makes a very literal translation of the BASIC program that serves as its input. This is part of the learning process. CBREEZE requires *you* to be aware of what types of arguments are being provided.

SUMMARY

Mathematical operations are carried out in C much as they are in BASIC. The main difference lies in the strict argument requirements of C compared with the more relaxed nature of BASIC. Again, know your variables. Know what variables are required by various math functions. Know what values they return. Beware of math operations that combine one data type in such a manner that another data type results. By adhering to the data type rules in C, it should take only a short time to have them become second nature whenever you are programming in this language.

CHAPTER SIX

C Language Statements

Any discussion of C language will make constant reference to functions. In BASIC, functions are not nearly as numerous as statements, and we are more familiar with dealing with the latter. However, C language functions become statements when they are used in a C language program. They become program statements made up from C functions.

C does contain a limited set of statements, many of which correspond to statements in BASIC. In this chapter we discuss the various C statements, which should be learned quite easily.

The standard C language statements are

```
if
if else
while
do while
for
switch
case
default
break
continue
return
goto
```

Many of these should be familiar to you. As a matter of fact, *if*, *if else*, *while*, *for*, and *goto* work in very much the same manner as they do in BASIC. The other statements are specially set up for the various C language routines they address.

48

C Language Statements   Chap. Six   **49**

While addressing the *if* statement, a brief discussion on logical operators will also be provided. In BASIC, IF-THEN statements often include a number of logical operators. As a matter of fact, these operators may be used with other statements as well, to shorten overall programming time. Logical operators are also used in C, but they are represented a bit differently. They are broken down into two discrete categories: logical connective operators and bitwise operators. Logical connective operators are discussed first. These include AND and OR. In BASIC, these operators may also be used for manipulation of bits in binary numbers, but this is not the case in C.

The logical connective operators AND and OR are expressed in C language programs by the symbols "&&" and "||", respectively. As bitwise operators, they would be expressed as "&" and "|", respectively.

Another set of operators that are relied on heavily in BASIC (and in all other languages as well) are the relational operators. These include the equals sign (=), more than (>), less than (<), more than or equal to (>=), less than or equal to (<=), and not equal to (<>). In C, many of the same operators apply, although there are some differences.

For instance, in C, the equals sign (=) is used as an assignment operator only. As an example,

$$a = b;$$

uses the assignment operator to assign the value of *b* to *a*. However, if we wish to compare the value of *a* with *b* and do something if the two are equal, the assignment operator (=) no longer applies. A BASIC program portion such as

```
50  B=75
60  A=B
70  IF A=B THEN (do something)
```

would be written in C as

```
b = 75;
a = b;
if (a == b)
      (do something);
```

This is a nonsense program (in both BASIC and C), but it illustrates the difference between the assignment operator (=) and the equality operator (==). They each mean something completely different. In the C language program portion, the assignment operator (=) is used to assign variable *b* the value of 75 and in the next line to assign to variable *a* the value of *b*. However, in the *if* statement line, the equality operator (==) is used. We can say that the equality operator is used whenever two values are to be compared (as opposed to one or the other being changed). In C, "=" and "==" have two completely different meanings. The first makes an assignment; the other makes a comparison.

50   C Language Statements   Chap. Six

Going one step further, the BASIC program line

```
100  IF A=B AND C=D THEN (do something)
```

would be written in C as

```
if (a == b && c == d)
   (do something);
```

In this example, the use of the two equality operators compares *a* with *b* and *c* with *d*. The connective operator "&&" takes the place of AND in the BASIC program. Both programs state that if *a* is equal to *b* *and* *c* is equal to *d*, then do something. This means that both expressions on either side of the logical connective operator must be true for the action to take place.

Here is another example:

```
100  IF A=B AND C=D OR E=F THEN (do something)
```

The C language equivalent line would be

```
if (a == b && c == d || e==f)
   (do something)
```

Both programs perform an action if *a* is equal to *b* and *c* is equal to *d*. If one or the other of these expressions is not true, but *e* is equal to *f*, the action is still performed. To put it simply, the logical connective operators work in C just as they do in BASIC. One does have to be careful of the equality operators to avoid some very sticky problems. For example, if the C program line

```
if (a = b && c = d)
   (do something);
```

were used, the action (do something) would take place every time. Instead of comparing *a* with *b* and *c* with *d*, this line would assign *a* to *b* and *c* to *d*. Such mistakes are common among programmers who are making the switch from BASIC to C (and even to those of us who feel that we have successfully made the switch), but after awhile, one begins more or less to think in C as opposed to thinking in BASIC and converting to C. As this transition takes place, problems such as these diminish in occurrence.

The inequality operator in BASIC is represented as "<>". In C, the inequality operator is "!=". Therefore,

```
100  IF A<>B THEN (do something)
```

C Language Statements   Chap. Six   **51**

would look like

```
if (a != b)
    (do something);
```

in C.

The remaining relational operators in C match those in BASIC. But be careful! In C, the "more than or equal to" operator must be expressed in exactly that order. "More than" comes first, followed by "equals." In BASIC, the "more than or equal to" operator may also be written as "equal to or more than." This is not legal in C. The following list shows what is legal and what is not:

Legal:

>=	More than or equal to
<=	Less than or equal to

Illegal:

=>	Equal to or more than
=<	Equal to or less than

Some C environments may recognize some of the illegal operators listed here, but many do not. Be on the safe side and always list all operators in standard C format.

The bitwise operators may be used only with integer values in C and are listed below:

&	Bitwise AND
|	Bitwise inclusive OR
^	Bitwise exclusive OR
<<	Left shift
>>	Right shift
~	One's complement (unary)

They must not be confused with their logical connective counterparts. The following programs demonstrate the use of the bitwise operators:

BASIC:

```
100  X=7 AND 1
```

C:

```
x = 7 & 1;
```

52   C Language Statements   Chap. Six

For bitwise manipulations, the AND operator is used just like a connective operator in BASIC. However, in C, the bitwise AND operator is represented by "&", and the connective operator is represented by "&&".

With all of this in mind, we are prepared to move on to a discussion of many of the C language statements and their relationships to similar BASIC language statements.

```
10  INPUT X%
20  IF X%=14 THEN PRINT "THAT IS THE NUMBER"
30  END
```

This simple program uses the INPUT statement to receive an integer value from the keyboard. If the value is equal to 14, a message will be printed; if not, the program terminates. The END statement is optional in this particular case, since BASIC will stop execution automatically when there are no more lines to execute.

```
main()
{

    int x;

    scanf("%d", &x);

    if (x == 14)
        printf("THAT IS THE NUMBER\n");

    exit(0);

}
```

In this program, variable x is declared an *int*, while *scanf* assigns the keyboard input to the memory location of x. The *if* statement is used to test for the occurrence of x being equal to 14. Note that the equality operator (==) is used rather than the assignment operator (=). The statement that immediately follows is executed when the *if* test proves true (nonzero). Then there is the *exit*() function, whose argument is zero (0) (value is unimportant most of the time). This argument is returned to whatever function called exit in the first place [in this case, main()]. In C, a value of −1 indicates a malfunction, whereas a value of 0 usually indicates that all is well. The value of the argument really makes no difference at all in this application. Most of the time, you will see exit functions used with arguments of 0.

```
10  INPUT X%
20  IF X%=14 THEN PRINT "THAT IS THE NUMBER":PRINT "I WAS
    LOOKING FOR"
30  END
```

C Language Statements   Chap. Six   **53**

This is a slight modification of the previous BASIC program. Here, multiple operations are carried out when the IF-THEN test proves true. The first phrase is written to the screen, followed by the second phrase. The program then terminates when line 30 is executed. If X% is not equal to 14, nothing is printed, and the program is terminated.

```
main()
{

    int x;

    scanf("%d", &x);

    if (x == 14) {
        printf("THAT IS THE NUMBER\n");
        printf("I WAS LOOKING FOR\n");
    }

    exit(0);

}
```

This program is quite similar to the previous C example, but more than the extra call to *printf* has been added. Note that at the end of the *if* statement line, there is another opening brace ({ points left). This is necessary when more than one statement is to be executed as a result of the *if* statement test. As stated earlier, whenever there is an opening brace, there is always a matching closing brace. This one is found following the last call to *printf*. Following standard C format, it is printed one line below the last statement line and directly beneath the calling function or statement (in this case, *if*). All statements that lie between the opening brace and the closing brace are executed when *x* is equal to 14. Braces may be used when only one statement is to be executed, but this is not required and was not done in the previous program examples. The *if* statement always expects at least one statement to follow. This is assumed. If more than one statement is to follow, the braces are required. If the braces are not included for multiple statement quantities, only the first statement (the function immediately following the *if* statement line) will be executed as the result of the *if* test proving true. All the remaining lines will be executed as if they were not a part of the *if* test.

```
10  INPUT X%
20  IF X%>=10 OR X%=5 THEN PRINT "CORRECT"
30  END
```

This program tests for the value of X% being more than or equal to 10 or being equal to 5. If either of these conditions is true (since the logical OR was used), the word "CORRECT" is printed.

54　　　　　　　　　　　　　　　　C Language Statements　　　Chap. Six

```c
main( )
{

    int x;

    scanf("%d", &x);

    if (x >= 10 || x == 5)
        printf("CORRECT\n");

    exit (0);

}
```

This illustrates the use of the relational and logical connective operators with the *if* statement in C. Note that the brace following the *if* statement line is not included because only one statement follows. The exit function, like the END statement in BASIC, is optional in this particular program, since execution will terminate automatically when there are no more lines to execute. In C, a program is always ended by a closing brace that matches the opening brace following *main*( ) [unless there is a premature termination created by *exit*( )]. This is the signal to terminate execution. Therefore, if the END statement were removed from the BASIC program, or the *exit*(0) function were removed from the C program, no run differences would be noted.

```basic
10   INPUT X%
20   IF X%=22 THEN END
30   PRINT "TRY AGAIN"
```

Although this program will run as is, it might be thought of as a portion of a BASIC program that terminates whenever X% is equal to 22, but does something else in other lines (not listed here) if X% is equal to anything but 22. When this program is run, any number other than 22 will cause the prompt "TRY AGAIN" to appear on the screen. One might assume that a GOTO statement or another routine would follow line 30; but this is enough for our discussion. Here the END statement in line 20 is extremely important, because it terminates execution of the program while there are still other lines that could be executed. In previous programs, the END statement was optional. In this one, however, it is mandatory.

```c
main( )
{

    int x;

    scanf("%d", &x);

    if (x == 22)
        exit(0);

    printf("TRY AGAIN\n");

}
```

If-Then-Else   **55**

This program does exactly the same thing as the BASIC version. The exit function is placed below the *if* statement line and is executed only when the value returned to *x* by *scanf* is equal to 22. Here the exit function is mandatory for a successful program run.

IF-THEN-ELSE

In this section we explore more fully the various *if* statement constructs.

```
10  INPUT X%
20  IF X%=20 THEN PRINT X% ELSE PRINT X%*X%
```

This program demonstrates the use of IF-THEN-ELSE. If X% is equal to 20, its value will be written to the screen. If it is not equal to 20, ELSE takes over and X% times X% is written. The C language equivalent of this program is

```
main()
{

    int x;

    scanf("%d", &x);

    if (x == 20)
        printf("%d\n", x);
    else
        printf("%d\n", x * x);

}
```

The *if-else* sequence in C is very clear cut. Note that a single statement is executed if the *if* test proves true. Therefore, no braces are needed. Also, a single statement is executed when *else* is in control, so no braces are needed with the *else* portion of this program. The first *printf* line is executed when *x* is equal to 20. If it is not equal to 20, the second *printf* statement is executed.

```
10  INPUT X%
20  IF X%=20 THEN PRINT X% ELSE IF X%=10 THEN
    PRINT X%-1 ELSE PRINT X%*X%
```

This program makes use of IF-THEN-ELSE and ELSE-IF. If X% is equal to 20, this value will be displayed on the screen. If X% is equal to 10, this value minus 1 is displayed. If neither of these conditions is true, the value of X% times X% is displayed.

56   C Language Statements   Chap. Six

```c
main()
{

    int x;

    scanf("%d", &x);

    if (x == 20)
        printf("%d\n", x);
    else if (x == 10)
        printf("%d\n", x - 1);
    else
        printf("%d\n", x * x);

}
```

The C language version follows the same route as the BASIC program, although it is a little easier to understand because multiple lines are used to express what was expressed in a single line in the BASIC program. From looking at the C version, we can see that the value of x is displayed when x is equal to 20. However, if x is equal to 10, $x - 1$ is displayed. If neither of these conditions is true, x times x is displayed. If multiple statements were to be carried out in association with *if*, a brace would follow the *if* statement line (opening). A closing brace would mark termination of the statements to be carried out under *if*. The same applies to *else-if* and *else*. Remember, *else-if* and *else* are not considered statements executed under *if*, and therefore are not included within the braces.

SWITCH

The following C program is quite tedious, but there is an easier way to handle so many conditional tests:

```c
main()
{

    int x;

    scanf("%d", &x);

    if (x == 1)
        printf("ONE\n");
    else if (x == 2)
        printf("TWO\n");
    else if (x == 3)
        printf("THREE\n");
    else if (x == 4)
        printf("FOUR\n");
    else
        printf ("FIVE OR LARGER\n");

}
```

Switch   **57**

This program uses the *if/else-if/else* construct to compare the value of *x* and print
a message based on its value. All of these *if* statements can cause confusion, especially
when a tree of comparisons must be made that may involve 10 or more possible
values.

Here is where the *switch* statement may be used to good advantage. The following
program works identically to the one above, but uses different statements to arrive
at the same result:

```
main()
{

    int x;

    scanf("%d", &x);

    switch(x) {
        case 1:
            printf("ONE\n");
            break;
        case 2:
            printf("TWO\n");
            break;
        case 3:
            printf("THREE\n");
            break;
        case 4:
            printf("FOUR\n");
            break;
        default:
            printf("FIVE OR LARGER\n");
    }


}
```

This program is easier to understand because it is less cluttered than the first. The
switch statement compares a single integer or character value with a series of *case*
statements. *Case* names a *constant* to which the argument to *switch* is compared.
If a match is found, the statement following the matched *case* is executed. In addition,
all subsequent statements within *switch* are also executed—unless a *break* statement
is encountered. As it does with loops, *break* causes an immediate exit from *switch*.
Notice that each *case* contains two statements, the last being a break. This assures
that the remaining *case* statements are not executed.

The last portion of *switch* contains the *default* statement. The statement(s)
contained in *default* is executed when no match is found. *Default*, then, is the equivalent of *else* in the preceding program.

Remember, a *switch* compares integer values or *char* values only. Strings, floats,
doubles, and so on, cannot be used. All *case* arguments must be constants, such as

58   C Language Statements   Chap. Six

65 or 'A', depending on whether you choose *int* constants or *char* constants. Do not use a variable argument with *case*.

When a match is detected, all statements following the matching *case* will be executed unless a *break* statement is encountered. This causes the *switch* to be exited.

The *default* statement controls statements that are executed only if no match occurs in the *switch*. It is found at the end of the *switch* and its use is optional, just as *else* is optional in an *if* conditional test.

When *int* or *char* values must be put through a series of conditional tests, the *switch* statement provides an efficient process by which this can be done with a minimum of confusion. If the number of comparison tests is small, *if-else* is probably preferred. However, if the tests form a long series, *switch* is the preferred route to take.

CONDITIONAL EXPRESSIONS

The *conditional expression* in C provides an alternative to *if* statement constructs. The following program will help to introduce the subject of conditional expressions:

```
main( )
{
        int  x,  y,  z;

        x = 4;
        y = 5;

        if (x < y)
                z = x;
        else
                z = y;

}
```

This program will assign *z* the value of *x* if *x* is less than *y*. If *x* is not less than *y*, then *z* is assigned the value of *y*. The next example uses a conditional expression to accomplish the same thing.

```
main( )
{
        int  x,  y,  z;

        x = 4;
        y = 5;
        z = (x < y) ? x : y;

}
```

Summary   **59**

The expression is found in the last program line. It uses two new operators, represented
by the question mark (?) and the colon (:). In plain language this line would read

$$z \text{ equals } x \text{ if } x \text{ is less than } y, \text{ else } z \text{ equals } y$$

The question mark and the colon together form what is known as the *ternary operator*.
This operator evaluates a series of expressions. In this example, $(x < y)$ is the first
expression. This returns a nonzero value if true and causes the second expression
to be evaluated. This is the one represented here by the variable x (following the
question mark). If the first expression is false, the third expression is evaluated. This
one is y (following the colon). Whatever expression is evaluated second is the value
of the conditional expression. In the example above, this value is assigned to z.

We can use the conditional expression in place of many *if-else* constructs and
in places where *if-else* will not work at all. For example,

```
main()
{

    int x, y;

    x = 10;
    y = 8;

    printf("%d\n", (x < y) ? x : y);

}
```

The call to *printf* could also have been written as

```
if (x < y)
        printf("%d\n", x);
else
        printf("%d\n", y);
```

This involves more program lines, a little more time at the keyboard, and is not
nearly as simple as the first example. The conditional expression is another example
of a C language shortcut that saves time and enhances program clarity.

SUMMARY

Most of the statements found in C closely resemble statements of the same or similar
names in BASIC. The idea of loops, of branches, and of conditional tests (using
IF) are certainly not foreign to any BASIC programmer with just a little bit of
experience. These statements, together with a few primitive functions, were the tools
used to build C language. More than any other aspect of C, these statements bear

the most direct relationship to BASIC operations. Your experience with BASIC equivalents of these will aid you in your transition to competence in C.

Every language requires a method of comparing values. In BASIC and in C, the IF (*if*) statement serves this purpose. This statement is used similarly in both languages, and most BASIC programmers will have no difficulty in mastering it. There are differences in the values that can be directly compared, but this is dealt with in a later chapter. For now, the *if* statement in C provides a special note of familiarity to the BASIC programmer. Additional C language statements are discussed in the next chapter.

CHAPTER SEVEN

Loops

In this chapter we discuss additional C language statements that are used to form and control loops. Just as they do in BASIC, loops play a crucial role in C language programs. The FOR-NEXT loop in BASIC is the best known and most often used. Its equivalent in C is called a *for* loop. In BASIC, we can also loop with a WHILE-WEND statement. In C, the *while* loop does the same thing. C also boasts a *do-while* loop, which is not used very often, but which can be very advantageous in certain programming situations. In BASIC, we can also create loops that are continuous or exitable with the GOTO statement. C language also has a *goto* statement, but it is rarely used since there are so many more efficient ways of accomplishing the same thing with *while*, *for*, and *do-while*.

The GOTO statement in BASIC is much used and abused. Most BASIC programmers would be lost without GOTO, but these same people may not take full advantage of the potential offered by the WHILE-WEND statement, which is rarely used. In C, however, the *while* loop is seen often; thus *goto*s are seldomly used. Only in rare instances are *goto*s truly advantageous in C, and the beginning C programmer should not rely too heavily on this statement, as it may hinder his/her future development.

```
10  FOR X%=1 TO 100 STEP 1
20  PRINT X%
30  NEXT X%
```

This is the standard FOR-NEXT loop demonstration program on which most BASIC programmers cut their teeth. Chances are that your first experience with a FOR-

NEXT loop included a floating-point variable (X) rather than an integer variable (X%); but this leads to inefficient use of memory, explained previously. This loop simply counts from 1 to 100 in steps of 1. The STEP value is not mandatory in this sample program, since when STEP is not included, FOR-NEXT loops increment in steps of 1 as the default. However, this is not true in C, and the inclusion of STEP should make for a clearer explanation.

```
main()
{

    int x;

    for (x = 1; x <= 100; x = x + 1)
        printf("%d\n", x);

}
```

The C language equivalent of the previous BASIC program uses the *for* loop. Several statements follow within the parentheses following *for*. These are separated by semicolons that mark the end of a statement line. The first statement assigns x a value of 1. The second statement says that x is less than or equal to 100. The next statement assigns x a value of x plus 1. One can easily see the relationship between this portion of the C program and the FOR-NEXT loop in the BASIC program. This loop will count from 1 to 100 and increment x by 1 on each pass. Each time the loop cycles, the *printf* function is executed, and the value of x is written to the screen. The first value of x determines the lowest value (in a positive stepping loop). The next value assigned to x in the *for* statement line sets its maximum value. The last statement assigns a step value. Any statements that follow this line will be executed within the loop. If more than one statement were to be executed in the loop, an opening brace would follow the *for* statement line, while a closing brace would be found at the end of the loop statements.

Although this program is correct, it does not follow standard C language format in one respect. When a value must be incremented or decremented by itself plus or minus another number, it is not usually written as $x = x + 1$ or $x = x - 1$. To follow standard C language format, the *for* statement line should have been written as

```
    for (x = 1; x <= 100; ++x)
```

The notation $++x$ is exactly equivalent to $x = x + 1$. In a negative stepping loop, the notation $--x$ is exactly equivalent to $x = x - 1$. This may seem a bit confusing at first, but as long as you know how these notations relate to what you have been doing in BASIC, you should have no problem. The notation $++x$ simply means that x is incremented by 1 each time this line is executed. The notation $--x$ means that x is decremented by 1 each time the line is executed.

Loops   Chap. Seven   **63**

```
10  FOR X%=1 TO 100 STEP 1
20  PRINT X%
30  PRINT X%+10
40  NEXT X%
```

This is the same program as before, except that an extra PRINT statement has been added to display the value of X% plus 10. Two PRINT statements are executed within the loop, so two screen writes will take place on each of the 100 loop passes.

```
main()
{

    int x;

    for (x = 1; x <= 100; ++x)  {
        printf("%d\n", x);
        printf("%d\n", x + 10);
    }

}
```

This C language program also contains one extra statement within the *for* loop. Notice also that two extra braces have been added. The one immediately following the *for* statement line indicates that the following collection of statements is to be executed. The closing brace in the line immediately following the last *printf* statement indicates the end of the statements that are to be executed within the loop. The last closing brace in the entire program marks program termination. This is the one that aligns with the opening brace that follows *main*().

To expand our knowledge of *printf* a little more, the C program could also have been written as follows:

```
main()
{

    int x;

    for (x = 1; x <= 100; ++x)
        printf("%d\n%d\n", x, x + 10);

}
```

Here only one *printf* statement follows the *for* line. Therefore, the extra braces are not required. However, the single *printf* call does exactly the same thing as two calls to *printf* in the preceding C program. In the control string, two newline characters are included in quotation marks. The first conversion specifier, %*d*, is followed by the newline character. Therefore, the value of *x* is displayed, and a carriage return/line feed takes place. However, we are not yet finished with the contents of *printf*. Another conversion specifier is encountered. It is replaced with a value of *x* + 10.

64   Loops   Chap. Seven

Still another newline character is generated. Remember, we can treat newline characters just as we do any other characters, but when they are printed, a carriage return/
line feed takes place. Used effectively, they can greatly decrease overall program
size when a great deal of formatted information must be written to the screen.

```
10  FOR X%=0 TO 100 STEP 2
20  PRINT X%
30  NEXT X%
```

This is a repeat of a previous BASIC program, except that X% is incremented by
2 instead of 1 on each pass.

```
main( )
{

    int x;

    for (x = 0; x <= 100; x = x + 2)
        printf("%d\n", x);

}
```

The matching C language program is shown just to indicate that when the
loop variable (or any other variable, for that matter) is to be incremented by more
than 1 or decremented by more than 1, we can use the standard BASIC notation.
However, x += 2 means the same as $x = x + 2$. This shorthand notation is seen
more often in C programs, as it decreases overall typing time:

```
10  FOR X%=100 TO 1 STEP -1
20  PRINT X%
30  NEXT X%
```

This is the same routine as shown earlier, except that X% counts from 100 to 1 in
steps of −1. When X% is less than 1, the loop terminates.

```
main( )
{

    int x;

    for (x = 100; x >= 1; --x)
        printf("%d_n", x);

}
```

The C language program is set up in much the same way as its BASIC counterpart. Since the loop is stepping in negative values, the first value assigned to x in

Loops   Chap. Seven   **65**

the *for* statement line will be its maximum value. In this case, the value is 100. In the next portion of this line, the relational operator "more than or equal to" is used to indicate that the value of x will be more than or equal to 1. When this condition is no longer true, the loop will terminate. The notation ––x decrements x by 1 on each pass of the loop. I think you will agree that *for* loops in C are closely equivalent in format to FOR-NEXT loops in BASIC. Most programmers making the transition from BASIC to C experience little difficulty with *for* loops.

```
10  FOR X%=1 TO 100 STEP 1
20  FOR Y%=100 TO 0 STEP -1
30  PRINT X%;Y%
40  NEXT Y%
50  NEXT X%
```

This illustrates the use of a nested loop in BASIC. The X% loop is called the outer loop, while the Y% loop is the inner one. On each of the 100 passes of the outer loop (X%), the inner loop (Y%) will run through all 101 of its passes. I say 101 because Y% counts backward from 100 to 0 rather than from 100 to 1. On each pass of the Y% loop, the values of X% and Y% are displayed on the screen in horizontal format (side by side).

```
main()
{

    int x, y;

    for (x = 1; x <= 100; ++x)
        for (y = 100; y >= 0; --y)
            printf("%d %d\n", x, y);


}
```

The C language version closely conforms to the BASIC example. There is nothing mysterious about placing a *for* loop within a *for* loop in C, although many readers may be wondering why an opening brace does not follow the first *for* statement line. It does appear that more than one statement is executed within the body of the outer loop. This includes the *for* statement and the *printf* function. However, extra braces are not necessary because the outer loop really sees only the *for* statement. The call to *printf* is associated with the *for* statement, which decrements y. In other words, when the nested *for* loop is executed, the *printf* statement is automatically associated with it. It is a single statement following a *for* loop. Therefore, no brace is necessary following the y loop. In fact, the *printf* statement is not really associated at all with the x loop. The only association with the x loop in this program is the y loop. In this usage, the entire contents of the y loop appear as one statement to the x loop.

66   Loops   Chap. Seven

```
10  FOR X%=1 TO 100 STEP 1
20  FOR Y%=100 TO 0 STEP -1
30  PRINT X%;Y%
40  PRINT X%+10;Y%+10
50  NEXT Y%
60  NEXT X%
```

This is the same program as before, except that an extra PRINT statement line has been added within the body of the Y% loop. Each time the Y% loop cycles, the values of X% and Y% will be displayed, followed by these values plus 10. In this BASIC program it is easier to see what I was alluding to in the explanation of the previous C program and the associativity of the statement contained within the *y* loop. Notice in the BASIC program that the two PRINT statements are enclosed within the Y% loop and bear no direct relationship to the X% loop.

```
main( )
{

    int x, y;

    for (x = 1; x <= 100; ++x)
        for (y = 100; y >= 0; --y) {
            printf("%d %d\n", x, y);
            printf("%d %d\n", x + 10, y + 10);
        }


}
```

In this program, braces have been added to enclose the multiple statements that are carried out within the body of the *y* loop. The *x* loop still sees the nested *for* loop as a single entity. Therefore, no braces are required to encompass the contents of this loop, which effectively represent a single statement. The two *printf* calls are associated only with the *y* loop. Note that the closing brace for this loop is located on the third line beneath the word *for*, which opens the *y* loop. This makes it easier for anyone viewing the program listing to see exactly which statements are being executed by which calls.

```
10  FOR X%=1 TO 100 STEP 1
20  FOR Y%=100 TO 0 STEP -1
30  PRINT X%;Y%
40  PRINT X%+10;Y%+10
50  NEXT Y%
60  PRINT "CYCLING OUTER LOOP"
70  NEXT X%
```

This program is similar to the previous BASIC examples. There is an addition, however, in that line 60 is a PRINT statement that is part of the outer, or X%, loop. Prior to the X% loop recycling, the message in line 60 is displayed on the screen.

Loops   Chap. Seven   **67**

The first two PRINT statements are associated with the nested, or Y%, loop. The last PRINT statement is associated with the outer, or X%, loop.

```
main()
{
    int x, y;

    for (x = 0; x <= 100; ++x) {
        for (y = 100; y >= 0; --y) {
            printf("%d %d\n", x, y);
            printf("%d %d\n", x + 10, y + 10);
        }

        printf("CYCLING OUTER LOOP\n");
    }
}
```

It seems as though there are braces all over the place; but it is fairly easy to see what is executed under control of each loop by noting the position of the closing braces. We can tell that the first closing brace is associated with the *for* statement controlling the inner loop. The next closing brace is associated with the *for* statement controlling the outer loop. The final closing brace is associated with *main*(). This is a representation of two nested loops, each of which contains more than one associated statement. Two statements are associated with the outer or *x* loop. First, there is the inner *for* loop and then the final *printf* statement line, which prints the cycling prompt. The outer loop again views the *for* loop and its components as it would a single statement. It views the final *printf* statement line as the second statement associated with it. The inner, or *y*, loop sees the two *printf* statement lines that follow as its associations. Note that the *x* loop braces contain its entire contents. The *y* loop braces encompass this loop's entire contents. If we really wanted to get technical, it could be said that the *x* loop braces encompass the *for* statement line *and* the contents encompassed by the braces of the nested *for* statement line and the final *printf* statement line.

I admit that this can be quite complex at first. It may be easier for some readers always to include opening and closing braces with any *for* statement line, regardless of whether multiple statements associated with the loop are to follow. However, be warned that many tutorials on C will not use unnecessary braces.

```
10  X%=0
20  WHILE X%<=100
30  PRINT X%
40  X%=X%+1
50  WEND
```

This program uses the BASIC WHILE-WEND statement to form a WHILE loop. The contents of the WHILE loop are executed until the test condition at the top of

68   Loops   Chap. Seven

the loop (following WHILE) is no longer true. WEND signifies the end of the loop. When WEND is encountered, the loop recycles. This program will print the value of X% as long as X% is less than or equal to 100. In line 10, X% is assigned an initial value of 0. In BASIC, this is not necessary, since any variable that has not been preassigned is equal to 0, or "" in the case of a string variable. However, in C, it is absolutely necessary to make initial assignments to all variables. An unassigned numeric variable will not necessarily be equal to 0. As a matter of fact, it rarely will.

```
main( )
{

    int x;

    x = 0;

    while (x <= 100) {
        printf("%d\n", x);
        ++x;
    }

}
```

This program incorporates the *while* statement. The program is very similar to the BASIC version, although, of course, there is no WEND. Here, *x* is declared *int* and is then assigned an initial value of 0. This assignment is mandatory in C language programs, whereas in BASIC, an unassigned numeric variable has a default value of 0. Note that an opening brace follows the *while* statement. This is necessary because more than one statement will be executed within the *while* loop. This is usually the case with *while* loops, but there are some exceptions. As with the *for* loop, if only one statement is to be executed within the loop itself, the *while* loop statements need not be enclosed by braces.

Each time the loop cycles, the value of *x* is written to the screen by *printf*, and *x* is incremented by 1 $(++x)$. At the beginning of each cycle, the value of *x* is tested to see if it is less than or equal to 100. If this is true, the cycle is completed and goes around for another. If it is false (i.e., *x* is more than 100), the loop is exited. The closing brace that falls beneath the *while* statement marks the loop termination point. Any lines that follow this closing brace are not part of the loop itself.

```
10  X%=100
20  WHILE X%>=0
30  PRINT X%
40  X%=X%-1
50  WEND
```

This is the negative-stepping version of the previous BASIC program. The WHILE loop again prints the value of X%, which is assigned an initial value of 100. On

Loops   Chap. Seven   **69**

each pass of the loop, X% is decremented by 1. When X% is less than 0 (−1), the
loop terminates.

```
main()
{

    int x;

    x = 100;

    while (x >= 0) {
        printf("%d\n", x);
        --x;
    }


}
```

This program is similar to the former C language version, except for the starting
value of *x*, which is 100. Also, *x* is decremented within the loop by the −−*x* notation.
This program will display the value of *x* starting at 100 and ending at 0. When a
value of −1 is detected, the *while* test proves false. The loop is then exited and
execution is terminated because no statements lie beyond the loop in this program.

```
 10  X%=0
 20  Y%=0
 30  WHILE X%<=10
 40  WHILE Y%<-5
 50  PRINT X%;Y%
 60  Y%=Y%+1
 70  WEND
 80  X%=X%+1
 90  Y%=0
100  WEND
```

This BASIC program demonstrates the use of a nested WHILE loop. The nested
loop steps the value of Y% from 0 to 5. The PRINT statement and the Y% increment-
ing routine are associated only with the Y% loop. The first WEND terminates the
Y% loop. At this point, X% is incremented by 1, and Y% is reassigned a value of
0. These last two lines are associated only with the outer, or X%, loop. When the
program is run, the changing values of X% and Y% are displayed on the monitor
screen.

```
main()
{

    int x, y;

    x = y = 0;
```

70   Loops   Chap. Seven

```
while (x <= 10) {
    while (y <= 5) {
        printf("%d %d\n", x, y);
        ++y;
    }

    ++x;
    y = 0;
}

}
```

There is nothing highly unusual about the use of nested *while* loops in C. Just make certain that you understand which braces surround statements associated with a particular loop. Variables x and y are declared *int*s. Both are assigned a value of 0 by the sequence x = y = 0. In most dialects of BASIC, this type of assignment is illegal, but in C it is perfectly correct. This line is equivalent to

```
x = 0;
y = 0;
```

The *while* loop that increments y is nested within the body of the *while* loop that increments x. The statements associated with the y loop are contained within braces, as are the statements associated with the x loop. In this example, the y loop, in its entirety, is looked upon as one statement by the x loop. The other two x loop statements are ++x; and y = 0;. The *printf* function and ++y; are the statements associated specifically with the y loop.

```
10  X%=0
20  WHILE X%<=10
30  FOR Y%=0 TO 5 STEP 1
40  PRINT X%;Y%
50  NEXT Y%
60  X%=X%+1
70  WEND
```

This program nests a FOR-NEXT loop within the body of a WHILE-WEND loop. When the for-next loop times out, X% is incremented by 1. When X% is incremented to 11, the WHILE test is no longer true, so the program terminates.

```
main( )
{

    int x, y;

    x = 0;
```

Loops   Chap. Seven   **71**

```
while (x <= 10) {
    for (y = 0; y <= 5; ++y)
        printf("%d %d\n", x, y);

    ++x;
}

}
```

Nesting a *for* loop within the body of a *while* loop in C is quite simple, probably even simpler than doing the same thing in BASIC. Note in the example above that no braces are required following the *for* loop, since only one statement is executed. Braces do surround the *while* loop statements, which include the *for* loop and the *x* incrementer. Both *x* and *y* are declared *int*s, and *x* is assigned an initial value of 0. It is not necessary to assign *y* a value of 0 at this point in the program. This assignment is made immediately following the *for* statement, where the lower and upper values of *y* are assigned.

```
10  X%=0
20  PRINT X%
30  X%=X%+1
40  IF X%<=20 THEN GOTO 20
```

This is an example of an exitable loop in BASIC. The value of X% is displayed on the screen, and X% is incremented by 1 as long as it is less than or equal to 20. If X% is more than 20, the program terminates. As mentioned previously, GOTO statements are often abused in BASIC. In other words, they are used when not absolutely necessary. Certainly, you have had the experience of trying to decipher a program that contained a large number of GOTO statements. The process can be quite tedious. This simple program example presents no problem, but remember that branch statements tend to hide the path of program flow. This is true in any language. Therefore, for program clarity, branch statements should be avoided where it is practical to do so.

```
main()
{

    int x;

    x = 0;

BR:
    printf("%d\n", x);
    ++x;

    if (x <= 20)
        goto BR;

}
```

72   Loops   Chap. Seven

This is the exact C equivalent of the BASIC program, although it could be handled in a far simpler manner without the *goto* statement. The use of *goto*s in C is usually frowned on, but there may come a time (rarely) when this statement can be put to practical use. This is sometimes the case when a program needs to be changed drastically for testing purposes. In some instances, it is far simpler to branch over program segments that are not to be used for these tests rather than to erase these portions from the source code. In any event, it is good to know how to use the *goto* statement, even though most program applications will not require or prefer it.

C language *goto* statements must be followed by a label name. In the example above, the label name is *BR*. The label itself is identified by a trailing colon (:). This is not to be a part of the label name when it is used with *goto*. The trailing colon indentifies this name as a label, as opposed to a function or a variable. When a *goto* statement is encountered during program execution, a branch is made to the point identified by the label that is named with *goto*. As in BASIC, branches may be made to a previous part of the program or to a portion that lies past the *goto* statement. With most C compilers and interpreters, a label must begin with an alphabetic character, but numbers may be embedded in the name. In the program above, the *goto* statement is contained within the *if* statement line. It names the label to which the branch is to be made. Note that the label name used with *goto* is not terminated with a colon but with a semicolon. The colon is used only to establish a label name, as discussed previously.

The following C language program demonstrates a better way of accomplishing the same operation without a *goto* statement. The program could have been written in practically the same way in BASIC for an improvement as well.

```
main( )
{

        int x;

        x = 0;

        while (x <= 20) {
            printf("%d\n", x);
            ++x;
        }


}
```

This program uses a *while* loop that executes a *printf* statement and increments x. When x is more than 20, execution terminates.

This is also a good point to introduce the *do-while* loop in C. This loop is not used very often, as it is very similar to the *while* loop. The *while* loop tests for a true-false condition at the top of the loop. The *do-while* loop tests for a true-false condition at the *bottom* of the loop. In the original BASIC and C language program

Loops   Chap. Seven   **73**

examples, an *if* statement was used to test for a true-false condition at the bottom
of the loop. The following C program uses *do-while* to effect a similar operation:

```
main( )
{
        int x;

        x = 0;

        do {
             printf("%d\n", x);
             ++x;
        } while (x <= 20);


}
```

This program is exactly equivalent to the previous C language example as far as
machine operation is concerned. Note that *do* is followed by an opening brace. This
indicates that more than one statement is to be executed as a part of the loop. As
with the other examples, if only one statement is included in the body of the loop,
braces are not necessary. The *do-while* loop more or less says "do the following"
(enclosed in braces). The while portion says "go back to *do* while the test line is
true." Notice that the closing brace for the *do* loop statements precedes the use of
while. One may think of *while* in this example as an *if* statement followed by a
goto. It says "while *x* is less than or equal to 20, goto *do*."

Again, *do-while* statements are used very rarely, but there are certain cases
where it is advantageous to test for a true-false condition at the bottom of the loop
rather than at the top. In these cases, *do-while* can be quite effective.

```
10  FOR X%=0 TO 100 STEP 1
20  PRINT X%
30  IF X%=20 THEN GOTO 50
40  NEXT X%
50  PRINT "LOOP EXITED"
```

This is a nonsense program, in that a loop is set up to count from 0 to 100, but an
IF-THEN statement is included to exit the loop when X% equals 20. However, it
makes an ideal example of a conditional loop exit that can be converted to a C
language demonstration program.

```
main( )
{

        int x;

        for (x = 0; x <= 100; ++x) {
             printf("%d\n", x);
```

74   Loops   Chap. Seven

```
                              if (x == 20)
                                  goto BR;
                     }
         BR:
                              printf("LOOP EXITED\n");

      }
```

The C language version closely copies the program in BASIC. Each time the loop cycles, *if* tests for a condition of *x* being equal to 20. When this occurs, the *goto* statement is executed and branches to label BR:. Here *printf* displays the closing message on the screen.

Again, a *goto* has been used, and in C, such statements are almost never necessary. In this example, a *goto* was used to break out of the loop and branch to the first statement immediately following the loop. In C, there is another statement that can take the place of *goto* in this particular example. The *break* statement is used to exit a loop prematurely. The following program is the equivalent of the program just presented but uses *break* instead of *goto*.

```
         main( )
         {

             int x;

             for (x = 0; x <= 100; ++x) {
                 printf("%d\n", x);
                 if (x == 20)
                     break;
             }

             printf("LOOP EXITED\n");

         }
```

We have no control over where *break* branches to. Its sole purpose is to exit a loop. Execution resumes at the first statement immediately following the loop. We can say, then, that *break* brings about early termination of a loop. In this example it has been used to take the place of *goto*, since all the latter statement did was branch out of the loop to the first executable line following the loop. Again, it is more efficient to avoid the use of *goto*.

This next BASIC program uses GOTO to start the loop on its next cycle based on a certain value of the loop variable:

```
         10  FOR X%=0 TO 100
         20  Y%=X%*2
         30  IF X%=10 THEN GOTO 50
         40  PRINT Y%
         50  NEXT X%
```

Summary

Naturally, it would have been easier to have used the IF-THEN statement to execute the PRINT statement whenever X% was not equal to 10, but this program makes for a good demonstration of a new C language statement. This loop counts X% from 0 to 100 and prints the value of Y% on each pass unless X% is equal to 10. When this is true, the GOTO statement branches to NEXT and the loop recycles.

In C, the *continue* statement can be used when it is necessary to start a new cycle without executing the remaining statements in the loop:

```
main( )
{

    int x, y;

    for (x = 0; x <= 100; ++x) {
        y = x * 10;
        if (x == 10)
            continue;
        printf("%d\n", y);
    }

}
```

The *continue* statement automatically branches to the top of the loop and causes the next cycle to begin. Any statements that are situated at a point past *continue* are not executed until accessed on the next pass. This is another example of how to avoid the use of *goto* in C.

SUMMARY

As is the case with BASIC, various types of loops are essential for writing many program applications in C language. Fortunately for the BASIC programmer who is learning C, the latter language sets up loops in a manner similar to the former. There is nothing especially mysterious about programming loops in C, nor in inserting statements into these loops. It seems that persons learning BASIC do a lot of playing around with FOR-NEXT loops; however, experimentation with WHILE-WEND is often ignored. In C, the *while* loop may be used more often than a *for* loop, so it is important to understand how both types work. The *do* loop is used far less often in C, but there are times when its use is advantageous, if not instrumental.

Although it is important to be intimately familiar with the standard loops in C, it is just as important to stay away from the *goto* statement. It may be used to advantage on rare occasions, but it is almost never used by good C language programmers. Such branches destroy the structure of C language programs, making them difficult to understand.

CHAPTER EIGHT

Character Conversion

In BASIC we are concerned primarily with two types of variables: numeric and string. Certainly, numeric variables can be broken down into integer, floating-point, and double-precision types. However, we have no such subcategories when dealing with string variables. In BASIC, a string variable may be used to hold a single number (in quotes), a single letter, or a string of letters, numbers, or a combination of both. The same is true in C, but C goes a few steps further and adds different variable types under what might be a major classification of "string" variables. As in BASIC, a character string array may be assigned a numeric value or an alphanumeric value. This value may consist of one or more characters. However, C also offers a *char* variable (as opposed to a *char* * or *char* array variable). Anytime you want a variable to contain a single character, you may declare it as *char* and use it to contain the character or the ASCII code of the character. In C, a *char* variable is handled like an integer. As a matter of fact, when you assign a specific character (by name) to a *char* variable, that variable contains the ASCII code of the character.

```
10  CH$="A"
20  PRINT CH$
```

This simple BASIC program assigns to string variable CH$ a value of "A." CH$ is then displayed on the screen using the PRINT statement.

```
main()
{

        char ch;
```

76

Character Conversion   Chap. Eight   **77**

```
        ch = 'A';

        printf("%c\n", ch);

}
```

This is one possible equivalent of the preceding program in BASIC using a *char* variable in C. We could also have used a string pointer, but why do this when a *char* variable will suffice? First, *ch* is declared a *char* type. This variable is assigned a value in the next line. Here the constant "A" is assigned as a single character. This is done using the apostrophe in place of the quotation marks. This means that *ch* is now equal to the character "A", or more accurately, *ch* is equal to the ASCII code (65) of the letter "A". The ASCII code is assigned from the computer set.

The *printf* function is used with a new type of conversion specification. The designator *%c* indicates that a character is to be printed (as opposed to a character string, floating-point value, or decimal integer). When the program is run, the capital letter "A" will be displayed on the screen.

```
        10  CH$="A"
        20  PRINT ASC(CH$)
```

This BASIC program uses the ASC function to cause the ASCII code of the first character contained in CH$ to be displayed on the screen. Since CH$ contains only one character, the letter "A", its ASCII code (65) will be displayed.

```
    main()
    {

        char ch;

        ch = 'A';

        printf("%d\n", ch);

    }
```

In C, there is no equivalent to the ASC function in BASIC, because none is really needed. As stated earlier, *char* types are treated just like *int* types for most operations, so conversion from character to ASCII code of character is handled within the *printf* line only. This program is identical to the preceding C program, except for the conversion specification in the *printf* line. We are supplying variable *ch* as the argument to *printf*. We already know that *ch* has been declared a *char* type. However, the conversion specification (*%d*) indicates that the value is to be displayed as an integer. Therefore, the integer value of *ch* (ASCII 65) is displayed on the screen.

```
        10  X%=65
        20  PRINT CHR$(X%)
```

78   Character Conversion   Chap. Eight

This BASIC program uses the CHR$ function to print the character whose ASCII value is contained in X%. ASCII code 65 represents the capital letter "A". Therefore, the CHR$ function will display "A" on the screen.

```
main( )
{

    int x;

    x = 65;

    printf("%c\n", x);

}
```

As was the case with the ASC function, there is no specialized function in C to convert a number to its character equivalent. None is necessary. In this program, *x* is declared in *int* type and is assigned a value of 65. Again the conversion is carried out using the *printf* function. The conversion specification used here (*%c*) means that a *character* is to be printed. The ASCII code of the character is contained in *int* variable *x*, which serves as the argument for *printf*. Therefore, the character represented by ASCII 65 (capital letter "A") is displayed on the screen.

To illustrate further the tie between *char* types and *int* types, the following C language program does exactly what the preceding one did:

```
main( )
{

    char x;

    x = 65;

    printf("%c\n", x);

}
```

Here, *x* is declared a *char* type and is then assigned the integer value of 65. The *printf* function uses a character-conversion specification and *char x* as its argument. Again, the letter "A" is displayed on the screen. Therefore, we know that a *char* type can be assigned a single character value by enclosing that character in apostrophes. It may also be assigned an integer value (0 to 255). Remember, even when a character type is assigned to a *char* variable, the variable actually receives the ASCII value of that character. There is nothing unusual about a *char* type being able to accept an integer value.

As discussed elsewhere, *putchar* can be used to display a single character on

Character Conversion   Chap. Eight   **79**

the screen, and *getchar* may be used to retrieve a single character from the keyboard. However, *putchar* will always output the character itself. It cannot be used to convert a character to its ASCII code value. *Putchar* can, however, be used to convert an ASCII value assigned to an *int* variable or a *char* variable to its character equivalent. The *scanf* function can also be used to retrieve a character from the console when used in the format

```
scanf("%c", &x);
```

where *x* has been declared a *char* type.

To avoid confusion, it is usually best to use an *int* variable anytime you need a variable to hold a single character or possibly an ASCII code of a character. Although *char* types can effectively be used in place of *int* types, and indeed, they are in certain specialized functions, this practice can cause confusion for the beginner.

```
10 I%=255
20 PRINT HEX$(I%)
```

This BASIC program uses the HEX$ function to print the hexadecimal value of the decimal value contained in I%. The HEX$ function will return the hexadecimal equivalent of decimal 255 in this example, which is "FF".

```
main()
{

    int i;

    i = 255;

    printf("%x\n", i);

}
```

As you may have realized by now, there is no equivalent of the HEX$ function in C. Again, none is needed. The conversion is accomplished using the *printf* function and the hexadecimal conversion specification (*%x*). The decimal value in variable *i* is converted to hexadecimal form being displayed on the screen. The displayed value will again be "FF".

```
10 I%=255
20 PRINT OCT$(I%)
```

This BASIC program uses the OCT$ function to print the octal value of I% on the screen. The octal value of decimal 255 is 377. This is the number that will be displayed.

80   Character Conversion   Chap. Eight

```
main()
{

    int i;

    i = 255;

    printf("%o\n", i);
}
```

Again, the *printf* function is used to make the needed conversion from decimal to octal in this example. The octal conversion specification (*%o*) is used to convert the decimal value of *i* to its octal equivalent of 377 before being displayed on the screen. The octal conversion specification is represented by "percent-oh" as opposed to "percent-zero."

The *scanf* function may be used to receive hexadecimal or octal values via the keyboard, as in

```
scanf("%x", &i);     "HEXADECIMAL"
scanf("%o", &i);     "OCTAL"
```

Remember to include the ampersand before each variable. All variables should previously have been declared as *int* types. As in BASIC, integers may be decimal, hexadecimal, or octal in base. Also, we may make assignments directly to *int* variables in hexadecimal or octal notation. Hexadecimal notation in BASIC requires that the value be preceded by "&H". This indicates that the value is hexadecimal. In C, a similar prefix is required to indicate a hexadecimal value, but in this case, it is "0x" (zero-*x*). Here, I am referring to the letter "*x*" preceded by zero. The letter *x* is a character, as opposed to a variable. The prefix notation for octal constants is simply the character zero. The following lines demonstrate such assignments:

```
int x, y;
x = 0xb800;     "HEXADECIMAL ASSIGNMENT"
y = 0377;       "OCTAL ASSIGNMENT"
```

SUMMARY

Hopefully, this chapter has cleared up some of the confusion experienced by BASIC programmers who are making the transition to C language. When first starting out in C, it seems that nearly everything you do is far more difficult than it is in BASIC. This would give the impression that C is a far more difficult language than BASIC. This is totally untrue. The C programming language is simply much more versatile than BASIC. We have already seen that performing numeric conversion is quite simple, and there is a brand new variable type (*char*) that can be used to hold single characters or integers. Most of the difficulty encountered by BASIC programmers

Summary   **81**

making the transition to C lies in the preconceived prejudices that have been garnered
by using BASIC exclusively. I have seen many BASIC programmers laboriously
convert hexadecimal numbers to decimal notation in order to input these values in
C programs. (Incidentally, these conversions were made using the HEX$ function
on a separate computer running under BASIC.) As you know, numeric variables in
BASIC can be directly assigned hexadecimal numbers, but for some reason, these
programmers thought the same was not true in C. C language does not offer all of
the conveniences found in BASIC statements through its standard set of functions,
but operationally, C is an easier language to use, and the equivalents of these BASIC
functions can usually be programmed quickly (if necessary at all).

The gist of this chapter is: Try not to treat new variable types or conversion
methods as problems, but rather as bonuses that only C can offer. In the long run,
these bonuses will make programming in C a much more pleasant experience. As a
matter of fact, whenever you return to BASIC, you undoubtedly will begin to miss
the flexibility of C.

CHAPTER NINE

C Language Arrays

Arrays in C language are formed and manipulated in a manner that should not be too foreign to BASIC programmers. The exceptions are CHAR arrays, of which there are no direct BASIC equivalents, and arrays of CHAR pointers, which correspond to BASIC's string arrays.

All C arrays must be declared before use and at the beginning of the program, as is true for all other types of variables. The following C program portion shows how an integer array of 40 elements is declared. This declaration takes the place of the BASIC DIM statement that dimensions an array:

```
int x[40];
```

which would be the same as

```
10 DIM X%[39]
```

in BASIC, assuming an OPTION BASE of default 0. In BASIC, the OPTION BASE statement declares the minimum value for array subscripts. The default value is zero. Therefore, the first element of an array is element zero. While the option base can be changed to 1 in BASIC, this does not apply to C. In the latter language, all array elements begin with position zero.

Notice that the C example specifies 40 elements, whereas the exact BASIC equivalent specifies 39. As we discussed in an earlier chapter, the value used in declaring a C array names a different quantity than the value used when DIMming a BASIC array. The C version names the total number of elements in the array (effectively), whereas the BASIC version names the highest array element position.

82

Multidimensional Arrays   **83**

In the C version, the first array position is 0 and the last is 39. This makes for a total of 40 elements (the value used in the declaration). In BASIC, the first element is 0 and the last element is 39. Again, there are 40 elements, but the value 39 in the BASIC array has named the last element position. Each array has 40 elements, which are counted from zero to 39. C requires the total number of elements when declaring an array, whereas BASIC requires the last element position.

The following BASIC program dimensions an array of 40 elements and assigns values to each element in a FOR-NEXT loop. It uses another loop to print each element value multiplied by 5:

```
10  DIM X%(39)
20  FOR I%=0 TO 39
40  X%(I%)=I%
50  NEXT I%
60  FOR I%=39 to 0 STEP -1
70  PRINT X%(I%)*5
80  NEXT I%
```

Each element is assigned a value of from 0 to 39 within the first loop, these values being counted by the loop. The second loop accesses each array position in reverse order and prints its value times 5.

The C language equivalent of this BASIC program is

```
main()
{

    int i, x[40];

    for (i = 0; i <= 39; ++i)
        x[i] = i;

    for (i = 39; i >= 0; --i)
        printf("%d\n", x[i] * 5);

}
```

This C language program duplicates the BASIC example. Note that brackets are used to enclose array subscripts in C. BASIC uses parentheses to do this, and it is common for beginning C programmers mistakenly to use parentheses instead of brackets in defining array positions. This usually leads to a jumble of error messages when the program is run or compiled. Some C environments will mistake an array for an undefined function when parentheses are used instead of brackets.

MULTIDIMENSIONAL ARRAYS

Multidimensional arrays in C are also handled along the same lines as those in BASIC. The C language equivalent of

84   C Language Arrays   Chap. Nine

```
10 DIM X%(39,39)
```

is

```
int x[40][40];
```

Both of these examples name a multidimensional array which contains a total of 1600 elements arranged in a 1×1 array table. The BASIC program line

```
40 X%(0,0)=14
```

is written in C as

```
x[0][0] = 14;
```

Although separate bracketed subscripts are used in C, this is not too great a transition to make from the subscripts being enclosed in a single set of parentheses, separated by commas in the BASIC designation. Note that, as in BASIC, arrays of other data types are handled in C exactly as the integer example above demonstrates. For instance, an array of doubles would be declared as

```
double x[40][40];
```

Arrays are often not used to good advantage in various programs written in both BASIC and C. There is nothing highly mysterious about their operation as long as one thinks of an array as a collection of data items stored in a predefined table and accessed according to these table coordinates.

CHAR ARRAYS

Char arrays were touched on in an earlier chapter, but for review purposes, these arrays in single-dimension form may be thought of as equivalent to string variables in BASIC. An array of characters may be accessed on a character-by-character basis or may be used as a complete string consisting of all characters from the first to the last. The end of the *char* string is signified by the NULL character (\0).

That is all fine and good, but what about the equivalent of string arrays in BASIC, as in

```
10 DIM A$(49)
```

We cannot write

```
char a[50]
```

Char Arrays   **85**

because this simply declares an array to hold a total of 50 characters, not 50 character strings. Here we resort to a multidimensional array, as in

```
char a[50][256];
```

This declares a multidimensional character array which is capable of holding 50 × 256 single characters. More important, it is capable of holding 50 character *strings*, each of which may contain up to 256 characters, including a NULL character signifying the end of the string. This value is chosen to align with BASIC's capability of holding a maximum of 255 characters in any character string.

Let's compare a BASIC program with a C program for fuller understanding:

```
10  DIM A$(49)
20  A$(14)="HELLO"
30  PRINT A$(14)
```

This BASIC program dimensions an array designed to hold up to 50 string values. The fifteenth element position, A$(14), is assigned a value of "HELLO". The last program line prints the value of A$(14).

The C language equivalent of this program is

```
main()
{

    char a[50][256];

    strcpy(a[14], "HELLO");

    printf("%s\n", a[14]);

}
```

It is not necessary to include the second dimension of the array as part of the argument to *strcpy()*. The argument of *a*[14] points to the start of the storage area at the fifteenth position (remember, we began counting at zero) in the array. Each array position names a memory location that will store up to 256 characters. The same is true when printing the value of *a*[14] using *printf*.

Now, how would we specify the first character in the string contained at *a*[14]? This requires access of the second array dimension, as in

```
x = a[14][0];
```

This assigns to *x*, which should have been declared a *char* or *int* variable, the ASCII value of the first character in the string pointed to by *a*[14]. The second character would be found at *a*[14][1], the third at *a*[14][2], and so on. The first dimension, *a*[14], gets us on the correct array line, so to speak. The second dimension takes us

86   C Language Arrays   Chap. Nine

through the character string on that line. In Chapter 11 we explain another way to declare an array that will hold many string values, but for now this is the way to program the equivalency of a BASIC language string array.

It is sometimes difficult to distinguish between an array of numbers and an array of characters. First of all, there is no basic difference. All of them hold numeric values, although in the case of a *char* array, these are integer values in the range 0 to 255. So although there is no difference in how these various arrays arrange their elements, there is a big difference in how they are accessed. For the most part, numeric arrays are accessed or read a single element at a time. But *char* arrays are usually read from beginning to end to extract a character string. Numeric arrays are usually "loaded" by reading in a single value at a time. This is also true of *char* arrays, but special functions are able to read in an entire string of characters as a unit. Functions such as *printf* are able to read them out in the same unit quantity.

Certainly, the characters that make up a string can be read individually. This is convenient for writing programs that mimic the MID$, RIGHT$, and LEFT$ functions in BASIC. However, when a program is accessing individual character positions, they will use the element brackets, as in $a[1]$. When the entire string of characters is being accessed, all that is used is the pointer to the beginning of the string, or a. This also applies to multidimensional *char* arrays, but the first-dimension brackets will usually be present. In such instances, a notation of $a[14][1]$ refers to the first element in the string pointed to by $a[14]$, whereas $a[14]$ without the second-dimension brackets is referring to the entire string pointed to by the $a[14]$ reference. Just remember, in a single-dimension *char* array, the presence of brackets refers to a single element. No brackets are a reference to the entire string as a unit. With double-dimension arrays, two sets of brackets access a single character, and a single set references the entire string.

The same criteria can also apply to numeric arrays, but not nearly as often. Sometimes it is necessary to pass an entire array to a function. In such instances, a single-dimension array name such as x is used as the argument. This will pass the entire contents of the array to the function, which can then access each individual element in the traditional manner. A multidimensional array can be passed in the same manner, or with the addition of the first-dimension element subscript, an entire row of values is passed.

In no instance can an entire array of numbers be printed as a string as would be the case with a *char* array. The latter is the only type of multielement array storage class that can be accessed as an entire unit. A numerical array is comprised of separate elements that, generally, must be accessed individually. *Char* array elements can be accessed individually or as a single string unit, depending on how the array argument is presented. For example,

```
main()
{

    char a[20];
```

Summary   **87**

```
        int x;

        strcpy(a, "STRING");

        for (x = 0; x <= 5; ++x)
            printf("%c\n", a[x]); /* Print individual characters */

        printf("%s\n", a); /* Print entire string as a unit */

}
```

This program declares a *char* array and copies "STRING" to its memory locations. Within the loop, each character is accessed individually and written to the screen as a *char* value. The last call to *printf* writes the entire string of characters to the screen as a single unit. This is not possible with any other type of array through the use of the standard C function set.

SUMMARY

With the exception of *char* types, arrays in C are very similar to those found in BASIC. The syntax is a bit different, but this can quickly be learned. It should take only a short while for you to become comfortable in handling array operations in C. We discuss managing arrays of character strings further in a subsequent chapter. This should enable you to grasp better the powerful text-handling capabilities of C language.

CHAPTER TEN

String Functions

C language offers a small set of portable functions that perform many of the most common string manipulations. Each function works with a sequence of characters that is terminated by a null byte (0), which is the definition of a string in C. C strings and strings in BASIC have many things in common, and some of the C functions used for string manipulation have direct equivalents in BASIC.

Strings and *char* arrays were briefly discussed earlier, but in this chapter we delve more deeply into this subject and explain each of the string utility functions found as a part of the standard C language function set.

STRCPY

The *strcpy()* function in C is the equivalent of the assignment operator (=) in BASIC when it is used to assign a value to a string variable. The BASIC program

```
10  A$="HELLO"
```

requires the *strcpy()* function when translated into C:

```
main()
{

        char a[10];

        strcpy(a, "HELLO");

}
```

88

Strcpy **89**

A char array is declared with 10 sequential bytes set aside for storing a character string. This will allow for a string of a maximum of nine printable characters and a null byte to signal the end of the string. The constant "HELLO" is stored somewhere in memory. *Strcpy()* locates the first byte in "HELLO", which is the letter "H", and copies it to the first storage location reserved for *a*. It then copies the second byte from the constant to the second storage position in *a*. This process continues until a null byte is copied. This terminates the *strcpy()* operation. The constant "HELLO" is stored by C as

H E L L O \o

When it is copied to the storage area reserved for *a*, the same sequence results. If you assume that the beginning storage location reserved for *a* is 100, then the sequence will be stored as

100	101	102	103	104	105	106	107	108	109
H	E	L	L	O	\o	**UNUSED STORAGE**			

Actually, the characters are stored as 1-byte integers with values of from 0 to 255, as in

100	101	102	103	104	105	106	107	108	109
72	69	76	76	79	0	**UNUSED STORAGE**			

Each of the integer values is the ASCII code for the characters in "HELLO".
The following example uses two *char* arrays:

```
main()
{

    char a[10], b[10];

    strcpy(a, "HELLO");
    strcpy(b, a);

}
```

The first array is assigned the value of the constant "HELLO". *Strcpy()* finds the storage location of the constant and copies it to the storage location set aside for *a*. Next, *b* is assigned the value of *a*, so the memory location of *a* is located and its contents are copied to the storage location for *b*. In each case, the source storage area is located and its contents copied to the target storage area.

Any time that a string value, be it a constant or contained in a *char* array, is to be assigned to a *char* array, the *strcpy()* function is used to handle this operation.

The assignment operator (=) does not apply in such cases as it does in BASIC or in C when numerical values are assigned to variables.

STRLEN

The *strlen*() function in C is equivalent to the LEN function in BASIC. Both return the total number of "printable characters" in a string. In C, the null character that terminates the string is not included as a part of the character count. *Strlen*() counts all characters up to the null byte. Like LEN, *strlen*() always returns an integer value. The following BASIC program will serve as a demonstration:

```
10  A$="HELLO"
20  X%=LEN(A$)
30  PRINT X%
```

This program will display a value of 5 on the screen, because there are five characters in "HELLO". The C equivalent is

```
main()
{

    int x;
    char a[10];

    strcpy(a, "HELLO");
    x = len(a);

    printf("%d\n", x);

}
```

The same value is displayed by this program, since the value of "HELLO" in *a* contains five characters prior to the null byte.

In each of the previous examples, arrays have been declared for 10-character storage. C requires *you* to determine the size of the maximum string length any array can hold. In BASIC, string variables are usually fixed at a maximum length of 255 characters. This is quite wasteful of memory storage, since the unused storage areas are still assigned to the variable. In C, the size of a *char* array will be determined by the maximum length of a string this array might be asked to store. A value of 10 was chosen for the previous examples, because this was more than adequate to store "HELLO". Actually, a value of 6 would also be adequate, since "HELLO" will be stored in 6 bytes of memory (including the null byte).

Strcat 91

STRCAT

BASIC allows strings to be added together in a mathematical way, as in

```
10  A$="PRO"
20  B$="GRAM"
30  A$=A$+B$
40  PRINT A$
```

This program displays the string "PROGRAM", which is the result of adding A\$ and B\$. We cannot do this in C or in most other languages. Such an operation is found only in BASIC. However, C does offer a utility function called *strcat()*, which can be used for this purpose. This function stands for *string concatenate*, which means to tack one string onto the end of another. The following program is a C language version of the one shown above:

```
main()
{

    char a[8], b[5];

    strcpy(a, "PRO");
    strcpy(b, "GRAM");

    strcat(a, b);

    printf("%s\n", a);

}
```

The arrays are declared with the absolute minimum of storage elements to properly effect the operation. Array *a* has eight elements and *b* has five. First, *strcpy()* is used to copy "PRO" to *a*. It is used again to copy "GRAM" to *b*. Then *strcat()* is called to copy the contents of *b* to the end of the string contained in *a*. After this call, *a* is equal to "PROGRAM\0". This is the value displayed on the screen.

Strcat() uses the null byte in the destination string (*a*) to determine where the concatenation occurs. Originally, this null byte is located at array position 3, which is the point at which *strcat()* begins copying the contents of *b*. This function copies *b* up to and including the null byte. The end result is a properly terminated string that includes the original contents of *a* plus the contents of *b*.

Suppose that you wished to add the values of several strings. The following BASIC program serves as an example:

```
10  A$="NEW"
20  B$="PRO"
30  C$="GRAM"
40  A$=A$+B$+C$
50  PRINT A$
```

92   String Functions   Chap. Ten

This time the string "NEW PROGRAM" is displayed. The first three characters
are assigned to A$, the next three to B$, and the last four are assigned to C$. Variable
A$ simply serves as a receptacle for the sum of B$ and C$. In C, this could be
written as

```
main()
{
    char a[12], b[4], c[5];

    strcpy(a, "NEW ");
    strcpy(b, "PRO");
    strcpy(c, "GRAM");

    strcat(a, b);
    strcat(a, c);

    printf("%s\n", a);

}
```

It is necessary to use *strcat()* twice in this example. After the first call, *a* is equal
to "NEW PRO". The second call to *strcat()* copies the contents of *c* onto the end
of the previously concatenated contents of *a*.

SPRINTF

The *printf* function has already been discussed in detail, but C also offers a version
that writes a formatted output to a string pointer or *char* array instead of the monitor
screen. The following BASIC program can be duplicated in C using *strcat()*, but a
more direct translation can be accomplished with *sprintf*:

```
10  B$="PRO"
20  C$="GRAM"
30  A$=B$+C$
40  PRINT A$
```

Here A$ simply acts as a receptacle for the sum of B$ and C$. The C version
could be written as

```
main()
{
    char a[8], b[4], c[5];

    strcpy(b, "PRO");
    strcpy(c, "GRAM");
```

Strcmp
93

```
sprintf(a, "%s%s", b, c);

printf("%s\n", a);

}
```

The *sprintf* function writes its formatted output to the char array named as its first argument. This is followed by the control string, which indicates that two string values are expected. These are provided by arguments *b* and *c*, which follow the control string. When *sprintf* is executed, *b* and *c* are written as a single string to *a*. The *sprintf* line could also have been written as

```
sprintf(a, "%s %s", b, c);
```

This would make *a* equal to "PRO GRAM". *Sprintf* works just like *printf* in that the control string determines the exact format of the write. For example,

```
sprintf(a, "%s%s", c, b);
```

would result in *a* being equal to "GRAMPRO". The *sprintf* function provides a great deal of flexibility in handling complex assignments to *char* arrays. It combines the traits of *strcpy*() and *strcat*() in a single function, which may have a multitude of different arguments. It is also ideal for converting numeric values to string values, as in

```
sprintf(a, "%d %f %d", 14, 28.3, 32);
```

This results in *a* being equal to "14 28.3 32".

STRCMP

The *strcmp*() function compares two string values and returns an integer value to indicate whether or not the strings match, whether the first is smaller than the second, or whether it is larger. In BASIC, we can use numeric operators such as $=$, $<>$, $<=$, or $>=$ to compare two strings. In C, this type of string comparison requires the *strcmp*() function.

In most implementations, *strcmp*() will return a value of zero (0) if the strings are identical. If the two are not equal and the first unequal character in the first argument has a higher ASCII value than the same byte in the second string, a positive value is returned. If the byte in the first argument is a lower ASCII value than that in the second, a negative value is returned.

The *strcmp*() function is used in a format of

```
x = strcmp(a, b);
```

94   String Functions   Chap. Ten

where *x* is an *int* variable and *a*, *b* are pointers to *char* arrays or pointers to character strings. For example,

```
main()
{

        char a[10], b[10];
        int x;

        strcpy(a, "HELLO");
        strcpy(b, "HELLO");

        x = strcmp(a, b);

        printf("%d\n", x);

}
```

will display the value of zero (0) on the screen, because *a* is equal to *b*. If the value of *a* were changed to "hello", then *x* would be equal to a positive value, because the letter "h" has a higher ASCII value than "H". If *a* were equal to "ARM", a negative value would be returned to *x*. It is usually not necessary to know the exact values returned (other than zero for a match), as the following program will demonstrate:

```
main()
{

    int x;
    char a[80], b[10];

    strcpy(b, "HELLO");

    gets(a);

    x = strcmp(a, b);

    if (x == 0)
        printf("The two are identical\n");
    else if (x < 0)
        printf("Smaller\n");
    else
        printf("Larger\n");

}
```

This program will indicate whether the string obtained from the keyboard is equal to, larger than, or less than "HELLO" on a byte-by-byte comparison.

SUMMARY

Although the standard set of string utility functions is small, most microcomputer implementations of C also offer additional functions that may be used to convert numbers to strings, compare only a portion of character strings, and so on. All of these probably use *strcpy*, *strlen*, *sprintf*, and *strcmp* as building blocks. With the basic string functions discussed in this chapter, hundreds of specialized functions that address string operations can be built. The standard set of string functions is small, but each is very powerful. Fortunately, their uses are quite easy to learn.

CHAPTER ELEVEN

Pointers and Memory Access

C language pointer operations encompass an area that generally tends to give the beginning programmer the most difficulty. Although pointers are used in BASIC, their implementation is hidden from the programmer. However, C language allows pointers to be specifically programmed and used to great advantage. Pointer operations in C are responsible for a major part of the versatility associated with this programming language.

Simply put, a pointer is a special type of variable that points to a specific place in memory. Typically, a pointer points to a part of memory where a value is stored or where one is to be stored. Remember, a pointer is not directly equal to any user-defined value, but rather the place in memory where such a value is stored.

In C, *character* pointers are used quite often. Such pointers are very similar in use to CHAR arrays, which were discussed earlier. As a matter of fact, CHAR pointers and CHAR arrays may be treated as one and the same in many C operations.

The following program example shows how a character pointer is declared and used within a simple C program:

```
main()
{

    char *a;

    a = "hello";

    printf("%s\n", a);

}
```

Pointers and Memory Access   Chap. Eleven   **97**

First, variable *a* is declared a CHAR pointer. This is done by using the unary operator, which is represented by an asterisk (*). The unary operator specifies a pointer as opposed to a standard CHAR variable. This special variable is now available to point to a specific place in memory, which will contain a *string* of values that represent printable characters (ASCII 0 to 255). The end of the string is signified by a null character (\0) just as it is when setting up a CHAR array.

When a character pointer is declared, it points to a random location in memory. To make proper use of a pointer, it is necessary to give it something tangible to point to. In this case, the word "hello" is provided. This is done just as it would be in BASIC, through the use of the assignment operator (=) and the string constant enclosed in double quotes.

Do not be misled into thinking that the pointer is somehow equal to the word "hello". It is *not*! Rather, *a* points to the location where the computer has stored the constant "hello". It should be remembered that a pointer must point to something that is already in existence. It differs from a standard variable in that it can hold nothing. It only points to something that is already stored in memory or to a memory location, which has been set aside for future storage. Standard variables, when declared, have storage space set aside for them. For instance, an INT variable automatically has 16 bits of storage set aside in memory when such a variable is declared, assuming the use of a standard MS-DOS microcomputer. However, such storage space is not set aside for a pointer.

The constant "hello" is actually written into the program, and when this program is run the computer must allocate a place in memory to store this constant. It is not important to know where the constant is stored as long as we know that *a* points to its location. When the *printf* function is called, notice that the pointer is treated just as though it were a CHAR array variable. The pointer points to the memory location that contains the first character in the string "hello". All following memory locations are read sequentially until the null character is detected. This marks the end of the string and *printf* is exited.

Let's examine pointers in more detail, using the previous program as a further example. Assume that the constant "hello" is stored in RAM memory at location 15,000. This means that the letter "h" resides at 15,000, while the letters "e", "l", "l", "o" are found at 15,001, 15,002, 15,003, and 15,004, respectively. There is also one additional character that is stored at 15,005. This is the null character (\0), which signifies the end of the character string in memory. Pointer *a* points to location 15,000. This is the start of the character string. When used to represent a string value (as opposed to each character that makes up the string), all memory locations from and including 15,000 are read until the null character is reached.

One can quickly see the relationship between character pointers and character arrays. This relationship is actual rather than symbolic, and this is the reason why character pointers and CHAR arrays may be treated as being the same in many C operations. These especially involve functions that accept character strings as arguments.

However, character pointers and CHAR arrays must also be thought of as

98 Pointers and Memory Access   Chap. Eleven

completely different within the context that one is a pointer with no storage space set aside, and the other is a variable with a programmed amount of space set aside for storage. The following program does the same as the preceding one, but in this case a CHAR array is used instead of a pointer:

```
main()
{

    char a[10];

    strcpy(a, "hello");

    printf("%s\n", a);

}
```

Here, the *strcpy* function is used to copy "hello" into the storage location set aside specifically for the CHAR array. From this point on, the access by *printf* is the same as before. We cannot make a direct assignment with a CHAR array (through use of the assignment operator) as we did with the pointer. In this example, the constant "hello" is contained in one memory location and the storage space set aside for the CHAR array is at another. In other words, the constant is copied into the storage area represented by the array. Using a pointer, no copying of storage area takes place. The pointer simply directs attention to the constant at its original place in memory.

The following is an example of the improper use of a pointer:

```
main()
{

    char *a;                    WRONG!

    strcpy(a, "hello");

    printf("%s\n", a);

}
```

This program mistakenly uses a pointer as though it were a CHAR array. The *strcpy* function copies data from one memory location to another. This assumes that the target location is large enough in sequential memory spaces to hold that which is obtained from the source. This works fine for CHAR arrays, but remember that pointers do not have space automatically set aside. When first declared, they point to a random location in memory. A better way of thinking of this is to say that unassigned pointers can point to any place in memory, including certain areas that are already in use. An improper use of pointers, as the program above demon-

Pointers and Memory Access   Chap. Eleven   **99**

strates, could result in valuable memory locations being overwritten. This can cause the entire program to "crash." At worst, it can write over that portion of memory which designates disk files and cause them to be lost. Frequently, the program will run just fine. In such instances the programmer has gotten off lucky, because the pointer was randomly directed to a safe area of memory.

Here is another program that shows improper use of a pointer:

```
main()
{

        char *a;                    WRONG!

        gets(a);

        printf("%s\n", a);

}
```

In this example, the *gets* function is used to read the keyboard input. The intention here is to *assign* the pointer the value of the keyboard string. Again, you may get away with this if the declared pointer happens to access an unused portion of memory, but this is bad and potentially disastrous programming. Some compilers and interpreters will detect such an error. Most will not. The *gets* function reads each character received from the keyboard into an area of memory. The pointer declaration does not set aside memory space for this purpose. If *a* had been declared a CHAR array, there would be no problem, assuming that there were enough array elements to contain the keyboard input. However, a pointer should not be used to "hold" anything. (*Note*: Later in this chapter we explain how pointers can be directed to point to a special area of memory set aside for storage using memory allocation functions. The rules outlined in this chapter apply to pointers that have been declared and point to "random" areas of RAM memory.)

From this discussion it should be clear that pointers are special variables that are used specifically to point to certain areas of memory. Actually, all variables, be they *int*, *double*, *char*, and so on, also point to areas of memory where their assigned values are stored. When any variable is declared, space is set aside to store whatever quantities they are designed to represent. On the other hand, a pointer may be thought of as a free agent. Upon declaration, it points to a random area of memory. But a pointer is not tied to a single area of memory as is a common variable. It can be made to point anywhere. A pointer carries no storage space with it, so it can be used to move all around RAM memory to allow retrieval of previously written data or to allow for data to be written at these locations.

Character pointers can be used to good advantage in many applications, especially where it is desirable to count through each character position. The following program will begin to demonstrate this principle:

100   Pointers and Memory Access   Chap. Eleven

```
main()
{

    char *a;

    a = "hello";

    printf("%s\n", a);
    printf("%c\n", *a);

}
```

In this example, a character pointer is declared and points to the beginning of "hello". The first *printf* line prints the string pointed to by *a*. The second *printf* statement prints **a*. Again, the unary operator is used, but this time it is not to make a pointer declaration. Notice also that the second *printf* line uses the *%c* conversion specification rather than *%s*, which appears in the preceding line.

When a pointer is used with the unary operator, this indicates that the memory contents (an integer) of one element in the string is to be read. The first *printf* line will cause the word "hello" to appear on the screen. The next line will display the letter "h", the initial character pointed to by **a*.

We can take this a step further and actually count through each element of the string accessed by the pointer. This is done using the increment operator (++). If **a* points to the first character in the string "hello", then **a++* counts the pointer to the second element. Another **a++* counts on to the third element, and so on, until the end of the string is reached. The following programs demonstrate this:

```
main()
{

    char *a;
    int x;

    a = "hello";

    for (x = 0; *a != '\0'; ++x)
        printf("%c\n", *a++);
```

or

```
main()
{

    char *a;
    int x;

    a = "hello";
```

Pointers and Memory Access   Chap. Eleven   **101**

```
            while (*a != '\0') {
                    printf("%c\n", *a)
                    *a++;
            }


    }
```

The result of either program is to print

                        h
                        e
                        l
                        l
                        o

on the monitor screen. Each character in the string is accessed individually, displayed, and followed by a linefeed.

It should be understood that *a++ points to the first character in the string and then counts *a by one. After this operation, *a now points to the second character in the string. With each incremental operation, *a points to the next character in the string. This is an exercise in changing the location in memory to which the pointer points.

The following program does the same as the preceding two:

```
    main()
    {

        char a[6];
        int x;

        strcpy(a, "hello");

        for (x = 0; a[x] != '\0'; ++x)
                printf("%c\n", a[x]);


    }
```

All of these programs demonstrate a method whereby each character in a character string may be accessed individually. This is somewhat reminiscent of the MID$ function in BASIC, which can access individual characters or subgroups of characters.

Pointers to character strings in C are actually much easier to use for manipulation of the individual characters than the previous pointer examples show. Instead of using a *for* loop to display the individual characters, a *while* loop makes for easier programming:

102 Pointers and Memory Access   Chap. Eleven

```
main()
{

    char *a;

    a = "hello";

    while (*a != '\0')
            printf("%c\n", *a++);

}
```

The *while* statement portion of this program could also have been written

```
while (*a != '\0') {
     printf("%c\n", *a);
     *a++;
}
```

The latter version may be a bit easier to understand, as it increments the pointer in a separate line. The former example prints the character pointed to and then increments *a* in one statement. This is typical of the versatility of C, but such versatility often makes certain C constructs difficult for the beginner to understand.

One must be cautious when assigning pointers. The following BASIC program will help to set up an example:

```
10  A$="hello"
20  B$=A$
30  PRINT B$
40  A$="goodbye"
50  PRINT B$
```

Here A$ is assigned an initial value of "hello", then B$ is assigned a value of A$. Therefore, when line 30 directs the printing of the value of B$, the string "hello" will appear on the screen. Next, A$ is reassigned a value of "goodbye". Again, B$ is printed and it still equals "hello".

In C we can do the same thing with pointers:

```
main()
{

    char *a, *b;

    a = "hello";
    b = a;
    printf("%s\n", b);
    a = "goodbye";
    printf("%s\n", b);

}
```

Pointers and Memory Access   Chap. Eleven   **103**

Again, the string "hello" will be displayed twice. However, let's try a slightly different approach:

```
main()
{

    char a[20], *b;

    strcpy(a, "hello");

    b = a;

    printf("%s\n", b);

    strcpy(a, "goodbye");

    printf("%s\n", b);

}
```

In this example, only one pointer is used. There is also a CHAR array or array of characters. The *strcpy* function is used to copy the constant "hello" into the array. Then pointer *b* is assigned to *a*. This means that *b* will point to the memory location set aside for the array. When *b* is first used with *printf*, the string "hello" is found at the location to which it points. Therefore, this string is displayed on the screen. However, another *strcpy* function is used to change the value of the array to "goodbye". Again, *printf* is used with pointer *b* as its argument. This time, the displayed string is "goodbye". The only assignment to *b* was the memory location of the array. By changing the value of the array(*a*), we have also changed what *b* points to. The assignment line of *b* = *a* is the same as saying that *b* will be equal to anything *a* is equal to.

This did not occur in the initial program, which used two pointers, because *a* was assigned the memory location of a constant. Here *b* was always equal to the constant that appeared at that memory location. When *a* was later reassigned another constant value, *b* still pointed to that memory location which held the word "hello". In the second example, *strcpy* was used to *copy* the contents from one memory location to another, the latter being that assigned to the CHAR array. The pointer, in turn, was assigned the memory location of the array and *not* that of the constant which was copied to the array. The end result was a pointer that pointed to whatever the array contents were.

Throughout this discussion, the fact that a pointer can point to any area of available memory has been stressed. We have learned that when a pointer points to a character string, it is possible to retrieve each character in the string individually. Since individual characters are stored as integer values in the value range 0 to 255, we could also display the memory contents of a string as integer values, as in

104 Pointers and Memory Access   Chap. Eleven

```
main()
{

    char *a;

    a = "hello";

    while (*a != '\0')
        printf("%d\n", *a++);

}
```

This program will display the ASCII values of the five characters that make up the word "hello". What has happened here? It may not be obvious, but the pointer has been used to PEEK into memory and return the values at the location where "hello" was stored. If a compiler or interpreter is used that allows free access to all portions of memory (instead of a 64K segment), then pointers may be used to PEEK into any area of memory and to POKE as well!

In order to peek or poke certain areas of memory, it is first necessary to direct a pointer to the desired area. All past examples of pointer operations have directed pointers toward areas of memory that were set aside to store constants. We do not know exactly where these areas are, because the compiler or interpreter simply sets aside space where it happens to be available. In these operations, it is not necessary to know the specific locations of this storage space in memory. However, for peek and poke operations, we must first "aim" the pointer at a specific location.

To direct a pointer to a specific memory location, we assign it the value of that location. It is really quite simple, as the following program demonstrates:

```
main()
{

    char *a;

    a = (char *) 14500;

    printf("%d\n", *a);

}
```

This is the C equivalent of the BASIC program

10 PRINT PEEK(14500)

assuming a DEF SEG value of 0. The pointer is first declared. It is then directed to point to absolute memory location 14500. Most compilers and interpreters will require the cast operator (*char* *) so as not to confuse the executing environment. Most compilers will generate a "warning" if the cast operator is omitted, but the program will execute properly. The RUN/C interpreter treats the absence as an

Pointers and Memory Access   Chap. Eleven   **105**

error and execution will halt. Now *a* points to memory location 14500. To read
the value at this location, we simply print *a*. From an earlier discussion, we learned
that this will return the value of the first character *a* points to. The conversion
specification in the *printf* line uses %*d*, which means that the value read at this
location will be displayed as an integer.

Using a pointer directed to a specific location in memory, this program has
been able to peek that memory location. Remember, the memory location must be
provided in absolute form. MS-DOS machines divide memory into 64K segments.
In BASIC, the DEF SEG statement is used to choose the segment within which
we wish to operate. For example, in

```
10 DEF SEG = &HB800
20 PRINT PEEK(14)
```

DEF SEG specifies the 64K segment beginning at 47104 decimal or &HB800, and
PEEK reads the memory location at byte 14 in this segment. This might lead one
to believe that the absolute memory location is 47104 + 14, or 47118. This is totally
incorrect, however, because MS-BASIC segment specifications use a truncated form.
BASIC adds a zero to the end of hexadecimal segment values to get the absolute
address. The addition of this zero is the same as multiplying the assigned segment
value by 16. So the absolute memory location of &HB800 + 14 is &HB800 * 16 +
14, or &HB8000 + 14. In decimal form, this would be 47104 * 16 + 14, or 753664.

The BASIC program shown above could be written in C as

```
main()
{

    char *a;

    a = (char *) 0xb80001 + 14;

    printf("%d\n", *a);

}
```

It could also have been written as

```
main()
{

    char *a;

    a = (char *) 0xb80001;

    printf("%d\n", *(a + 14));

}
```

106 Pointers and Memory Access Chap. Eleven

The latter representation causes the pointer to point to the fourteenth character or element from 0xb8000. Notice that both programs follow the hexadecimal specification with the letter "*l*". This tells the compiler or interpreter that this constant is a long integer. An uppercase "L" is also acceptable, but one or the other must follow any long constant. This gets back to an earlier discussion in which we stated that C likes integers best. If we use values other than integers, we usually must specify that the constant being assigned is other than an integer. In some interpreters or compilers it is not necessary to specify a long constant when an assignment is being made to a previously declared long variable. However, it is good to get in the habit of following *all* long constant values with an "*l*" or "L". It cannot hurt to do so.

The following program will peek 1000 consecutive memory locations starting at absolute location 0xb8000. This is the start of the graphics screen for the IBM Personal Computer and most compatibles:

```
main()
{

    char *a;

    for (a = (char *) 0xb80001; a <= (char *)
        0xb80001 + 1000; ++a)
        printf("%d\n", *a);

}
```

This program uses a simple *for* loop which assigns pointer *a* the memory locations that we desire to peek. On each pass of the loop, the integer value of the character pointed to by *a* is displayed on the screen. The program could also have been written as

```
main()
{

    char *a;
    int x;

    a = (char *) 0xb80001;

    for (x = 0; x <= 1000; ++x)

        printf("%d\n", *(a + x));

}
```

In the second example, *a* is initially set up to point to the beginning memory segment. This initial location never changes. However, integer variable *x* is counted from 0 to 1000 by the *for* loop. The *printf* function accesses the memory location of *a*

Pointers and Memory Access   Chap. Eleven   **107**

with an offset of x. This is more similar to the method by which a succession of locations are peeked in BASIC.

We can also poke memory locations using pointers in C. The following program demonstrates this:

```
main()
{

        char *a;

        a = (char *) 14500;

        *a = 255;

}
```

This is the same as the following BASIC program:

```
10  POKE 14500,255
```

assuming that DEF SEG is equal to 0. This is very similar to C language peek operations using pointers, but instead of reading the value pointed to by $*a$, the value is assigned. Earlier, you were cautioned that pointers contain no memory storage of their own and that assignments to pointers can cause memory locations to be overwritten. This is exactly what is being done with the poke operation. One memory value is being overwritten by another.

The following program will fill the IBM PC graphics screen with solid white by poking each of the 16,385 memory locations with character 255. *Note*: To perform these types of operations using the RUN/C interpreter, you must first use the command SET TRUST ON. This will deactivate the safety feature and allow you to access any area of memory:

```
main()
{

        char *a;
        int x;

        a = (char *) 0xb80001;

        for (x = 0; x <= 16384; ++x)
                *(a + x) = 255;

}
```

Here the start of memory is at absolute location $0xb8000l$. This serves as a reference point throughout the rest of the program. Variable x is counted from 0 to 16384, which marks the beginning and ending offsets of the graphics screen. Within the

108 Pointers and Memory Access Chap. Eleven

for loop, the value of *x* is added to the value of *a*. A value of 255 overwrites whatever is currently found at the accessed memory location. Note that this program is very similar to a previous one that read 1001 successive memory locations. Again, for any of these peek or poke operations to work properly with the RUN/C interpreter, the TRUST mode must be set to ON. Make absolutely certain that the programs are input as shown in these pages, and do not go poking into random memory locations.

Most C compilers and interpreters do offer *peek* ( ) and *poke* ( ) functions, although these were not a part of the original language. Such functions were and still are necessary, because the most efficient microcomputer implementations of C on MS-DOS machines restrict memory access to a 64K segment. The *peek* ( ) and *poke* ( ) functions allow access to memory outside this segment. This is usually handled by machine language routines called from C rather than by functions written in C proper. Nevertheless, the RUN/C *peek* ( ) and *poke* ( ) functions could be written as follows, assuming that the TRUST mode is on, giving free access to all memory:

```
peek(x)
long x;
{

        char *a;

        a = (char *) x;

        return(*a);

}

poke(x, y)
long x;
int y;
{

        char *a;

        a = (char *) x;
        *a = y;

}
```

With the TRUST mode set to ON, these functions would work just like those already contained in the RUN/C function set. It can be seen that pointers and memory access go hand in hand. Later in this chapter you will see how pointers play a role in memory allocation.

Although *char* pointers have been discussed to this point, C allows the programming of pointers of any type. Therefore, we may have *int* pointers, *float* pointers,

Pointers and Memory Access   Chap. Eleven   **109**

double pointers, *long* pointers, and so on. The following program demonstrates the use of an *int* pointer:

```
main()
{

    int *x, y;

    y = 14;
    x = &y;

    printf("%d\n", *x);

}
```

This program declares *x* to be an integer pointer (i.e., pointer to a place in memory sized to contain an integer value). A standard *int* variable, *y*, is also declared. It is assigned a value of 14. Next, *x* is directed to point to the memory location set aside for *y*. We get the memory address of *y* by preceding this variable with an ampersand (&). After this assignment, *x* points to the same place in memory that *y* does. The next line prints the value in memory to which *x* points. This will be 14, since this was the value assigned to *y*.

    Here is another demonstration:

```
main()
{

    int *x, y;

    y = 22;
    x = &y;

    printf("%d\n", *x);

    y = 18;

    printf("%d\n", *x);

}
```

This follows the same routine as the last program, but after *x is displayed the first time, the value of *y* is reassigned. When *x is displayed again, it will be equal to the new value of *y*. The pointer assignment line *x* = &*y* means that *x will always be equal to the value of *y*, regardless of how many times *y* is assigned or reassigned. Pointer *x* points to that location in memory which is used to store all assignments made to *y*. We can do the same thing with other types of pointers, as in

110 Pointers and Memory Access Chap. Eleven

```
main()
{

        double *x, y;

        y = 13.228;
        x = &y;

        printf("%lf\n", *x);

}
```

Both the variable and the pointer have been declared double. Therefore, a larger area of memory is set aside to store a double-precision floating-point value (64 bits on most MS-DOS implementations). Once the proper pointer assignment has been made, pointer x will point to the memory location reserved to hold assignments to y.

Remember, when a standard numeric variable is preceded by the ampersand (&), this is a signal to the compiler or interpreter to return or reference the memory location of that variable. The designation $&y$ is a pointer in itself. It discloses the memory location of y. To actually see this memory location access, the following program is presented:

```
main()
{

        int x;

        x = 14;

        printf("%d\n", &x);

}
```

The *printf* function argument is $&x$ or the start of the memory location set aside for integer variable x. Using RUN/C on my IBM Personal Computer, the value of 21754 is displayed on the monitor screen. It may be different on your machine, but in any event, this is the start of the memory location set aside when x was declared. Memory locations will always be integer values, but often they are long integers.

The following program shows another trick:

```
main()
{

        int x;

        x = 22;

        printf("%d\n", peek((long) &x));

}
```

Memory Allocation Functions   **111**

or

```
main()
{

    int x;
    char *a;

    x = 22;
    a = (char *) &x;

    printf("%d\n", *a);

}
```

Both of these programs peek at the contents of memory set aside for holding values assigned to int x. In the first example, the RUN/C *peek*() function is used. A cast operator coerces the integer memory location of x to a long integer in order to fulfill *peek*()'s argument requirements. The value returned by *peek*() will be the same as the value assigned to x, since *peek*() is reading storage space assigned to x. In the second example, the same thing takes place, except that a *char* pointer is used instead of the *peek*() function. *Char* *a* is made to point to the same memory location assigned to x. Again the value of x is returned.

   Note: These programs will return the actual value assigned to x provided that this value is not more than 255. Either PEEK routine returns only a single byte from memory, whereas RUN/C uses 2 bytes to represent integer values. If a value is greater than 255 (the maximum value of a single byte of memory), the second byte is used. For instance, if $x = 256$, the accessed memory location would be equal to 0 and the next sequential byte would be equal to 1. This is the 2-byte code for integer 256.

MEMORY ALLOCATION FUNCTIONS

Closely tied with pointer operations are the memory allocation functions. As has been stated again and again, pointers can be made to point to any area of memory. Typically, pointers are "aimed" at portions of memory that have already been written to or where space has been set aside for storage. But suppose that we want a pointer to point to an area of memory that can be set aside specifically for storage and use the pointer to access this area. Here is where the memory allocation functions come into use. These are especially desirable when it is necessary to set aside a large portion of memory, supposedly to store a lot of data. Now this can be done by declaring a large *char* array, but array space is limited, as a certain amount is set aside for this purpose. Once it has been used up, the space set aside must either be enlarged (if possible) or you must resort to another means of storage.

   The UNIX memory allocation functions allow areas of memory to be set aside

112   Pointers and Memory Access   Chap. Eleven

and accessed by a pointer. We do not specify what locations in memory are to be used for this storage, only that we want so many bytes of storage space. These functions attempt to locate such an area that is not currently allocated to some other purpose. When an area or "block" is found, the function allocates the desired number of sequential bytes and returns a pointer to the first byte in this block.

The standard memory allocation functions include *malloc*() and *calloc*(). Many compilers designed for microcomputers may have others that are more efficient than these, as they are designed for a particular type of computer or hardware configuration. Generally, these specialized functions are not portable. However, *malloc*() and *calloc*() are a part of the standard C language function set and should be supported by every compiler and interpreter.

Malloc() allocates a block of memory in a way that is compatible with the UNIX operating system. Admittedly, *malloc*() can be quite inefficient when many small blocks of memory are allocated from a single program, but it provides a universal function with which to base a discussion on memory allocation.

Calloc() does about the same thing, except that it clears or sets to zero each byte in the block allocated. *Calloc*() might be used in place of *malloc*() if it is necessary to know the length of a string of data that is written to the allocated memory location with the count stopping at the first cleared byte. Otherwise, the two are identical.

The following C program demonstrates the use of *malloc*():

```
main()
{

    char *a, *malloc();

    a = malloc(800);

    strcpy(a, "Now is the time");

}
```

This example calls *malloc*() to set aside a block of 800 bytes. A *char* pointer, *a*, is assigned the return location from *malloc*(). This names the location of the first byte in the reserved block.

The next line uses *strcpy*() to copy the string argument to the memory location pointed to by *a*. You will remember an earlier discussion in this chapter that warned against copying anything to pointers because they do not necessarily point to an area of memory large enough to hold a value. This could cause a dangerous overwrite of memory currently in use. However, this case is different. Pointer *a* now has size. It points to an area of memory that contains 800 bytes set aside for access by this pointer only. It is now perfectly safe to copy data to the pointer's location, just as would be done with a declared *char* array.

This brings up another and more efficient way to program the equivalent of a string array in BASIC. The following program will set up this discussion:

Memory Allocation Functions **113**

```
10  DIM A$(50)
20  FOR X%=0 TO 50
30  INPUT A$(X%)
40  NEXT X%
```

This example dimensions an array that will hold up to 51 strings. A loop is entered, and on each pass user input is received from the keyboard and read into each array element. We can accomplish the same thing in C by using a multidimensional char array, but a better way might be to establish an array of *char* pointers. The following program does just this:

```
main()
{

    int x;
    char *a[51], *malloc();

    for (x = 0; x <= 50; ++x)
        gets(a[x] = malloc(256));

}
```

The declaration *char* *a*[51] sets up an array of *char* pointers. On each pass of the *for* loop, *gets* is used to read the keyboard input. The argument to *gets* is *a*[*x*]. But another operation takes place before data are actually read into *a*[*x*]. The location in memory to which *a*[*x*] points is returned by *malloc*(). This function sets aside a maximum storage area of 256 bytes per pointer. This matches BASIC's ability to assign up to 255 characters to a string variable. The extra byte is for the NULL terminator character. Each pointer is "sized" or directed to a place in memory with adequate storage to hold the input string at the keyboard.

This program duplicates the BASIC example and is the way CBREEZE would handle the translation, but it is a bit wasteful. After all, the input string probably will not be 255 characters in length. The following program demonstrates a more efficient way of doing the same thing:

```
main()
{

    int x;
    char *a[51], b[256], * malloc();

    for (x = 0; x <= 50; ++x) {
        gets (b);
        a[x] = malloc (strlen(b) + 1);
        strcpy(a, b);
        }

}
```

114   Pointers and Memory Access   Chap. Eleven

An array of pointers is still declared but so is a *char* array of 256 character positions, maximum. The *gets* function reads its input in the *char* array, then the pointer is sized using *malloc()*. The number of bytes that *malloc()* sets aside is determined by the length of the string in *b*. If the input read to *b* is 40 characters in length, the pointer is sized to 40 plus 1 bytes. (Note: the extra byte is for the null character.) The contents of *b* are copied to the pointer's allocated area of memory, which is the exact size to store those contents. Of course, this assumes that you will not be performing any other operations on the pointer, such as copying another string to the end of what is already there. The pointer is not sized to accept a larger string.

The following C program demonstrates another use for pointers and memory allocation functions in C. It sets aside a large block of memory and then writes information to fill the screen. The screen is then saved in this allocated memory block, a byte at a time. Later, the screen is cleared, but the saved screen still resides in that block of memory. The last stage of the program restores the erased screen by reading bytes from that block back to the screen memory location:

```
/*  BE  SURE  TO  SET  TRUST  MODE  TO  ON  */

main()
{

        char *a, *b;
        int x;

        a = (char *) 0xb00001;   /*Beginning of video memory */
        b = malloc(4000);

        for (x = 0; x <= 23; ++x)
            printf("Filling screen with data\n");

        for (x = 0; x <= 3999; ++x)
            *(b + x) = *(a + x); /* Read screen bytes to *b bytes */

        cls();

        for (x = 0; x <= 3999; ++x)
            *a++ = *b++; /* Put bytes from block back on screen */

}
```

This program was written especially for the RUN/C interpreter when used with the IBM PC monochrome monitor. Note that *malloc()* is not declared a *char* pointer, because this is not legal in RUN/C. This declaration will be mandatory for most other C environments.

The two *char* pointers are declared and *a* is made to point to the beginning of video memory at 0xb0000. This is a long integer value and the letter "*l*" follows it to let the environment know that the constant is not an integer. *Malloc()* is called and returns a pointer to a block of 4000 bytes of memory to *b*. Next, the screen is

Memory Allocation Functions

filled with a quoted phrase, repeated over and over. Once the write is complete, another loop is entered. This one steps *a* through 4000 successive memory locations comprising the screen. The byte at that screen location is read into *b*, which is also stepped a byte at a time. When this loop is exited, each of the screen memory bytes has been copied to the memory block.

The screen is now cleared and is supposedly lost forever. However, the next loop performs a reversal of the previous one. During this stage of the program, the contiguous bytes from the allocated block of memory are read into the screen memory. Put simply, the block contains a copy of the original screen, so the block contents are transferred back to screen memory. The end result is the recreated screen display that was present before *cls*() was executed.

The read and write will take a few minutes because of the slow speed of the interpreter, but the screen is, indeed, captured, stored, and called back when needed. The same thing would have taken place if *calloc*() were used instead of *malloc*(). *Calloc*() accepts a two-part argument in the format

```
calloc(number of elements, element length)
```

The first argument is simply multiplied by the second to arrive at the total number of bytes to reserve, but this type of notation allows the second argument to be the *sizeof*() function, which returns the bytes required for storing various data types. This allows for more portability, since one system may use 2 bytes to store integers and another may use 4. A call such as

```
calloc(100, sizeof(int));
```

sets aside enough memory to store 100 integer values. If a system requires 2 bytes for each integer, a total of 200 bytes are set aside. But if a program using this line were transferred to a system that used 4-byte integers, *sizeof*() would return a value of 4 and a total of 400 bytes would be reserved. This function is more portable than is *malloc*(), although the latter could be made more portable by expressing it as

```
malloc(100 * sizeof(int));
```

This brings about the same portability.

Of course, there are times when it is desirable to have a whole block of memory containing null bytes (those that have been set to zero). *Calloc*() allocates and clears memory in this fashion. A null block could be used to fill a video screen, thus erasing or clearing it. This might serve in lieu of a *cls*() function, which is not available in many C implementations.

The previous C program, which saved a screen in a memory block and then called it back after the original screen was cleared, performed what is known as a *block move*. A block of memory from the video screen location was transferred to

116   Pointers and Memory Access   Chap. Eleven

another area reserved by *malloc()*. Technically, the video memory was not moved, but copied, from the source location to the destination block. Another block move was performed when the memory from the destination block was copied back to the cleared screen. This was a very slow process when run under an interpreter, and it is still less than rapid even when a compiler is used.

Fortunately, there is a function that was not described as a part of the original C language, but which has become fairly standard in C environments for microcomputers, that does the same thing. It is called *movmem()*, and its purpose is to move a block of memory from one location to another. In most implementations, *movmem()* is written in machine language and is called from C programs. This makes the block transfer as fast as it can be on any particular hardware configuration.

The latest version of RUN/C does contain the *movmem()* function, and since it is a machine language routine called from the C interpreter, it runs very rapidly. Using this function, the block move described previously, which took several minutes, can now be done in less than a second. The following program uses *movmem()* to accomplish the same thing that the preceding example did:

```
/* BE SURE TO SET TRUST ON */

main()
{

    char *a, *b;
    int x;

    a = (char *) 0xb00001; /* Screen address */
    b = malloc(4000);

    for (x = 0; x <= 23; ++x)
        printf("Filling screen with data\n");

    movmem(a, b, 4000); /* Copy screen */

    cls();

    for (x = 0; x <= 200; ++x) /* Time delay */

    movmem(b, a, 4000); /* Retrieve screen */

}
```

The portion of the program up to the point where the phrases are written to the screen is the same as before. However, the *movmem()* function is called after the screen is written, and it almost instantly copies the video screen memory to the allocated block. The screen is then cleared. The next loop is a simple time-delay routine. *Movmem()* works so fast that you might not notice that the screen had been cleared before it was written again. This delay loop will accentuate the fact that the screen is cleared. Suddenly, the screen will appear again. It is not slowly

Summary   **117**

written, but seems to have been "zapped" back on. In fact, each byte of data was
written as before, but due to the machine language nature of *movmem*(), the write
takes place at the fastest possible machine speed.

CLEARING ALLOCATED MEMORY

After a block of memory is allocated and used, it may be desirable to release that
block so that it may be reallocated to another pointer or used for some other purpose.
It is not efficient to keep allocating block after block of memory when one or two
blocks would be sufficient. This would apply when a block is used for a singular
purpose and then no longer needed. The UNIX-compatible memory release function,
standard with most C interpreters and compilers, is *free*(). It is used in a format of

$$x = free(p)$$

where *x* is an integer variable and *p* is a pointer to a previously allocated block of
memory. The call above will attempt to free the block, making it available for other
allocation calls. When *free*() is called, it returns a code to *x*. The value of *x* after
the call will be zero (0) if the release was successful and equal to some other value
(usually, −1) if there is a release problem. If a problem exists, this is usually a sign
of some turmoil within the computer's memory management segment, or a sign that
the pointer used as an argument to *free*() does not point to an allocated block of
memory.

SUMMARY

Pointers create a lot of confusion for BASIC programmers who are trying to learn
C. However, they are nothing more than special variables that can be used to point
to anything in memory. Think of a pointer as being a *free agent*. When initialized,
it points to a random location in memory. This might be thought of as pointing to
nowhere in particular. But this new type of variable can be assigned the address of
something already in memory, giving access to that location at any time. There are
pointers to strings, pointers to integers, and pointers to floats. There can even be
pointers to pointers.

   Pointer operations in C make up a large part of the touted versatility of this
language. Owing to the unusual nature of pointers as seen by BASIC programmers,
many people shy away from delving fully into this subject. Do not be afraid of
pointers. True, they are different types of variables than those with which the BASIC
programmer is accustomed to working. Nevertheless, they should be no stranger
than string variables were when you were first learning BASIC.

   It should be obvious from this chapter how closely pointers are connected with
memory allocation and management. Every computer is different from all other makes,

so the time will come when you will need to use C to program some highly machine-dependent operations. In such cases it will be necessary to tap your computer's internal architecture. This will certainly require the use of pointers. Once you begin to understand pointers, you will see just how much power and versatility they provide. If you are ever programming again in a BASIC environment, you will miss them.

CHAPTER TWELVE

Structs
and Unions

STRUCTS

There are a number of data types in C that have no equivalents in BASIC, whatsoever. A *structure* falls into this category. Structures are *collections* of one or more variables, often of different data types, and grouped together for access by a single variable name. The variables contained in a structure are called *members*. Unlike arrays, where all elements are of the same data type, structure members may be composed of any and all C data types.

A structure is defined by using the *struct* keyword. The following construct defines a structure named *examp*:

```
struct examp {
       int x;
       double y;
       char a[20];
};
```

Here *examp* is called the *structure tag*. It is the name of a new pseudo data type called *examp*. The following program uses this structure:

```
main()
{
    struct examp {
          int x;
          double y;
          char a[20];
    };
```

119

120   Structs and Unions   Chap. Twelve

```
struct examp ref;

ref.x = 14;
ref.y = 22.5;

strcpy(ref.a, "hello");

printf("%d %lf %s\n", ref.x, ref.y, ref.a);

}
```

In this example, the structure *examp* is defined. It contains three members, of data type *int*, *double*, and *char*, respectively. We now need some method of accessing this *struct* of pseudo data type *examp*. This is done by declaring *ref* a variable to access the *examp* struct members. Again, *struct* is used in making this declaration.

A new operator enters the picture at this point. It is represented by a period (.) and is called the *member* operator. The notation *ref.x* accesses the *struct* member named *x* or *int x*. The program could have declared another variable named *x* outside the structure, and this would be a separate variable from *ref.x*. Declarations inside a structure can be accessed only by the structure variable. Even though structure members may bear the same name as variables used elsewhere in a program, they are completely separate entities.

All structure elements are accessed (i.e., assigned or read) by using the *struct* variable followed by the *member* operator (.) and the name of the member itself. The following program presents a more practical use of *struct* in setting up an employee record:

```
main()
{

    struct employee {
        char name[20];
        char address[100];
        int age;
        float salary;
    };

    struct employee rec;

    strcpy(rec.name, "John Jones");
    strcpy(rec.address, "213 Elm St.");

    rec.age = 27;
    rec.salary = 337.50;

}
```

In this example, *struct employee* is a structure that contains a collection of information that profiles an employee. Different elements are aptly named to contain the name,

Unions   **121**

address, age, and salary of the employee. There are several data types in the *struct*, but all are tied together under a single general reference.

All previous examples of structures in this chapter have used structure tags. These are optional, and it is perfectly legal to drop the tag and define a structure in the following manner:

```
struct {
      int x;
      double y;
      char a[20];
} examp;
```

Here *examp* is the variable that accesses the structure, not a structure tag. Any reference to this structure must use *examp* ahead of the member operator, as in

```
examp.x = 22;
```

This means that it is no longer necessary to declare a structure variable, as in

```
struct employee rec;
```

from the preceding program example. However, without a tag, it is not possible to declare other variables to name the structure reference. In the preceding program, several variables could have been declared to reference the same structure, as in

```
struct employee rec;
struct employee mat;
struct employee ref;
```

Here *rec*, *mat*, and *ref* are variables that are declared to access the same structure. These names can be used interchangeably. This is possible because a structure tag was used. Without the tag, you are stuck with the variable name that followed the structure declaration, such as *examp* in the example above.

UNIONS

A *union* is a special type of collection that has the same form as a structure, but all members of a union share a *common* area of memory. This allows one block of memory to store several different data types, but only one at a time. Therefore, the last assignment to a union is the one currently stored in memory. Any previous assignment is overwritten.

Each union member overlaps the next in the same area of memory. The union memory location is accessed by referencing the proper union member through the member operator. The amount of memory allocated to a union is determined by the size of the largest member in the union.

122   Structs and Unions   Chap. Twelve

A union is declared in the following way:

```
union examp {
      int x;
      double y;
      char a[20];
};
```

This is the same format used with *struct*s, except that the *union* declaration heads the construction. As is the case with *struct*s, *union* tags are optional. When a tag is used, a program accessing the union must declare a variable for that union, as in

```
union examp ref;
```

Remember, a union looks like a structure as far as source code format is concerned. However, a union is not capable of holding several different data types at one time. It can only represent a single quantity, be it *char*, *long*, *float*, *double*, *int*, and so on. Anytime a value is assigned to a union, it is stored at a specific memory location. The next assignment to this union is stored at the same location and overwrites the previous assignment. The most recent assignment is the only one that is available when reading a union member.

SUMMARY

*Struct*s and *union*s offer a convenient method of grouping a number of different data types in one collection that can be referenced by a single variable in combination with the member operator and member name. Certainly, any operation that can be carried out by using a structure can also be performed using separate variables. However, the grouping of related information of different data types and accessing it by a common variable adds more form to a program. It is easier to keep track of what the program is doing with these various data types from observation of the source code.

CHAPTER THIRTEEN
Input/Output

In previous chapters we have discussed writing to the standard output (the monitor screen) and receiving information from the standard input (the keyboard). In this chapter we compare the two sets of functions (input and output) and show how modifications of these may be used to read and write information to and from other input/output devices.

The input functions discussed to this point include *scanf*, *gets*, *getchar*, and *getch*. Each of these has an equivalent function that addresses output. The following chart shows the various functions and their matches:

Input	Output
gets	puts
getchar	putchar
scanf	printf

We know that *gets* is used to read a string from the standard input. *Puts* is a special output function (or macro) that writes a character string to the output. It will not write any other type of data, only a character string. *Gets* terminates its keyboard scan when a newline is received (<return>). *Puts* ends its writing of characters to the monitor with a newline. The line

```
puts(s);
```

is identical to

123

124   Input/Output   Chap. Thirteen

```
                    printf("%s\n", s);
```

assuming that *s* has been declared a char array. The following program uses *gets* and *puts*:

```
main()
{

    char s[80];

    gets(s);

    puts(s);

}
```

The *gets* function retrieves input from the keyboard until the <return> key is pressed. The terminating newline character is replaced by a NULL character, which signals the end of the string. The *puts* function works in reverse. It writes characters to the screen until the NULL is reached. It then replaces the NULL with a newline.

Getchar reads a single character from the keyboard, halting execution until the <return> key is pressed (in most implementations). *Putchar* displays a single character (as a character) on the monitor screen and terminates it with a newline. The following program demonstrates the interaction of these complementary functions:

```
main()
{

    int x;

    x = getchar();

    putchar(x);

}
```

The *putchar* line in this program could also have been written as

```
        printf("%c\n", x);
```

However, *putchar* is far simpler, and we know that it will display a character based on an argument which is the ASCII value of that character.

The *scanf* function scans the keyboard for formatted information, based on instructions provided by the control string that contains the conversion specifications. *Printf* writes formatted output to the monitor screen, based on the same control criteria. The following program shows the complementary usage of these two functions:

Input/Output   Chap. Thirteen   **125**

```
main()
{

    char a[80];
    int x;
    double y;
    long z;

    scanf("%s %d %lf %ld", a, &x, &y, &z);

    printf("%s %d %lf %ld\n", a, x, y, z);

}
```

The symmetry is easily seen. Each set of functions includes one that is designed to read and another designed to write. Each set shares the same, basic format. While each of the functions discussed is designed to read the standard input or write to the standard output, each also has a counterpart that can read or write from and to other input/output devices, such as printers, files, and communications ports.

BASIC works along these lines as well. To accept input from the keyboard, INPUT is used. To accept input from a file, INPUT# is used. From the output standpoint, we use PRINT to write formatted output to the screen and PRINT# to write formatted output to a file.

C offers these advantages as well. As a matter of fact, *printf* is a dedicated function that writes only to the standard output, but it is built from another function called *fprintf*. The leading "f" stands for "file," so *fprintf* means "file print."

Let's assume that *fp* is a special type of variable that points to an opened disk file. Then

```
                      fprintf(fp, "%s\n", "hello");
```

writes "hello" followed by a newline character to the file named by *fp*. All *printf* really does is open the monitor screen as a file and call *fprintf* to write to that file.

Scanf has its equivalent in the latter category as well. It is called *fscanf*, and retrieves formatted information from a file. Assume again that *fp* points to an open file. Then

```
                      fscanf(fp, "%s%d", a, &x);
```

retrieves the first two data types from this file, the first being a single word followed by a space and then an integer value. This line assumes that *a* has been declared a *char* array and *x* is an integer variable. For implementation of *scanf*, the standard input is opened as a file and *fscanf* is called to read that file.

The other pairs also have their generic file equivalents, such as

fgets	fputs
fgetc	fputc

The latter two are the file equivalents of *getchar* and *putchar*.

126   Input/Output   Chap. Thirteen

There is even another type of output function called *sprintf*. This stands for "string printf" and is used to write formatted information to a *char* array instead of to a file or the standard output. *Sprintf* is somewhat equivalent to the STR$ function in BASIC. STR$ is used to convert numeric values into string values. Assuming that *a* has been declared a *char* array:

```
sprintf(a, "%d %d", 14, 28);
```

this line will assign *a* a string value equivalent to "14 28". CBREEZE uses *sprintf* to mimic BASIC's ability to add strings, as in

A$=B$+C$+D$

which is translated as

```
sprintf(a$, "%s%s%s", b$, c$, d$);
```

FILEKEEPING

Next to the standard input/output, filekeeping makes up the majority of input/output operations in C as in many other computer languages. In this section we provide an overview of C language filekeeping, although it will not entail a complete tutorial. Filekeeping in any language is a complex subject, but you have already learned enough about C to understand the basics. This discussion will include sequential filekeeping practices only.

The first thing to do when attempting to read or write files in BASIC is to open the desired file. To do this, the OPEN statement is used in a format like

10 OPEN "TST.FIL" FOR OUTPUT AS #1

This opens a disk file named "TST.FIL" for a write operation. The file reference is #1. In C, there is an *open* function, but this is a primitive usually incorporated to build another function, called *fopen*. *Fopen* is used to open a "buffered" file, and this is what we are looking for in this discussion. The C equivalent of this BASIC program is

```
#include "stdio.h"
main()
{

    FILE *fp, *fopen();

    fp = fopen("TST.FIL", "w");

}
```

Filekeeping   **127**

Note: It is not necessary or even legal to declare *fopen*() when programming under RUN/C, nor to *#include stdio.h*.

This program introduces a new data type. Actually, it is a new data NAME called FILE. This declares *fp* and *fopen*() as pointers to files. The *fopen* function returns a file pointer and *fp* is declared as such a pointer as well, just as *char ∗a* declares *a* to be a pointer to a character string. The standard header file *stdio.h* defines the FILE data type and other functions used in filekeeping routines.

The next line uses *fopen* to open a file named "TST.FIL" for a write operation due to the *lowercase* letter "w". *Fopen* returns a pointer to the open file and *fp* points to the same place in memory. The *fp* pointer is equivalent to the #1 designation in the BASIC program example. If for some reason the file cannot be opened, *fp* will be equal to NULL, which is usually defined as zero on most machines. For this reason, it is important to check the return value in *fp*. Most often, you will see a file opened in the following manner:

```
#include <stdio.h>
main( )
{

        FILE *fp, *fopen( );

        if ((fp = fopen("TST.FIL", "w")) == NULL)
            printf("Can't open file");

}
```

The *if* statement line does several things. First it executes *fopen*, which attempts to open the file as instructed. This line also tests the value of *fp*. If it is equal to NULL (defined as 0 in the *stdio.h* header file), the error message is written to the screen. If *fp* is not equal to NULL, execution can continue.

Most C functions that write or read return some type of value to indicate whether the operation was successful. This applies to *printf*, *scanf*, and so on, as well as to the filekeeping functions. It is not actually necessary to check these return values as far as a successful execution run is concerned, and in most instances, examples in this book do not incorporate them. This is especially true when the standard input is read or there is a write operation to the standard output. However, standard input/output is often reassigned in some applications. For instance, the CTTY command in MS-DOS can be used to change the standard input/output to the serial port for modem or remote control. In such circumstances it is advantageous to test functions that read and write the standard input/output to see if these operations are successful.

When it comes to filekeeping, a test of return values should be mandatory to make certain that files are, indeed, being written or read. The foregoing test of a file-opening routine makes certain that the file can be opened before any write takes place.

128   Input/Output   Chap. Thirteen

The following program opens a disk file for write and writes a quoted phrase to the file:

```
#include "stdio.h"
main()
{

        FILE *fp, *fopen();
        char a[80];

        if ((fp = fopen("TST.FIL", "w")) == NULL) {
            printf("Can't open file\n");
            exit(0);
        }

        if ((fputs("Writing to file\n", fp)) == NULL)
            puts("Can't write to file");
        else
            fclose(fp);

}
```

This program looks more complex than it really is because of the checks that have been made for errors upon attempting to open and to write the file. In its simplest form it would be written as

```
#include "stdio.h"
main()
{

        FILE *fp, *fopen();

        fp = fopen("TST.FIL", "w");

        fputs("Writing to file\n", fp);

        fclose(fp);

}
```

Either program will open a file named TST.FIL and write the phrase "Writing to file" followed by a newline character. The file will then be closed and the program will terminate. However, the first example is far better, because it assures that the status of the file write is known by generating error prompts if something goes wrong.

The following program opens this file again, this time for a read operation:

```
#include "stdio.h"
main()
{

        FILE *fp, *fopen();
        char a[80];
```

Filekeeping

129

```
fp = fopen("TST.FIL", "r");

fgets(a, 79, fp);

printf("%s", a);

fclose(fp);

        }
```

Again, *fopen* is used to open the file. Notice that the second argument to this function is "*r*". A lowercase "*r*" indicates that the file is to be opened for read operations. The *fgets* function, reciprocal of *fputs*, reads the information from the file into *char* array *a*. The second argument to *fgets* is an integer value that specifies the maximum length of the input received. *Fgets* will continue to read characters from the file until the string reaches this length or until a newline character is read. You will notice that a newline character was purposely placed at the end of the string written to the file in the preceding program.

Fgets will place the phrase "Writing to file\n" in array *a*. A *printf* statement writes the contents of *a* to the monitor screen. The final action of this program is to close the file with the *fclose* function. Its only argument is the pointer to the open file.

This program was written in its simplest form. The proper way to write this program appears below. This one includes all of the necessary checks to make certain that the file is properly opened and read:

```
#include "stdio.h"
main()
{

        FILE *fp, *fopen();
        char a[80];

        if ((fp = fopen("TST.FIL", "r")) == NULL) {
            puts("Can't open file");
            exit(0);
        }

        if ((fgets(a, 79, fp)) == NULL) {
            puts("Cannot read file");
            fclose(fp);
            exit(0);
        }
        else
            printf("%s", a);

        fclose(fp);

    }
```

130   Input/Output   Chap. Thirteen

These two programs correspond to the BASIC programs that follow:

```
10  REM WRITE FILE
20  OPEN "TST.FIL" FOR OUTPUT AS #1
30  PRINT #1, "Writing to file"
40  CLOSE #1


10  REM READ FILE
20  OPEN "TST.FIL" FOR INPUT AS #1
30  INPUT #1,A$
40  PRINT A$
50  CLOSE #1
```

If a file is to be opened for append, *fopen* is called with a new second argument:

```
fp = fopen("TST.FIL", "a");
```

will attempt to open an existing file and seek through to the end. Any writes that take place after this will be added to the end of the file. As is the case in BASIC, opening a file that does not currently exist for append will cause the file to be created, as though it had been opened for write.

The following program uses *scanf* to read input from the keyboard and *printf* to write the same output to the screen:

```
main()
{

        char a[90];
        int b;
        double c;

        scanf("%s %d %lf", a, &b, &c);
        printf("%s %d %lf\n", a, b, c);

}
```

If the keyboard input is

                    hello 14 22.345

this same line will be displayed on the monitor. The following program is the disk file version of the one above:

Summary   **131**

```c
#include "stdio.h"
main()
{
    char a[90];
    int b;
    double c;
    FILE *fp, *fopen();

    fp = fopen("TST.FIL", "w");   /* Open file for write */

    fprintf(fp, "%s %d %lf\n", "hello", 14, 22.345);/*Write file*/

    fclose(fp);                /* Close file */

    fp = fopen("TST.FIL", "r");   /* Reopen file for read */

    fscanf(fp, "%s %d %lf", a, &b, &c);  /* Read data to a, b, c */

    printf("%s %d %lf\n", a, b, c);  /* Display data */

    fclose(fp)               /* Close file */
}
```

The file is first opened for write, and the formatted output function *fprintf* writes its arguments to the file. The file is closed for write and reopened again, this time for read. The formatted input function *fscanf* reads the information from the file into the memory locations of its arguments. Finally, *printf* displays the retrieved file information. This is exactly what was done in the previous program, except that a disk file was used for input/output instead of the standard input/output.

This exercise should prove the common link between all input/output functions in C. Once you know how to use the basic read and write functions, you will find that you can easily access any input/output device.

SUMMARY

In C, reading and writing files is almost the same as reading and writing the keyboard and monitor. All of the functions designed to address the standard input/output have sister functions that address any legal input/output devices. This allows for a speedy learning process and should ease the fear that many students have when filekeeping or writing to and reading from communications ports is necessary. As you gain a better grasp of C, you will marvel at the ease with which seemingly complex operations can be carried out by using functions that share a definite commonality.

CHAPTER FOURTEEN

Writing Your Own Functions

C is a small language in comparison to most others. It consists of very few statements, but it does have an adequate assortment of functions. These functions have been made from the built-in statements and mathematical operations to form a set of tools from which more elaborate operations can be constructed.

One of the most advantageous features of C (especially when compared to BASIC) is that it allows the programmer to build specialized functions not addressed by the standard set of functions. In this chapter you will learn how to write your own functions, which can then be called from any C language program. One must remember that the standard functions, such as *printf*, *strcpy*, *strlen*, and so on, were built using C language primitives. The standard function set encompasses the minimum tool set that this language's developers felt necessary. As a programmer, you will find it necessary to build still other functions using this basic set.

A C language function is sometimes compared with a subroutine in BASIC. Such subroutines are accessed using the BASIC statement GOSUB. However, this comparison is a poor one. In C, a function is indeed a type of subroutine, but it is one that is separate from the calling program. This means that standard variables used within the calling program are completely unknown to the function unless they are specifically passed as a function argument. Similarly, the variables that are used internally by the function are completely separate and unknown to the calling program unless their values are specifically passed back to the calling program. Admittedly, this will sound confusing at first, but a few examples should clear this up.

The following BASIC program uses a subroutine to implement a time-delay loop:

132

Writing Your Own Functions   Chap. Fourteen   **133**

```
10  PRINT  "HELLO"
20  GOSUB  70
30  PRINT  "GOODBYE"
40  GOSUB  70
50  PRINT  "ENDING  PROGRAM"
60  END
70  FOR  X%=0  TO  1000
80  NEXT  X%
90  RETURN
```

After each PRINT statement line, the subroutine is entered which causes a delay in executing the next PRINT statement line, while the FOR-NEXT loop within the subroutine counts from 0 to 1000.

We can do the same thing in C with the following program:

```
main()
{

        printf("HELLO\n");
        dlay();
        printf("GOODBYE\n");
        dlay();
        printf("ENDING PROGRAM\n");

}
dlay()
{

        int x;

        for (x == 0; x <= 1000; ++x)
                ;

}
```

In this example, a C language function has been created and named *dlay*. You will notice that the function resides *outside* the body of the calling program, the latter being the program portion headed by *main*(). Within the body of the function, an integer variable is declared and this variable is counted from 0 to 1000 within a *for* loop. All that is necessary to call the function is to use its name. Within the calling program, you will see *dlay*(); used twice. Each time this function is encountered within the calling program, it is executed. The function figuratively takes control and the calling program is not in control until the function has finished executing. After a return from a function call, the next line within the calling program is executed. This also occurs after a return from a BASIC GOSUB.

There are distinct differences, however. In the BASIC program example, the value of X% is known outside the subroutine. At any time within this program the value of X% could have been displayed on the screen (using PRINT). At no time in the C program is the value of *x* known by the calling program. It is usually

134   Writing Your Own Functions   Chap. Fourteen

best to think of a C function as a completely separate program which is called by another program. Although comparisons are made between GOSUB in BASIC and C functions, a better comparison can be made between the BASIC CHAIN statement and the program CHAINed to and C functions.

Now, let's try another example, first in BASIC and then in C:
BASIC:

```
10  INPUT X%
20  GOSUB 50
30  PRINT X%
40  END
50  X%=X%*2
60  RETURN
```

C:

```
main( )
{

    int x;

    scanf("%d", &x);          WRONG!
    mult( );
    printf("%d\n", x);

}
mult( )
{

    x = x * 2;

}
```

The C language example is utterly and completely wrong, but it does illustrate the type of error that many beginning C programmers make when dealing with personally written functions. Here a function has been named *mult*(), and its purpose is to multiply the value of x times 2 just as the subroutine in the BASIC example did. However, this C program will not return the value of x multiplied by 2. As a matter of fact, it will not even compile or run at all on the interpreter, because x will show up as an undeclared variable.

Variable x in the calling program is a different variable altogether from the one found in the function. The function has no way of knowing what the value of x is within the calling program.

For a function to know the value of one or more variables within the calling program, the value or variable must be passed to the function. This is called an *argument* to the function. The following C program is another incorrect attempt at duplicating the BASIC example presented earlier, but it is closer to a working program than the preceding C example:

Writing Your Own Functions   Chap. Fourteen   **135**

```
main( )
{

    int x;

    scanf("%d", &x);
    mult(x);                        WRONG!
    printf("%d\n", x);

}
mult(c)
int c;
{

    c = c * 2;

}
```

In this example, *mult*( ) is called with an argument (*x*). This variable represents the value retrieved from the keyboard by *scanf*. The value is passed to the function named *mult*. Notice that *mult* is defined by name at the bottom of the program and that a variable is inserted within the declaration line. The variable used in the *mult* declaration is arbitrarily named *c*. It could just as well have been any other variable name, including *x*. If it were *x*, however, this would be a completely different variable from the one named *x* in the calling program. Either way, the variable named in the function declaration line will be equal to the value of the argument that was passed when *mult* was called from the main program.

Within the function, *c* is declared an *int*. It is absolutely essential that arguments passed to functions be properly declared within the function body. Now variable *c* in the function is equal to variable *x* in the calling program, since the value of *x* was passed by the calling program to the function.

However, this program still will not work properly, although it will compile or run without an error message. Indeed, the function will assign *c* a value of 2 times *x*. However, the calling program has no way of knowing the value of *c*. Remember, we are dealing with two separate programs here.

The following C language program will work just like the original BASIC program example. It is the correct C language version of this BASIC program:

```
main( )
{

    int x;

    scanf("%d", &x);
    x = mult(x);
    printf("%d\n", x);

}
```

136   Writing Your Own Functions   Chap. Fourteen

```
mult(c)
int c;
{

    c = c * 2;
    return(c);

}
```

This program does meet all the criteria to do what we originally wanted—to multiply the value input at the keyboard by 2. Within the function body, a *return* statement is used and *c* is its argument. Just as we passed a value *to* the function from the calling program, it is necessary to pass a value *from* the function to the calling program. In BASIC, a RETURN statement is mandatory for a *proper* exit from a subroutine. In C, the *return* statement may be used with an argument to return a value to the calling program. It is sometimes used without an argument should a condition warrant the *premature* return from a function when an argument value is incorrect. However, a *return* statement is not mandatory to get out of a function. In C, the function will return control to the calling program when there are no more function lines to execute *or* when a *return* statement is encountered.

In the program above, the function will return a value that is equal to *c*. You will remember that *c* was used to represent the argument passed from the calling program. This value was then multiplied by 2 within the function body. Therefore, from the standpoint of value alone, *c* is equal to $x * 2$. This is what we desired. When control is returned to the calling program, the function, *mult*(*x*), will be equal to $x * 2$. This value is assigned to *x* and displayed on the screen by *printf* in the main body of the program.

The *mult*() function was called from the main program. This caused control to fall on the function. When the function finished executing, it returned control to the main program, together with a value that was the result of its operations.

The following C functions perform other types of mathematical operations:

```
sub(a, b)
int a, b;
{

    return(a - b);

}


add(a, b)
int a, b;
{

    return(a + b);

}
```

Writing Your Own Functions   Chap. Fourteen   **137**

These simple functions subtract or add two integer values that are passed to them from the calling program. They might be used in the following manner:

```
main()
{

    int x, y;

    x = 10;
    y = 4;

    printf("%d %d\n", sub(x, y), add(x, y));

}
/* This program body would be followed by the
    source code of the functions shown above */
```

This program calls the *add*() and *sub*() functions, which return the result of their mathematical operations to be used by *printf*.

It can be seen that functions allow often-used routines to be programmed only once, named, and then called by that name anytime they are needed. This not only speeds programming time but makes the C program far easier to understand. In BASIC, it would be necessary to track down various GOSUB branches to trace the flow of a program that operated similarly to the C example above.

C functions can accept any legal argument. This includes *char* arrays and pointers to character strings. The following BASIC program will be converted to C in order to show how a function may manipulate string values:

```
10  A$="hello"
20  GOSUB 50
30  PRINT A$
40  END
50  A$=A$+"-goodbye"
60  RETURN
```

This program calls a subroutine to alter the value of A$. In C, this program could be written as

```
main()
{

    char a[40];

    strcpy(a, "hello");

    alter(a);

    printf("%s\n", a);

}
```

138 Writing Your Own Functions   Chap. Fourteen

```
alter(c)
char c[];
{

    strcat(c, "-goodbye");

}
```

In this example the *alter*() function is used to add "-goodbye" to the end of its string argument. No return statement is necessary, because control will return to the calling program at the logical end of the function. We are not passing a value back to the program, but changing the value of a string already in memory. Notice that the argument to *alter*() is declared within the function as a *char* array. However, this declaration uses empty brackets where one would expect to find an integer constant, specifying the number of elements or bytes.

This is not necessary when an array is passed to a function. Here *c*[] is a pointer to the memory location of *a* in the calling program. This function could also have been written as

```
alter(c)
char *c;
{

    strcat(c, "-goodbye");

}
```

since char arrays and char pointers may be interchanged in functions.

Instead of returning a value to the calling program, the *alter*() function changes the contents of the memory location assigned to the array. Since this memory location is also known by the calling program, no return is needed. This demonstrates the value of pointers in C. Do not be mislead into thinking that this same procedure will work with standard numeric variables, as in

```
main()
{

    int x;

    x = 14;

    alter(x);
                                    WRONG!
    printf("%d\n", x);

}
```

Writing Your Own Functions   Chap. Fourteen   **139**

```
alter(a)
int a;
{


    a = 24;


}
```

This will not change the value of *x* as seen by the calling program. The screen display from this example will be 14. The *alter*() function did nothing to change the value of *x*. Its variable *a* was assigned a value of 24, but the calling program has no contact with this variable or value, since it was not returned. Only pointer arguments allow functions to alter values in memory. All other types of arguments can be used only to return a value to the calling program.

Of course, it is quite easy to pass a pointer to a numeric quantity to a function. The following program is a proper modification of the last, incorrect example:

```
main()
{

    int x;

    x = 14;

    alter(&x);

    printf("%d\n", x);

}
alter(a)
int *a;
{

    *a = 24;

}
```

Here the *address* of variable *x* in the main program is passed to *alter*(). Within the called function, *a* is declared a pointer to an integer. This is the memory location of the quantity stored in *x*. The memory location is assigned a value of 24 by the expression, *a = 24;. Control is then returned to the calling program, where the value of *x* is displayed on the monitor screen. The original value of *x* was 14, which was stored at the memory address set aside for *x*. However, the function was passed this memory address, as opposed to the *value* of *x*, and this was changed to a new value. When control is returned to the calling program, variable *x* is now equal to the new value stored at its memory location.

140   Writing Your Own Functions   Chap. Fourteen

C LIKES INTS BEST

The heading of this section should look familiar. Again, C likes to assume that a quantity is an integer, unless it is told otherwise. This applies especially to functions. C assumes that all functions return integer values. An integer return is the default. However, if a function is to return a float, a double, a long, or even a pointer to a string, this noninteger return must be specially declared. As a matter of fact, it must be declared twice. Previously, it was stated that such functions as *log()*, *sqrt()*, *exp()*, and so on, must be declared as doubles within the calling program. (*Note:* This does not apply to RUN/C.) These are functions that do not return integer values. They return doubles and the calling program must be specifically instructed to expect this type of return. C also requires that a noninteger return be specified with the function name in the source code that makes up a function. The following program demonstrates this procedure:

```
main( )
{

    double x, y, add( );

    x = 14.1;
    y = 72.16;

    printf("%lf\n", add(x, y));

}
double add(a, b)
double a, b;
{

    return(a + b);

}
```

This is another version of the *add()* function discussed previously, and accepts arguments that have been declared double and returns a double-precision value. In the calling program, *add()* is declared double. This alerts C to expect a double-precision return from *add()* instead of an integer. When the source code for the function is written, the name is preceded by *double*. Again, this is a signal that the function returns a double-precision value. Without these necessary declarations, the function will return an integer value to the calling program.

This rule applies for all other types of returns. If a function returns a long integer, it must be declared *long* within the body of the calling program and preceding the function name. Although RUN/C does not allow built-in functions that return other than integer values to be declared in standard form, this is a requirement for all functions that you may write. If such a function returns other than an integer,

BASIC Functions in C   **141**

you must go through this declaration procedure in RUN/C and in almost every
other C programming environment.

BASIC FUNCTIONS IN C

The title of this section is a bit misleading, but it is possible to write certain functions
in C that will mimic the *operation* of useful BASIC functions. The CBREEZE translator offers versions of MID$, RIGHT$, and LEFT$ in specialized C functions. These
are not a part of the standard C function set, so they must be specially programmed.
All of these functions extract a portion of an argument string and write it to another
array or return the extract value. The following function was obtained from CBREEZE
and duplicates BASIC's LEFT$:

```
left$(a, b, x)
char *a, *b;
int x;
{

        int i;

        i = 0;

        while (i++ < x)
                *a++ = *b++;

        *a = '\0';


}
```

In this function, *a* and *b* are pointers to *char* arrays passed to *left$*(). Variable *x*
represents the passed value of the number of characters to be extracted from the
left side of the string. The passed string (actually, the address of the string) is represented by *b*, while *a* points to an array that will hold the result of *left$*().

Within the function, *i* is declared an *int* variable with an initial value of zero
(0). A *while* loop reads each character in *b* to *a* and increments *i* by one on each
pass. As long as *i* is less than the number of characters to be extracted, the loop
continues to cycle. You must remember that *x* specifies the total number of characters.
This means that character 1 is located at *a*[0], character 2 at *a*[1], and so on. If *x*
is equal to 5, the loop must count from 0 to 4. On each pass both pointers are
accessed for their character positions and then incremented to the next position.
When the loop is exited, *a* points to a string of characters equal to the leftmost
characters in *b*. However, this is not a true string yet, because the newly generated
row of characters is not terminated by the required null byte. The last line in the
function makes this assignment and control is returned to the calling program.

Other BASIC functions that do not have direct counterparts in C are pro-

142   Writing Your Own Functions   Chap. Fourteen

grammed along the same lines in CBREEZE and their source code is included as a
part of the program. CBREEZE has no hidden functions that must be included
with the program to obtain a successful run. If any special functions are needed to
translate a BASIC program, their source code is included as well.

CBREEZE goes to great lengths to translate BASIC into C by using the standard
C function set. It is only when a BASIC function has no C counterpart that additional
functions are added, just as they would be by a C programmer who needed a special
function.

Suppose that you wished to write a C function that would emulate the BASIC
INPUT statement used in a format of

```
INPUT "prompt";VARIABLE$
```

First, the prompt message would have to be fed to a *printf* or *puts* function
in C, then *gets* would be used to read the keyboard input into memory. The following
function would perform this emulation in C:

```
input$(a, b)
char a[ ], b[ ];
{

      printf("%s ", a);
      gets(b);

}
```

This function has two arguments. The first would be the prompt string and the
second would be the char array that was to accept the keyboard input. Within the
function, *a* is displayed with *printf*() and *b* is assigned with *gets*. This function
might be called by the following program:

```
main( )
{

      char c[30];

      input$("Input your name", c);
      puts(c);

}
/* Source code of input$() goes here */
```

This would be the equivalent of

```
10  INPUT"Input your name";C$
20  PRINT C$
```

Summary   **143**

The *puts* function in C is very convenient when a single character string is to be displayed on the screen followed by a carriage return/linefeed. In C, *puts*(*a$*); corresponds to BASIC's PRINT A$. However, *puts* works only with strings. If we wish to display a numeric value, it is necessary to use *printf*() together with a control string conversion specification and the argument itself. The following function was written to easily display integer values followed by a newline character:

```
printd(x)
int x;
{

        printf("%d\n", x);

}
```

Notice that the content of *printd*() is simply the *printf*() function line that would normally be used to display a single integer value. However, it is easier to type *printd*(*x*); while writing source code than it is to use the longer *printf*() method. A function that would print a single float value would be written as

```
pntf(x)
float x;
{

        printf("%f\n", x);

}
```

This is almost the same function as before, but it accepts a floating-point argument and uses the *%f* conversion specification within *printf*().

SUMMARY

C language functions are quite easy to understand once you realize that they are separate miniprograms that are called from a master program or another function. They may receive arguments from the calling program and return values to it; or they may receive memory locations (pointers) as arguments and directly change the contents of these locations for use by the calling program.

Writing C functions is an excellent training aid. The exercise you gain from this practice will speed you along your course toward proficiency in C. Fortunately, C language tutorials usually provide a wide assortment of specialized functions from which to learn. CBREEZE emulates several BASIC functions that have no direct counterparts in C through special C functions. All C functions follow the general format of standard C programs, so once you learn to write simple programs, you should also be able to write simple functions.

CHAPTER FIFTEEN

Programming Mistakes

At this point in the discussion, the reader should have gained a fair amount of knowledge about C, its functions, and its relationship to BASIC. It was mentioned earlier that C is a very flexible language, both in what it can do and how the source programs are written. For the most part, C is independent regarding the actual format of the source code. This relates directly to white spaces and the general way in which the program lines are laid out. All programs in this book have followed the standard C programming format, which will at first seem a bit strange to readers with experience in BASIC only. In this chapter we explore further the proper way to write a C language program. Specifically, program examples are shown in several different "workable" formats. Also, examples of improperly written programs are given; these examples address the errors that many beginning C programmers make.

The following C language program is written in what might be classified as the standard format. The call to *main*() begins the program, and *main*() is written at the left margin. The opening brace is written immediately below *main*() and also at the left margin. Usually, the first assignment in writing a C language program is to declare all variables. In this example, I have indented five spaces and named *x* an *int*. When all variables have been declared, the next step is to assign values to variables. Again, I have indented five spaces and have also skipped a line between the declaration and the assignment. The skipping of a line here is done simply to differentiate between program blocks. The first block is the opening call to *main*() and its opening brace; the second is the declaration of variables; the third is the assignment of variables. The fourth block in this particular program is the first function line, which is also indented five spaces. A line has been skipped here to differentiate this block from the assignment block.

144

Programming Mistakes   Chap. Fifteen   **145**

The end result is a program whose key blocks or elements are clearly defined. C is not always an easy language to understand, but by clearly defining program blocks in this manner, C programs can be more easily understood.

```
main( )
{

        int x;

        x = 5;

        printf("%d\n", x);

}
```

Such formatting is done so that a program you write in C can be comprehended by someone else. As programs take on more complexity, it is quite easy to lose track of what you have done if you do not follow such a format. Also, since your learning experience will involve reading materials and viewing programs written by others, it is good to get in the habit of writing your programs in the standard format. By doing this, you will become accustomed to the way C programs are normally presented.

From the compiler's point of view, such formatting is totally unnecessary. The program above could just as well have been written as follows:

```
main( )
{

        int x;
        x = 5;
        printf("%d\n", x);

}
```

Here the indentations from the preceding program have been maintained. However, the line spacing is not the same. This simple program is still quite easy to understand when presented in this format, but the same will not hold true for a complex program. In this example, no blocks are clearly defined, and everything seems to run together.

The next program example is in a format that many BASIC programmers use when starting out in C. This format is definitely to be avoided, since it tends to further muddy the waters of source program understanding.

```
main( )
{
int x;
x = 5;
printf("%d\n", x);
}
```

146   Programming Mistakes   Chap. Fifteen

In this example, all lines begin at the left margin. Because of the many symbols used in C (braces, brackets, ampersands, and so on), it is quite easy to omit a brace or other symbol and not be able to spot the error. This format may seem more comfortable to a BASIC programmer at first, but it will soon become unwieldy as programming experience increases.

Multiple statement lines are quite common in BASIC. Most dialects of BASIC support multiple statement lines and usually use colons as separators. Multiple statement, or, more appropriately, multiple block, lines are also permitted in C, as demonstrated by the following program:

```
main( )
{

    int x; x = 5; printf("%d\n", x);

}
```

Here the separators are semicolons. There is no real problem in this example, but one must remember that several C language statements, including *if*, *while*, and *for*, are not normally terminated with semicolons; real problems can be encountered when they are included on one line.

As an extreme example, another version of the original program is shown below:

```
main( ){ int x; x = 5; printf("%d\n", x); }
```

If you include many lines like this in any C language program, it will probably have meaning only to you.

Again, to the compiler, formatting is of no consequence, but to the person learning C, it is absolutely essential for a steady transition from the novice level upward. Each time you write a C language program, compare the finished product with a similar example in this or other books about C. If you notice a format deviation, make the necessary changes so that your program will conform. I will admit that at first, sticking to this format is difficult because it seems to slow you down. However, after a fairly short period of time, you will automatically begin writing all C language programs using the standard format. In other words, after a bit of practice, this highly useful format becomes quite comfortable.

You certainly have noticed by now that most mathematical operations in C are programmed using white-space differentiators between elements. For example, the BASIC program line

$$X=4*2$$

would appear in a C program as

$$x = 4 * 2$$

Programming Mistakes   Chap. Fifteen   **147**

This is not the case all the time, but it should be. The reason for the use of lowercase letters to name functions and, for the most part, variables in C is purely convention. In C, uppercase letters are reserved for symbolic names and constants. Everything else is normally written in lowercase letters. The spacing between the equals sign (=) and the mathematical operators (the asterisk for multiplication in this case) tends to highlight a mathematical operation. Using this format, the asterisk, when used to indicate multiplication, is not readily confused with the asterisk that is used to indicate a pointer. Mathematical operations are sometimes performed on pointers, and it is possible for two asterisks to appear back to back, as in

```
x=*p**z;
```

This is a little difficult to understand. However,

```
x = *p * *z;
```

provides a little more differentiation, and thus better clarity.

The following program in C is far more complex than the preceding one. Actually, the complexity has more to do with appearance than with the actual operation of the program itself. This program is very clearly defined by the C programmer's eye, however, because it follows standard format.

```
main( )
{

    int x, y;

    for (x = 0; x <= 100; ++x) {
         y = x * 2;
         printf("%d\n", y);

    }

    while (y <= 0) {
         --y;
         printf("%d\n", y);
    }

}
```

The declarations are handled in an individual block, and there is adequate indentation and line spacing. This program forms two loops using the *for* and *while* statements. Notice that each of the loops is separated by a line, which provides good differentiation. Notice also that the elements of each loop are indented five spaces from the start of the loop statement name. This makes it easy to see which program lines are a part of which loop. You can see that a space follows the *for* and *while* statements before the opening paren. This accentuates the fact that *for*

148 Programming Mistakes   Chap. Fifteen

and *while* are C language statements as opposed to functions. In C, the opening paren for a function argument immediately precedes the last letter of the function name. C language statements, however, use a white space following the last letter and the opening paren. Since each loop contains more than one statement, an opening brace follows each argument line. A closing brace marks the end of the loop. You can see that each closing brace is indented five spaces and falls a few lines beneath the first letter of the loop statement. In complex programs, such formatting makes it easier to tell which closing brace is coupled with which loop.

The following program better demonstrates the usefulness of proper closing-brace formatting:

```c
main()
{

    int x, y, z;

    for (x = 0; x <= 100; ++x) {
        y = x * 2;
        printf("%d\n", y);

        for (z = 0; z <= 20; ++z) {
            z = z * 3;
            printf("%d\n", z);
        }
    }

}
```

This program uses two loops, one of which is nested. At the end of the first *for* statement line is an opening brace. The same is true of the next *for* statement line, which is a part of the first loop. We know that it is a part of the first loop because no closing brace is vertically aligned with the opening *for* statement prior to the inclusion of the second *for* statement. Near the end of the program, you can see three closing braces. It is obvious that the first one is aligned with the nested *for* statement. The next closing brace is vertically aligned with the opening *for* statement. The final closing brace is on the left-hand margin and aligns with the call to *main()*. Opening and closing braces delineate program blocks, or in BASIC terminology, routines that operate more or less independently. This makes for far easier understanding of a program, because the viewer can quickly break down a complex program into individual blocks and determine the operation of each block on a separate basis.

EXAMPLES OF PROGRAMMING MISTAKES

The next portion of this chapter is a quiz. The reader will be shown several different C language programs, many of which contain errors. However, some are correct as presented. The errors referred to do not involve format but are of the type that

Examples of Programming Mistakes   **149**

will cause the compiler or interpreter to generate an error message and probably bring about a cessation to execution. The answers are given following each program example.

```
main()
{

    x = 24;

    printf("%d\n", x);

}
```

At first glance, this program may seem to be okay. A close examination of the *printf* line indicates that everything is in its place. This program is totally incorrect, however, because a variable has been used (x) that has not previously been declared. To make this program executable, the declaration *int x;* must be included prior to $x = 24;$. This is a common mistake, but fortunately, most environments will pick up this error and generate an appropriate message telling you what the problem is. Compilation or execution can then be halted in midstream, allowing you to make corrections to the program. Remember, all variables must be declared prior to their use in a C language program. Sometimes, you may add variables during a programming sequence. These are additional variables that were not declared previously. This is often done with the intention of returning to the declaration block and adding them. All too often, this step is forgotten. Again, any error message should indicate that one or more variables have not been declared. There will probably also be an indication of which program lines contain the undeclared variables.

```
main()
{

    int x, y;

    x = 1.2;
    y = 44;

    printf("%d %d\n", x, y);

}
```

There is definitely an error in this program, although it is one that most compilers or interpreters will not catch. Both variables have been declared, and the *printf* line is in proper order. However, both variables have been declared *int* types, and variable x has been assigned a floating-point value of 1.2. This program will execute, but the value of x will be converted to an integer. Therefore, x will be equal to 1 instead of the intended 1.2. This program is corrected by declaring only y an *int* type and declaring x a float. The *printf* function line must also be modified. The first *%d*

150   Programming Mistakes   Chap. Fifteen

designation must be changed to *%f* to indicate conversion to a floating-point value. Problems of this type create the most difficulty, since the compiler or interpreter does not usually indicate the error. In complex programs, such an error can mean hours of debugging, since what is intended to be a floating-point value is being fed to other program portions as an integer. When this bogus integer is passed to other program formulas, the resulting output answer is incorrect, and it may not be obvious just where the problem lies. A similar experience occurs when a special function is written that is intended to return a floating-point value but was not previously declared a float or double. Most of the time, the arguments will be worked through the function, but an integer value is always returned.

```
main( )

    int x, y, z;

    x = 13;
    y = 2 * x;
    z = y - 1;

    printf("%d %d %d\n", x, y, z);

}
```

The problem with this program may be obvious to many, but to others it will not be. Depending on the interpreter or compiler, several different error messages may be generated, none of which will clearly define exactly what the problem is. Looking at the program, we can see that all variables have been declared. It would also seem that proper assignments to these variables have been made. Also, there is no problem with the *printf* line. The problem is a simple one. The opening brace following *main* () has not been included. This throws the whole program out of whack. More than likely, your compiler will simply halt and indicate that compilation has been terminated. Alternatively, every program line may be listed as being in error. The entire situation is corrected simply by adding an opening brace immediately following *main* (). Remember, error checking in most C compilers is done on a very elementary basis. In many instances, the true nature of the error is defined, but in others, the compiler goes on its best assumption, which is often incorrect. After a bit of experience with a specific compiler, however, you will begin to identify certain error messages with certain program errors. It takes a while to learn this, however, so these problematical exercises should be helpful in speeding along your transition from BASIC to C.

```
main( )
{

    int x;

    scanf("%d", x);
    printf("%d\n", x);

}
```

Examples of Programming Mistakes   **151**

Here is a simple program that allows you to input an integer via the keyboard and then writes its value to the screen. The program, however, is incorrect. Some environments will catch this; many will not. The error here is the one most often made when using the *scanf* function. When *scanf* is used to retrieve a number, the holding variable (in this case, *x*) must be preceded by an ampersand to indicate its memory location. The variable must be a pointer, and the exclusion of the ampersand means that it is not. Therefore, this program will not execute properly, even if it makes it through the compilation process. A correction is made simply by preceding variable *x* in the *scanf* line with an ampersand (&).

```
main( )
{

     int x, y, z;

     for (x = 0; x <= 14; ++x) {
          y = 2 * x;
          z = 3 * y;
          printf("%d %d %d\n", x, y, z);

}
```

This program uses the *for* loop, which steps *x* from 0 to 14. The elements within the loop assign variables *y* and *z* and write them to the screen. The error found in this program will probably cause your compiler to generate an error message. Using the Lattice C compiler, the message will be "unexpected end of file". This means that the program terminated before the compiler expected it to. To help you find the error here, let me give you a clue. Look at the braces. In this program, you will see a total of three. This is an automatic error, since braces come in pairs. Whenever there is an opening brace, there must also be a closing brace. What has happened here is that an opening brace was used following the *for* statement line. No closing brace was included at the end of the loop elements. The closing brace at the end of the program is apparently paired with the opening brace following *main*( ) (because of its format position in the program). However, the C compiler or interpreter treats this last closing brace as the one that matches the opening brace following the *for* statement line. It thinks you included a closing brace following the *for* statement elements, but forgot to include a closing brace matched with the opening one following *main*( ). If you did include a closing brace following the loop and forgot to include a program termination brace, the same error message would be generated. This program can be fixed by simply adding one more closing brace at the end of the program. But to follow proper C programming format, the closing brace to the *for* loop should precede the left-margin closing brace and be indented five spaces. This will align it vertically with the opening *for* statement.

Anytime you complete a C language program, especially one that uses a lot of braces, you should perform a quick check to make certain that you always have

152   Programming Mistakes   Chap. Fifteen

an even number of braces. If you end up with an odd number, you have omitted a
closing brace or added an unneeded opening brace. This situation must be corrected
before a successful run can be obtained.

```
main( )
{

    int x;

    while (x < 100)
        ++x;


}
```

This program is intended to count x from 0 to 100 using a *while* loop. It will not
work, however, because of a serious error quite common to BASIC programmers
making the transition to C. The glaring error here is the fact that an initial value
of x has not been made. We do not have to do this in BASIC, since a variable is
always equal to 0 if it has not been assigned previously. This is not true with AUTO
variables in C. As a matter of fact, in this example, x can be equal to anything
within the range of legal integer values. To make this program work properly, an
assignment line must precede the *while* loop, setting x to its initial or starting value.
The compiler will not catch this error in most instances, and you can never be sure
just what value an unassigned variable will assume. Remember, a *for* loop assigns
its stepping variable within the loop commands, but a *while* loop of this type must
use a variable that has already been assigned a value within the main body of the
C program.

This type of error can be quite perplexing, especially if the initial value of x
assigned by the computer (as opposed to within a program) falls somewhere within
the legal test range of the *while* loop. This means that the count might start midway
between the intended beginning and ending points. If the computer-assigned variable
value lies outside the legal test range of the *while* loop, the loop terminates. Remember,
assign all variables before they are used, or the computer will assign them with
bogus values that have no meaning whatsoever as far as the intention of your program
is concerned.

```
main( )
{

    int x;

    for (x = 0; x =< 50; ++x)
        printf("%d\n", x);

}
```

Examples of Programming Mistakes   **153**

You may have to look hard to discover the error in this program. Some compilers and interpreters may not even see an error, and the program may run fine. However, there is an error of intent here, and it can be found in the second portion of the *for* statement line. Specifically, the problem lies with $x =< 50$. In C, the evaluation for this type of assignment must include the "less than" symbol first, followed by the equals sign. This is not true in BASIC, where we can legally specify "equal to or less than." In C, it is always "less than or equal to." In most instances, this type of error will cause early termination of the loop. Remember that in C, the equals sign always comes last.

```
main()
{

    int x;

    x = 0;

    while (x <= 100) {
        ++x;

        if (x = 50)
            printf("Variable x equals fifty\n");
    }

}
```

As pointed out earlier in this chapter, many of the program examples will contain errors, but some will not. Maybe you think that this one does not contain any errors. Wrong! This one contains a very serious error. It is serious because most environments will not catch it, and it can create havoc during the program run. If you are a beginning C programmer, chances are you just cannot find the error. The error is in the *if* statement line, specifically with $x = 50$. One must remember that in C, there are two types of equals operators. The single equals sign (=) is the assignment operator. It assigns the value on the right to the variable on the left. The comparison operator is two equals signs (==). This means that the values on either side of the comparison operator are evaluated. This is what we want in the *if* statement line. As written, the *if* statement test is always true, because x is assigned a value of 50. To make this program run properly, you must change the assignment operator to the double-equals comparison operator. Then the value of x will be compared with 50 instead of x being assigned a value of 50. Again, this is a serious error because no problem will be indicated via error messages. The program will be executable, but it will not execute in the manner intended. In BASIC, there is only one equals symbol, and it is used for both assignment and comparison. Unintentionally replacing the comparison operator with the assignment operator in C is a common mistake made by many beginning C language programmers.

154   Programming Mistakes   Chap. Fifteen

```
main()
{

    int x;
    float y;
    char c[80];

    scanf ("%d %s %f", &x, &c, &y);
    printf("%s %f %d\n", c, y, x);


}
```

This simple program uses the *scanf* function to retrieve an integer, a string, and a floating-point number from the keyboard input. The *printf* function is then used to display all three values. There is an error in this program, and it involves the *scanf* line. All variables have been properly declared, and ampersands have preceded each one in the *scanf* line. However, we do not use an ampersand to precede a character array value. These are already pointers. Only the numeric variables declared as *float*, *int*, *double*, and so on, need to provide pointers (by inclusion of the ampersand) in *scanf* arguments. Sometimes you can get away with including an ampersand preceding a character array variable, but not with a *char* * value. In any event, neither a *char* * value nor a character array value should be preceded by the ampersand when used with *scanf*. In this case, a compiler will probably perform its conversions without any error messages, and the executable program will seem to run properly until an attempt is made to write the value of *c* in this example. Chances are that it will come up blank. The program is corrected by removing the ampersand preceding variable *c* in the *scanf* line.

```
main()
{

    printf("Hello,\nHow are you?\nI am fine.");

}
```

This program is used to print phrases on the screen. At first glance, it appears quite odd, but in reality there is nothing wrong with it. It is correct as shown. This program will display

```
Hello,
How are you?
I am fine.
```

We are accustomed to seeing the newline ($\backslash n$) character at the end of a quoted phrase or conversion specifier. This is, however, not mandatory. A newline character

Examples of Programming Mistakes   **155**

may occur anywhere within the quoted string, and at this point, the carriage is returned and a new line is generated. This single *printf* line takes the place of three *printf* lines: the first two terminated by newline characters and the last one not. Again, this program is correct and should execute perfectly.

```
main( )
{

        int  x,  y;

        x = 23;
        y = 27;

        printf("The  numbers  are  %d  %d"\n,  x,  y);

}
```

This program is intended to print the phrase "The numbers are" followed by the values of *x* and *y*. As written, though, it will generate an error message because of a problem in the *printf* line. This illustrates another common mistake made by many beginning C programmers. Note that the quoted phrase and the conversion specifiers are contained within quotation marks. However, the terminating newline character (\n) is found outside the quotes. This is incorrect. The newline character has the same significance as any other character and must be included within quotes. The program is corrected by inserting the final quotation mark following the newline character.

```
main( )
{

        char  c[40];

        strcpy(c,  "COMPUTER");

        printf(%s  "is  the  word\n",  c);

}
```

You probably spotted the problem with this program almost immediately, due to our discussion of the previous program. The problem here also lies in the *printf* line. The conversion specifier (*%s*) is contained outside the quotation marks. Like the newline character, the conversion specifier must be included within the quotes. In BASIC, we are not accustomed to seeing arguments or variables included as part of a quoted phrase line. However, in C, they are intermingled. This program is corrected by inserting the opening quotation mark prior to the conversion specification.

156   Programming Mistakes   Chap. Fifteen

```
main( )
{

    int x, y, z;
    char c[40];

    x = 43;
    y = 2 * x;
    z = 2 * y;
    strcpy(c, "Hello");

    printf("%d %s %d\n", x, y, c, z);

}
```

This C language program uses three *int* variables and one *char* array, which are duly assigned proper values. The *printf* function is used to display each on the monitor screen. This program, however, does have an error—one that will not be caught by most compilers or interpreters. Look at the conversion specifiers in the *printf* line. The first indicates an integer value and, indeed, variable *x* has been declared an integer. The second specifier indicates a character string value, but its matching variable (*y*) is an integer. The next specifier names an integer, but its matching variable (*c*) has been declared a *char* array. This mistake is the result of a simple typing error. Obviously, the programmer intended that variable *c* be matched with the %*s* conversion specification. If this program were executed as shown, erroneous screen data would be displayed due to the mismatch. The extent of the display error would depend on the type of environment and the computer itself. This program is corrected by reversing variables *c* and *y* in the *printf* line.

```
main( )
{

    int x;

    x = 43;

    print("%d\n", x);

}
```

At first glance, this program appears to be perfect, but a programmer who had never learned BASIC and was beginning to learn C would probably spot the error immediately. The error in this program is aimed directly at BASIC programmers, who may tend to overlook it. Variable *x* has been properly declared an *int*. It has also been properly assigned an integer value. Therefore, the problem must lie in the next line. Look closely. Instead of *printf*, a standard C function, *print*, has been used. The compiler or interpreter will look for a personalized function named *print* and generate an error message. With the Lattice C compiler, this type of error would not generate

Summary   **157**

an error message. However, when the object file generated by the compiler is passed
through the linker, upon output of the executable program, the linker will generate
an error message "UNRESOLVED EXTERNAL DEFINITION". This means that
the linker could not find a function named *print* in the C library file. RUN/C will
detect it immediately and halt execution. What you end up with is an executable
program that will not do anything. Obviously, the program is corrected by changing
print to *printf*.

```
main()
{

    int x;
    char c[40];

    strcpy(c, "Diskette");
    x = strlen(c)

    printf("%d\n", x);

}
```

This problem contains a very simple and common error, although it may not be
obvious at first glance. Most compilers or interpreters will generate an error message
which would indicate that the line immediately following the error line contains a
miscue. The error message will be "omission of semicolon" or something similar.
Indeed, a semicolon has been omitted at the end of the line that uses *strlen*. With
some compilers, this is not a fatal error. The compiler may add that missing semicolon
for you. In others, the compiler may crash. Remember, a semicolon following a
function converts that function to a program statement. This program is corrected
simply by adding a semicolon at the end of the *strlen* line.

SUMMARY

This chapter has dealt with two subject areas that are crucial to the beginning C
language programmer. Proper formatting is absolutely essential in order to gain a
clear understanding of C programming from the onset. To stray substantially from
this format is to invite disaster in the form of a slow complex learning process and
an unclear understanding of what is taking place within a given program. Using a
nonstandard format may suffice for your own personal needs, but it will tend to
blur comprehension and make your programs almost useless to those who may want
to learn from you. Proper adherence to the standard C language format is not essential
from an execution point of view, but it is mandatory that you follow it in order to
go as far as you possibly can in learning to program in C.

Beginning as well as seasoned programmers will always make certain errors
when writing C programs. However, beginners tend to make mistakes that fall into

158   Programming Mistakes   Chap. Fifteen

the category of syntax errors. These are easily spotted by the experienced programmer, but are difficult for the beginner to detect. This chapter has dealt with some of the most common programming errors made by beginners, and it is hoped that the examples presented will allow you to be on the alert for similar errors in your programs. The error messages generated by your C environment are a help, but often, these messages are crude "guesstimates" of the real problem. Fortunately, beginning C programmers usually write a large number of very short, simple programs at the onset. By detecting bugs in these small programs, the syntactical problems usually do not carry over to more complex constructs that are written after a bit of practical experience has been obtained.

CHAPTER SIXTEEN

The RUN/C Interpreter

The RUN/C interpreter from Lifeboat Associates is among the first of the C interpreters that offer the full C programming language in interpretive form and at a price that is affordable by any programmer. Traditionally, if you wanted to program in C, a C compiler was the only route open. These can cost up to $500 and do not offer the user friendliness that the RUN/C package does. On the other hand, RUN/C retails for about $125 but is commonly advertised in software discount houses for slightly less than $100.

RUN/C offers a very pleasant programming environment for the BASIC programmer who is taking his/her first steps in C. Many of the commands for editing programs are the same as those found in Microsoft BASIC. The language set also contains some familiarities with such BASIC statements as CLS and LOCATE. These are special functions that are not a part of the standard C language function set, but are set up especially for RUN/C and aimed directly at BASIC programmers.

The following excerpt is from the Preface of the RUN/C user's manual. I think it speaks to the tailoring of RUN/C for the BASIC programmer:

RUN/C combines many of the best features of two popular computer languages: BASIC and C. Like BASIC, RUN/C is *interpreted*, meaning that you can quickly write a program, run it, change it and run it again—all within a single consistent environment. As an implementation of the C programming language, RUN/C interprets pure, unadulterated K&R C. A library of more than 100 C functions is built into RUN/C and the ability to load additional functions and source code libraries is also provided.

If you are familiar with microcomputer languages at all, you probably are familiar with BASIC. Perhaps you have even written programs in BASIC or at least looked at a few in books. BASIC has very wide appeal for several reasons:

159

1. It is comparatively easy to learn, since the words in its vocabulary are quite common: PRINT, LIST, RUN, GOTO.

2. Many sample programs are available, making it easy to find out how some previous explorer might have done the things you are now trying to do.

3. Lines are numbered, for easy reference.

4. Most importantly, BASIC is interpreted. This makes it possible for beginners to try their hand at creating or editing a BASIC program without having to spend several minutes waiting for a special computerized process to be completed before finding out if the program runs and if not, *why not*.

Despite these obvious advantages, BASIC is not ideal. Its GOTO and GOSUB system makes it difficult for even professional BASIC programmers to keep track of what a moderately sophisticated program is doing. Another problem is that programs written in BASIC tend to be large and run very s-l-o-w-l-y—even after they have been *compiled*. A third problem is that there is really no accepted definition of BASIC. There are BASIC+, MBASIC, PC BASIC, Apple BASIC, Commodore BASIC, True BASIC and ANSI BASIC, to say nothing of hybrids like RATBAS. These dialects do not share the same keywords in many cases; in others, the same keywords have different meanings. The result: a program written in one BASIC is not easily portable to other BASICs—a major problem.

The C programming language, developed in 1972, is an increasingly popular alternative to BASIC, to the teaching language Pascal and other professional languages such as COBOL, FORTRAN, PL1, Modula II and FORTH.

Just as Wheaties has been called "The Breakfast of Champions," C might well be called "The Programming Language of Champions"—or at least that of master programmers.

C was intended to have a logical design, so that once a program or program fragment was developed it could easily be understood by other programmers. It was designed to be concise, so programs could be written with the minimum of "keyboarding" associated with many other programming languages. It was designed to follow the newest concept in computer language design, taking full advantage of logical programming structures such as FOR and WHILE loops and IF-THEN-ELSE statements. And it was designed to allow programmers to get at the very basics or "guts" of the computer, making it much less necessary to resort to machine-specific assembly language.

Another factor is speed. Compiled C is very fast—operating within the speed range of assembly language programs. C is also quite portable, since the original K&R definition of the language has never been seriously challenged.

But until recently C has been handicapped by two things:

1. There were very few books on C and those that existed assumed the student was already familiar with other computer languages.

2. The only way to learn C was to buy a C language compiler. For a student this was equivalent to having to buy a Boeing 747 to learn how to fly! To add insult to injury, compiler manuals generally seem written for other writers of C compilers.

The fact is that the problem in learning and working in C is not with the language, it is with its lack of user interface. If you are already a C programmer, you are surely

The RUN/C Interpreter   Chap. Sixteen   **161**

all too familiar with the edit-compile-link-run-start again cycle in program development, and know what an investment in time goes into even the smallest program change. You're also well aware that editor, compiler and linker each has a command language all its own.

In considering a means for relieving this handicap faced by the users of C, it occurred to us that the interpreted environment and, in particular, the BASIC interpreter as developed by Microsoft and further refined by IBM had much to recommend it. Therefore, we modeled RUN/C after the now familiar BASIC-to-user interface.

But enough . . . we could spend pages telling you of the glories of RUN/C. But the proof is in the program, not the prose. Suffice to say that it is our hope that with the introduction of RUN/C, enthusiasts and students of this excellent language will enjoy the same immediate feedback and excellent debugging environment as has been enjoyed by users of BASIC for many years. We also hope that you will agree that an interpreted environment is as appropriate for C as for BASIC.

RUN/C was designed and written by Stephen Walton, a journalist and software author. His software publications include: SKETCHMODE, a graphics manager, and STARCLASH, a strategy game (Hayden, 1980); PROSET, a system for coding files for typesetting (Cromwell Graphics Corp., 1982); THE ELECTRIC DRAGON, a computerized version of the ancient Chinese oracle the *I Ching*, STARCLASH II, and FORCE 400, another original strategy game (Baen Software and Simon & Schuster Electronic Press, 1984). THE EXPERT, an expert system, awaits publication.

Steve's well-received novel, *No Transfer* (Vanguard Press, 1967), was published while he was a student at Michigan State University.

Peter Brooks, a C specialist with a love for mathematics, served as "language lawyer" and debugging specialist for the project. In addition, he wrote the line editor and other major I/O facilities for RUN/C.

Peter is also Executive VP of The Instructor Set, a company which teaches seminars on C and UNIX throughout the U.S.

RUN/C is based on a concept developed by John Reaves, our VP of Marketing. While a consultant at Lifeboat in early 1983, John also developed the initial Lattice C ad campaign and marketing strategy.

Also a successful playwright, several of John's plays were produced in New York in 1984.

This preface is very indicative of the style of the RUN/C manual. Unlike most C language documentation, which is extremely dry for beginners, the RUN/C manual presents the needed information in a very relaxed manner. The necessary facts are presented in a way that can only be described as "easy reading." I think most BASIC language programmers who are trying to learn C will find that the documentation, as well as RUN/C itself, conforms to many of the conventions that BASIC programmers have come to expect.

It is extremely easy to get started with RUN/C. The software is not copy protected, so it only takes a few minutes to copy the original diskette and use the backup for all programming applications. The copying process will probably take five minutes or more, because the master diskette contains a large number of C language files. Only a few of these provide the programming environment itself. The others are sample programs used to illustrate most of the C functions and statements supported by RUN/C.

Each function and statement is described briefly in the manual and a sample C program listing is included with each. For the most part these listings are the same as the sample programs contained on the diskette. Although the RUN/C manual is not a tutorial, as such, it does provide a wealth of information that will compliment any tutorial that may be used by the student learning C.

Version 1.32 of RUN/C was used for researching this book. Undoubtedly, a newer version will be out by the time you read these words, but the changes should not be so significant as to affect the accuracy of the discussions surrounding RUN/C. A liberal update policy is in effect, so if you wish to update to a new version, the cost should be minimal.

I was fortunate enough to have received the original version of RUN/C shortly before it was released to the general public. This was dubbed the "pioneer" version and was not nearly so supportive of the full K&R C language as were later versions. [K&R refers to the book by Brian Kernighan and Dennis Ritchie, *The C Programming Language* (Englewood Cliffs, N.J.: Prentice-Hall, 1978).] Also, the original RUN/C did not contain any functions that would allow access to more than 64K memory or input to the IBM PC BIOS.

However, each new version of RUN/C that was offered came closer and closer to being a full interpretive version of the famous Lattice C compiler. Today, RUN/C offers full access to the IBM BIOS and contains most of the same functions (specialized and standard) as the Lattice C compiler. There are still a few minor differences in the two, but anyone who learns to program in C using the RUN/C interpreter will have no problem in switching over to the Lattice C compiler or most other full-range C programming environments.

ABOUT RUN/C AND ITS CREATORS

In researching the origins of the RUN/C interpreter, I was fortunate enough to be able to interview Todd Katz, president of Age of Reason Company, and Peter Brooks. Todd was originally the new products manager of Lifeboat Associates for the Lattice C compiler. This company planned the marketing strategy for the Lattice C compiler, which has become known as one of the best in the business.

Mr. Katz explains, "As soon as [Lattice C] took off, it became obvious from talking with the people who were trying to learn C that an interpreter for C was needed." These thoughts were taking place during the middle of 1982 at a time when C language compilers for microcomputers were scarce and interpreters were nonexistent. Mr. Katz continues:

> I received word from a book publisher in New York City that he had located someone who wanted to write an interpreter for C. We at Lifeboat Associates immediately contacted Lattice, Inc. (authoring company of the Lattice C compiler), telling them about this.

About RUN/C and Its Creators
163

Their response was to the effect that an interpreter for C should not and could not be written. To make a long story short, this idea didn't go anywhere. We talked further with Ed Currie, president of Lifeboat Associates, and he continued to press Lattice, Inc. for a C interpreter. Apparently, they were not able to find anyone to write this interpreter. I understand that someone was put on the project, but after six months the conclusion was reached that an interpreter could not be written, or, at least, it would be more difficult to write an interpreter for Lattice C than it was to write the compiler, a five-year project itself.

About this time, another company leaked the fact that they would be offering a C interpreter in the near future. I went out and talked to them about their project and did some preliminary work with Dr. Currie. We realized that neither the development nor their marketing strategy was along the lines that we had envisioned at Lifeboat. Their package was aimed at a very low level user. They sort of wanted it to be a C interpreter for housewives. Therefore, they didn't feel that it needed to come anywhere close to approaching the full C language. They also had a lot of oddball, "nonstandard" features in their package.

Shortly after this, Todd Katz left Lifeboat Associates to form Age of Reason, Inc., but the idea of a C interpreter continued to be a major goal. A short while later, he hooked up with Steve Walton, also a former Lifeboat employee. Steve was approached with the idea of writing a C interpreter and after much consideration decided he would like to do it. Age of Reason, Inc. still maintained close contacts with Lifeboat Associates, and the latter company was still interested in a C interpreter. Lifeboat provided the front money to develop the project, but this advance was based on the completion of a marketable C interpreter.

Katz continues:

We originally planned an interpreter which followed the C language standard, but which was really quite limited, as it would contain no structure or union operations. Floating-point operations would also be bypassed. This was not uncommon in those earlier days when the majority of the limited number of C compilers in existence supported integer-only operations. But as the work on this project progressed, we realized these facets that we were not going to support could be done and should be done. The first line of code for the RUN/C interpreter was written in April 1984, but we kept expanding upon our original intentions to try and build as much into this project as possible. Our first goal of building a somewhat limited C interpreter was quickly changing into a C interpreter which fully supported the entire C language and more specifically would do everything the Lattice C compiler would.

In September 1984, Peter Brooks joined the C interpreter team. Peter is another alumnus of Lifeboat Associates and is known in Manhattan as an expert on both C language and the UNIX operating system. Peter was sufficiently intrigued by the interpreter project, which was still a closely guarded secret, and joined Age of Reason as a combination advisor and troubleshooter.

When Peter was asked about his thoughts upon joining this project, he replied:

I had been developing C programs for many years, and I was always irritated by the very slow turnaround time on all C compilers: the time between conception of the program and actual execution. As a matter of fact, whenever I had a small, quick, and dirty programming job to do, I would do it in an interpretive language such as BASIC rather than in C. By using an interpreter, I could generate code out of my head and into the machine and get immediate feedback on such things as syntax errors, execution time, and even logic errors. Through an interpreter I could develop my initial code about five times faster than I could with a compiler. Of course, for large jobs, BASIC is just not sufficient, and C was the language I had chosen for most serious development. I chose it for its flexibility and power, but there was still a large turnaround time. I could see no solution to this problem, so I simply lived with it, as do all C programmers.

I knew Todd Katz and Steve Walton from Lifeboat Associates, and when I was approached about the C interpreter, I realized what a difficult assignment it was, but also how useful it would be. At the time I was contacted, a large part of the C interpreter was already up and running. The code had already been written and debugged, there were still major difficulties to be overcome, but their concept was sound.

I was very enthusiastic about the notion of a C interpreter, especially from the standpoint of it being something that I would want to use, personally.

With the addition of Peter Brooks to the project, the first version of RUN/C was finished in late December 1984. RUN/C was written entirely in Lattice C. This first release was called the Pioneer version. From start to finish, the project had taken about eight months. It was marketed by Lifeboat Associates in early January 1985. This first version was by no means the end product long sought by Age of Reason. It was a somewhat limited C interpreter in that structures and unions were not permitted. However, it did support floating-point operations and the rest of the standard C programming language. It seems that every few months after this point, new updates of RUN/C were being made available, and each offered more and more. In addition to structures and unions, RUN/C supported full-memory PEEK and POKE as well as access to IBM BIOS and interrupts. The latest versions allowed direct access of all memory while in the unprotected mode. This would be the equivalent of the large-memory model of the Lattice C Compiler.

While talking with Todd and Peter, I asked if there was ever a time during the RUN/C project when they became so bogged down that they felt the project would never be completed. Todd answered: "Yes! There were about five or six different times when we reached apparently insurmountable problems. However, we plowed on and found a way around them. Even after Peter joined the effort, we still had a few rough periods."

Peter adds:

As we got close to apparent completion, it dawned on us that we had not taken multidimensional arrays into account. We did have a major difficulty in this area. We were finally able to work that one out. Still, there were points of confusion. In other words, "How do we do this? We don't have a clue at this point!" However, for the most part it was not a question of "Can we do it?" but "Can we do this comfortably and elegantly?" rather than through some brute-force mechanism. I still hold to the theory that reads: "In programming, all things are possible." It just boils down to a matter of how much

About RUN/C and Its Creators

time it is going to take to figure out how to do it and if the expenditure and hours are worth it.

At this point in the interview, I began to ask questions relating to C language in general, especially about BASIC programmers who want to learn C. Todd Katz emphasized that RUN/C was directed toward the BASIC language programmer as well as to the person who happens to stumble on to C and wants to learn the language. This direction toward lower-level users is manifest mostly in the documentation that accompanies RUN/C. There are a few special functions that mimic BASIC statements and functions, but other than these, RUN/C is used like most other C programming environments. For these reasons, RUN/C is ideal for the beginner and is also an excellent tool for the seasoned C programmer who wants fast turnaround time between program development and execution.

I have long contended that there is a certain elitist attitude among persons who know how to program in C. These persons seem to feel superior in the knowledge that they can program in a language most people do not know. I have also noticed an aura of protectiveness in this area, in that some C programmers do not like the idea of, or wish to see, lower-level programmers (such as those who know BASIC) moving into their exclusive arena of influence.

When I expressed these opinions, Peter Brooks responded with:

> I wouldn't go so far as to say that C programming is protected from outsiders. Given that the language is difficult to learn and it is powerful, those who have learned it, do, indeed, have a sense of superiority over everybody else. However, this is also true of LISP programmers. C programming is, in a sense, a priesthood. What we were trying to do by writing RUN/C was to demystify the language by providing a protective environment where programming errors could be made without costing so much in turnaround time.

Along the same line of questioning, I also expressed an opinion I did not agree with but had heard many times in C language circles. This opinion states that a person who knows no programming language can learn C easier than one who knows BASIC. Brooks stated:

> I can give you a professional answer, because I teach C professionally. There are two levels of people interested in learning C: (1) they are interested in learning C as a second language, or (2) they are interested in learning C as a first language. The second group is going to have more difficulty learning C than will the first. Knowing any computer language is always more advantageous than knowing none when learning C or any other language. I have taught a large number of people who know either BASIC or COBOL to program in C. Those tend to be my industrial audiences. The syntax of C is very new to them, but they understand the notion of what computers do. This gives them an enormous advantage over people who have never interacted with a computer before. The notion of a procedural language, of different types of variables, and of variables

that change are all contained in BASIC. Admittedly, those who know BASIC have to learn a different syntax, but those who know nothing about computers have to learn an entirely new way of thinking. I would far prefer teaching C to someone who knows BASIC than to someone who doesn't know any computer language.

Now, if I had my preference for someone else's first language, assuming I would be teaching them C, I would prefer this first language to be something like ALGOL or PASCAL. But again, anyone with any kind of first language is far ahead in their ability to learn C in comparison to someone with no language at all. BASIC provides you with all the major computer science constructs. The difficulty in teaching C to persons who already know BASIC lies in the fact that they are accustomed to a level of convenience not offered by the standard function set in C. To BASIC programmers, C is a step down in programming environment, despite C's high power. RUN/C is a special programming environment that offers some of the conveniences BASIC programmers are accustomed to, and it gives them an opportunity to compare apples to apples, regarding some attributes in both languages. With RUN/C, BASIC programmers do not have to give up something in order to learn the C programming language. I would hope that within the next 5 to 10 years, there will be no such thing as a compiler from the programmer's point of view. Certainly, there might be a compilation process hidden deep inside the system. In other words the compilation process will be transparent to the user. As for now, the programming environment in which you have an interpreter is far, far easier for the programmer.

I next asked Todd Katz how RUN/C was first received by the general public. He stated:

I think they were surprised. The people I showed it to at Comdex were quite amazed to see it work. After the initial surprise, I think most of the people who used RUN/C were very excited to have such an easy and efficient C programming environment at their disposal. Experienced C programmers stated their belief that this was really going to help many more people learn C. Admittedly, we have had some negative responses from a few people who think that they know C backwards and forwards (and usually they do not). We have had two people in this category who have told us that RUN/C is not satisfactory in comparison with their compilers. Quite frankly, initial sales of RUN/C more than fulfilled our optimistic expectations. RUN/C is being sold worldwide and people seem to be enjoying it in every country from Canada to Malaysia. It has recently been translated into Japanese and is selling in record numbers in Japan.

I hope this interview has shed some light on the history of RUN/C and some background on the people who developed and wrote the project. It is interesting to note that all of them were at one time or other connected with Lifeboat Associates, generally acknowledged to be the leading distributor and promoter of C language products in the world. It is easy to see why RUN/C is so friendly to BASIC language programmers, in that the major advisor and troubleshooter for this project teaches C language, often to BASIC language programmers.

Extended Line Editor   **167**

In summation, RUN/C was designed to be a C language environment which envelopes the user in a protective shell that allows the full C language to be used quickly and efficiently while providing protection from the cost of making serious errors. The concept has already proven to be a good one by the demonstrated world-wide popularity of RUN/C. RUN/C continues to grow in popularity, and it changes periodically by offering more and more features. I still hold to my prediction that it will introduce more people to C in a comfortable manner than will any other C language environment.

EXTENDED LINE EDITOR

RUN/C contains its own built-in editor, as does Microsoft BASIC; however, the RUN/C version is an *extended line editor* as opposed to a screen editor. To write your first C program, you first enter RUN/C by typing

RC <RETURN>

After the program is loaded, the RUN/C logo will appear at the top of the screen. Now type

AUTO <RETURN>

The AUTO command works just as it does in BASIC. This is the area of the editor that automatically generates line numbers. The RUN/C editor generates line numbers in increments of one instead of default increments of ten as is the case with MS BASIC. Line numbers are not actually a part of a C program. These numbers are simply references to allow you to make changes within a program once it is written.

From this point on, you proceed just as you would if you were writing a program in BASIC. You can insert characters by using the <Ins> key while the Del key deletes characters. The sequence of Ctrl-End will erase an entire line or all characters on that line starting at the cursor position. Hitting the End key will advance the cursor to the end of the line. RUN/C uses the line editor as opposed to a full-screen editor, so you cannot use the up and down arrow keys to move to other program lines. To edit a specific line, you must type EDIT followed by the line number. This can also be done in BASIC. When a program is finished, you simply hit the Esc key.

To insert lines, simply type INSERT followed by the line number above which the insertion is to take place. New line numbers will be generated and all that follow will be updated so that the finished program is sequentially numbered. The following is a summary of the various editing keys and their use with the RUN/C extended line editor:

Key	Function
Home or Ctrl-e	Moves cursor to the beginning of the logical program line.
End or Ctrl-x	Moves cursor to the end of the logical program line.
\<up arrow\>	No effect (beep).
\<down arrow\>	No effect (beep).
\<left arrow\> or Ctrl-s	Moves the cursor one position "backward" toward the beginning of the line. If the cursor is at the beginning of the logical program line, this command will have no effect. If the cursor is at the beginning of the second or third screen lines in a logical line, the cursor will "wrap" to the end of the preceding screen line. (See above for a description of the differences between *screen* and *logical* lines.)
\<right arrow\> or Ctrl-d	Moves cursor one position "forward" toward the end of the line. If the cursor is currently at the end of the screen line, it will "wrap" to the next line. It is not possible to move the cursor beyond the last character in a logical line.
Ctrl-\<left arrow\> or Ctrl-a	Moves the cursor to the beginning of the next word to the *left* of the current cursor position on the logical line. A *word* in this context is defined as a character or group of characters that begin with a letter or a number. Words are separated by blanks or special characters such as punctuation marks. Thus the effect of this command is to move the cursor backward past the preceding group of nonalphanumeric characters to the start of the next group of alphanumeric characters. (See the examples below.)
Ctrl-\<right arrow\> or Ctrl-f	Moves the cursor forward to the beginning of the next word to the *right* of the current cursor position on the logical line. A "word" is defined as a character or group of characters that begin with a letter or number. Words are separated by blanks or special characters such as punctuation marks. Thus the effect of this command is to move the cursor past the first group of continuous nonalphanumeric characters to the next alphanumeric character. It is not possible to move the cursor beyond the last character in a logical line.
Ctrl-Home or Ctrl-w	Deletes all characters from the cursor position to the beginning of the logical program line.
Ctrl-End or Ctrl-z	Deletes all characters from the cursor position to the end of the logical program line.
\<Ins\> or Ctrl-v	Toggles between the Insert and Overtype modes. On the IBM PC and PC compatibles, the shape of the blinking cursor indicates which mode is active: rectangular for *Insert Mode*, an underline for *Overtype Mode*. On MS-DOS systems which are running under systems other than native PC DOS (such as ANSI.SYS), the word **INSERT** will appear on the twenty-fourth screen line when the Insert Mode is active. The initial condition on entering the RUN/C editor is Overtype Mode. In Overtype Mode, any character typed will be placed in the line at the current cursor position. If a character is currently in that position, it will be overwritten. The first time the \<Ins\> key is depressed, Insert Mode is selected and the shape of the blinking cursor will become rectangular, covering the lower half of its current position.

Extended Line Editor

Key	Function
	When in Insert Mode, a character that is typed is inserted at the current cursor position. The character which had occupied that position, the cursor, and all characters to the right of the inserted character are moved forward to make room for the new character. When the end of the screen line (the eightieth character) is reached, characters "wrap" to the next line on the left side of the screen.
	Insert Mode can be turned off in two ways: either by pressing the <Ins> key or its control equivalent or by using any other active control or function key.
Del or Ctrl-g	Deletes the character at the current cursor position. All characters to the right of the deleted character move left one position. The cursor remains in its current position. Line wrapping occurs; that is, if a logical line extends beyond one screen line, characters on subsequent lines will move to the previous line. If you are at the end of the line, the <Del> command has no effect.
<backspace> or Ctrl-h	Deletes the character to the left of the cursor. All characters to the right of the deleted character and the cursor move left one position. The cursor also moves left one position. Line wrapping occurs. If the cursor is at the beginning of the logical line, the backspace key will have no effect.
Esc or Ctrl-c	Cancels any editing changes that may have been made in the current line, and redisplays the unaltered original line and the message **Line n unchanged** **Ok** Control passes from the RUN/C editor to the Command level.
<enter> or Ctrl-m	When pressed anywhere in the line, causes the entire logical line to replace the same logical line in memory. *Note*: If <enter> is pressed by mistake, the only way to modify the condition is to reedit the line.
<tab> or Ctrl-i	Moves the cursor to the next tab position in Overtype or Edit Mode. However, in Insert Mode all the following text will be moved forward to the next tab position. In Overtype Mode, the cursor will merely "move over" existing text to the next tabular position. Tabs are adjustable. The default setting is every five spaces beginning with column 1. Thus tab positions are columns 0, 5, 10, and so on.

If you decide to change something that is on the current line, there are many ways to make the change. For example, if the change is to the left of your current cursor position, the <left arrow> key will move the cursor to the left character by character. If the change is to the right of your current cursor position, the <right arrow> key will move the cursor to the right. If the item you wish to change is at or near the end of the line, the End key will move the cursor to the end of the line. If the item you wish to change is several words away, the Ctrl-<left arrow> and Ctrl-<right arrow> will move you backward or forward in the line a single word at a time.

Although there are many similarities between MS-BASIC editor and the RUN/C extended line editor, the two are of different types. You might think of the RUN/C editor as being a cross between the MS-DOS line editor (EDLIN) and the one found in MS-BASIC. It should take only a short while for you to become accustomed to using the extended line editor.

DOCUMENTATION

When one rates documentation of C language software, it is first necessary to consider who will be using that software. I have reviewed several C compilers whose documentation could be rated as excellent, provided that it is aimed at a knowledgeable C language readership. However, this same information would rate as poor if it were aimed at a reader who knew BASIC and was only beginning to learn C. Fortunately, the RUN/C documentation is excellent and is aimed at the beginner to C language. The RUN/C manual is by no means a BASIC-to-C tutorial, but it briefly explains each C function or statement and provides one or more actual program examples. This is of immediate help to the student, in that it fully explains proper syntax, argument data types, and return data types. The RUN/C manual will not take the place of a good tutorial, but it is certainly a complementary adjunct.

STANDARDIZATION

For the most part, RUN/C is a full K&R implementation of C language. However, it is more. In addition to the standard C functions, there are others that mimic several BASIC statements and functions, both in name and in operation. It should be understood that C was designed as a portable language. Such functions as CLS, LOCATE, TAB, and so on, are machine dependent. Although these are not standard C functions, they can be programmed from the functions already available. Such specialized functions, however, will be machine-dependent. The RUN/C interpreter contains the specialized functions named above. These make programming much easier, especially for the beginner, who will not have the knowledge to program the machine-dependent functions.

The original C language contained no PEEK or POKE functions. None were really needed, since pointers could address any area of memory on the minicomputers. However, when C was first implemented for microcomputers, most versions were restricted to a 64K area. This allowed no access to memory locations outside the program and data areas through pointer operations. Later versions implemented machine language PEEK and POKE functions that were called from C. Still later versions (often called large-memory models) allowed pointers to directly access any area of memory.

The pioneer version of RUN/C did not contain PEEK and POKE functions and there was no way to access memory outside the RUN/C data segment. However, RUN/C followed the same transitions that the earlier C compilers went through. The next version did indeed contain PEEK and POKE functions and a later rendition allowed all of memory to be directly accessed by pointers. The latter capability is put into effect by a special command (SET TRUST ON). Beginning C programmers are urged not to open RUN/C to unlimited memory access, since a programming error could cause important information to be overwritten and permanently destroyed. This could be disastrous if a disk file control block is inadvertently de-

Standardization

171

stroyed, as information already on disk could be lost forever. In the "safe" mode (SET TRUST OFF), it is far more difficult to create a disastrous memory overwrite through errors in pointer operations. In this mode, the only access to memory outside the RUN/C data segment will be through PEEK and POKE functions.

This speaks to the versatility of RUN/C. It makes an excellent learning environment, especially for BASIC programmers who want to move up to C. However, as these students become more experienced, the interpreter can be set to a mode that will allow them freer access. Experienced programmers will also find RUN/C quite acceptable. I have used C compilers for several years now, but I often test programs using RUN/C, because I can immediately correct a programming error and go through a rerun without having to recompile. Once the program is fully debugged, it can be compiled with greater assurances of a satisfactory run.

Because of its versatility, I do not think anyone who owns RUN/C will ever outgrow it. Nor will RUN/C ever take the place of a C compiler. A main advantage of the C language is execution speed, which often borders on that of assembly language programs. RUN/C, like all interpreters, is quite slow. In many instances it is slower than a BASIC interpreter. I tend to think of it as a programming tool rather than a programming language used to write practical applications that will be executed under RUN/C. It is a learning tool foremost, but it will be a tremendous boon to any serious C language programmer, by helping him/her to quickly debug a new application and prepare it for compilation.

As of this writing, I am currently BETA testing a new version of RUN/C, which is called RUN/C Professional. It is my understanding that the professional model will be a separate product that is an expansion of standard RUN/C. This new model, when completed, will have the capability of loading previously compiled routines and running them at the rapid speed that compiled programs produce. This means that specialized graphics libraries, precision mathematics libraries, and so on, will be open to the RUN/C Professional environment.

My only real complaint with RUN/C may no longer be a factor by the time you read these words. Newer versions of RUN/C may have eliminated this all together. The complaint lies in the declaration of standard functions which return values other than integers. A standard K&R implementation of C would require that such functions as *log*(), *sqrt*(), *sin*(), *exp*(), and *pow*() be declared as doubles in any program or function that calls them. RUN/C does not require this and it is an error to do so. Again, I am speaking of Version 1.32 and all others that have gone before it. Also, #INCLUDEing *stdio.h* is necessary in a standard implementation when filekeeping routines are programmed. It is an error to do this in RUN/C. My complaint is not in how they are declared, but involves the fact that they *cannot* be. The experienced C language programmer will undoubtedly appreciate this, since it involves less typing. But the beginner could get into a bad habit. It is important to understand that C expects all functions to return integer values unless specifically told otherwise. With the absence of these declaration lines, this general necessity in other C environments is overlooked. When the student moves on to a C compiler, problems might develop.

This one disadvantage is offset by many, many advantages. Unlike most C compilers which offer very primitive error detection during the compilation process, RUN/C offers excellent error detection. The error messages generated when an incorrect program run is attempted will be of great aid to the beginner in seeing just where he/she went wrong. For instance, if you use an integer argument with a function that requires a double argument value, execution will halt and RUN/C will tell you that it was expecting a different type of argument at a specific line. You can then edit the contents of this line and see where your mistake was made. MS-BASIC offers reasonably good error detection and error prompt lines. This same style is carried over into RUN/C.

USING RUN/C

Once you have learned to use the extended line editor discussed earlier, actually using RUN/C is no problem at all. You will find that all of the C language programs in this book will execute nicely in the RUN/C environment, although you may find it necessary to delete the declaration lines from the examples that name functions internal to RUN/C [i.e., *log*(), *sin*(), *exp*(), *sqrt*(), etc.].

The latest version at the time of this writing (Version 1.32) is capable of using user-built functions that return pointers, something earlier versions did not feature. However, a strong point is made for RUN/C being used by BASIC programmers learning C by looking closely at the "familiarities" found in the MS-BASIC interpreter. As mentioned previously, programs are begun by typing AUTO, which triggers the automatic line-number generator. If you need to edit a program line, you simply type EDIT followed by the line number. The left and right cursor keys work as they do in MS-BASIC editing operations.

When a program has been entered, you simply hit the escape key and type RUN to execute it. Or you can run it by hitting the F2 function key on the IBM PC keyboard, just as you do in BASIC. The big surprise about RUN/C is that there are no surprises! The environment seems to have been specially tailored for the BASIC programmer. If you have dabbled in C with a C compiler, you should be very pleased with the friendlier environment of RUN/C.

To put RUN/C through its paces, several benchmark tests were run. RUN/C will never take any prizes in the speed category, but it does run all standard C programs properly. This is more than could be said of many compilers a few years ago. RUN/C adheres to the true C programming language and offers no unpleasant surprises for the beginner, who will depend heavily on printed program listings from tutorials to become acquainted with this new language.

On the other hand, do not expect RUN/C to react to a C program the way a compiler would. It has been stated previously that integer operations will execute far faster than floating-point equivalents. Also, C converts all floats to doubles before processing, and this conversion requires time. Therefore, doubles offer more precision and execute faster than do floats. However, a lot of this does not apply to RUN/C. The following program serves as a good example:

Using RUN/C   **173**

```
main()
{

    double x;

    for (x = 0; x <= 500; ++x)
        ;


}
```

This simple *for* loop counts double *x* from 0 to 500. It will require approximately 12 seconds from start to finish on a standard IBM PC operating at 4.77 MHz. Normally, you could expect a significant speed increase if you declared *x* an *int* and left the rest of the program as is. However, it will not make the slightest difference in RUN/C. The program will still take about 12 seconds from start to finish. The same speeds were also clocked when *x* was declared a float.

Again, speed is not nearly as important a factor in such a translator as is its ability to run standard C programs. In the latter, RUN/C excels. Except for the fact that no internal functions that return other than integers need to or can be declared, RUN/C seems to be a standard implementation of C. There are few, if any, surprises. As a matter of fact, with only a few minor modifications to the CBREEZE source code, the entire program could run under RUN/C. This is a theoretical evaluation, because RUN/C could not possibly handle the number of code lines that make up CBREEZE, but each element of the complex CBREEZE program, written in Lattice C, is a standard C construct and fits RUN/C's code criteria. RUN/C was used for debugging many of the modules that eventually wound up in CBREEZE, which speeded development time considerably.

The following C program is a translation of a BASIC program published in *PC World* magazine to allow the IBM PC to display 16 simultaneous colors in low-resolution mode. This mode is alluded to in the IBM Technical Reference Manual but was never documented. To set up a low-resolution screen and write to it in BASIC is a fairly complex ordeal, but CBREEZE was able to translate this program into C, and RUN/C was fully capable of running it. The program follows:

```
long defseg;

main()
{

    double datanum();
    int modereg, colorreg, modesave, colorsave, crtreg, crtdata,
hires, graph, bw, video, gok, blink, mode, regare, regdata, cher,
attr, pixcol, y, t, x, pixel, pixeladdr, nibble;

    modereg = 0x3d8;
    colorreg = 0x3d9;
    modesave = 0x465;
```

```
colorsave = 0x466;
crtreg = 0x3d4;
crtdata = 0x3d5;
hires = 1;
graph = 2;
bw = 4;
video = 8;
gok = 16;
blink = 32;
defseg = 0L;
mode = 0;

poke(defseg + modesave, mode);
outp(modereg, mode);
poke(defseg + colorsave, 0);
outp(colorreg, 0);

for (regare = 0; regare <= 11; ++regare) {
    regdata = datanum();
    outp(crtreg, regare);
    outp(crtdata, regdata);
}

mode = hires + video;

poke(defseg + modesave, mode);
outp(modereg, mode);

defseg = 16L * 0xb800L;

for (cher = 0; cher <= 15998; cher += 2)
    poke(defseg + cher, 0xde);

for (attr = 1; attr <= 16000; attr += 2)
    poke(defseg + attr, 0);

pixcol = 0;
y = 0;

for (t = 1; t <= 39; ++t) {
    y = y + 1;
    if (t % 5 == 0)
        pixcol = pixcol + 1 % 15;

    for (x = 1; x <= t; ++x) {
        pixel = x + (y * 160);
        pixeladdr = (pixel & 0xfffe) + 1;

        nibble = pixel % 2;
        if (nibble == 0)
            poke(defseg + pixeladdr, (peek(defseg +
pixeladdr) & 0xf) + pixcol * 0x10);
        if (nibble == 1)
```

Using RUN/C

```c
                    poke(defseg + pixeladdr, (peek(defseg +
pixeladdr) & 0xf0) + pixcol);
        }


    }


    x = 1;
    pixcol = 8;

    for (t = 1; t <= 39; ++t) {
        x = x + 1;
        if (t % 5 == 0)
            pixcol = pixcol + 1 % 15;

        for (y = 1; y <= t; ++y) {
            pixel = x + (y * 160);
            pixeladdr = (pixel & 0xfffe) + 1;
            nibble = pixel % 2;
            if (nibble == 0)
                poke(defseg + pixeladdr, (peek(defseg +
pixeladdr) & 0xf) + pixcol * 0x10);
            if (nibble == 1)
                poke(defseg + pixeladdr, (peek(defseg +
pixeladdr) & 0xf0) + pixcol);
        }


    {


    exit(0);


}
int _ddata = 0;
double datanum()
{

    double x;

    static double y[] = {
        113,
        80,
        90,
        10,
        127,
        6,
        100,
        112,
        2,
        1,
        32,
        0,
        427.010511
    };
```

176   The RUN/C Interpreter   Chap. Sixteen

```
if ((x = y[-ddata++]) == 427.010511) {
    printf("Out of Data");
    exit(0);
}
else
    return(x);
```

```
}
```

This is a fairly complex program, yet it follows the standard route that such a program would follow if it had originally been written in C instead of BASIC. This CBREEZE translation runs perfectly under RUN/C, although it does take quite some time to write the graphic display, due to the slowness inherent in interpreters. CBREEZE conversion time was about 90 seconds on a standard IBM PC and total execution time under RUN/C is approximately 12 minutes.

The familiar BASIC functions that are built into RUN/C make for a more familiar environment for beginners. Take the following program, for example:

```
10  LOCATE 10,10
20  PRINT"My name is Thor."
```

This simple BASIC program would be a problem with most C compilers, because the LOCATE statement in BASIC is hardware-dependent. No such standard function exists in C. Programmers in the language are expected to be familiar enough with the internal architecture of their machines to program these using interrupts and system calls from C. However, the average beginner to C does not know how to do this. Chances are that he/she has never even explored the mechanics of moving the cursor about the screen, because this has never been necessary in BASIC, with its built-in conveniences.

RUN/C allows you to take some of these conveniences with you. The RUN/C version of this BASIC program is

```
main()
{

    locate (1, 1, 0);
    printf("My name is Thor.\n");

}
```

The same is true of CLS in BASIC. Again, this is a machine-dependent operation and most C environments do not provide a special function to handle this. CLS is definitely not a part of the standard C language, because C was always meant to be portable. Such machine dependencies could be specially programmed after the major portion of a program was brought up on a new machine.

Again, RUN/C takes you under its protective wing. The *cls*() function clears the screen just as CLS does in BASIC. You will also find built-in printer functions

Using RUN/C   **177**

such as *lprintf*, which is the printer version of *printf*, just as LPRINT is the printer
version of PRINT in BASIC. Other special features include access to the communica-
tion port (modem) through a single call. Traditionally, these functions would be
written by the programmer who had need of such access, and each would require a
considerable amount of C code.

RUN/C can run most programs designed for execution under a compiler, as
long as program length is not massive and the complexity of single lines of source
code is not too great. RUN/C can sometimes get confused in the midst of such
complexities that would present no problem to a compiler. Also, functions such as
printf and *sprintf*, whose number of arguments are not fixed, are restricted to seven
total arguments. This applies to Version 1.32 of RUN/C and may have been expanded
in the version currently available as you read these words.

RUN/C does present a few deviations from standard when it comes to displaying
special characters. However, a chart is provided in the documentation to help you
through this. For instance, if you wanted to display a phrase surrounded by quotes,
standard C would allow you to write

```
printf("\"Phrase in quotes\"");
```

which would display

```
"Phrase in quotes"
```

However, RUN/C will read the quote characters (\") as an improperly quoted phrase.
The proper method for accomplishing the above under RUN/C is

```
printf("\042Phrase in quotes\042");
```

The \042 designation uses 42, which is the octal value for the ASCII code of the
double quote (") character. An apostrophe or single quote is printed by the code
\047.

These are minor inconveniences that will have no bearing whatsoever on the
great majority of persons who use RUN/C as a learning environment. Any nonstandard restrictions are well documented in the RUN/C manual, which was written
for beginners. Some of us who are better versed in C appreciate the clear-cut style
of this manual as well. Reading most C documentation is a "dry" experience at
best. RUN/C documentation is a bit lighter and very informative.

It is my opinion and one shared by others that RUN/C is currently the friendliest
and best C environment for BASIC programmers who want to learn C programming.
There are enough familiar commands and functions that the student does not feel
completely isolated from his/her normal programming environment, and it is difficult
to make a costly mistake. This is not to say that you can simply sit down in front
of the computer and program easily in C. But you can sit down and begin inputting
some printed program examples or load them from disk files in much the same
manner you have been doing for some time in BASIC.

178   The RUN/C Interpreter   Chap. Sixteen

This is not true if you are going directly from a BASIC interpreter to a C compiler, especially if you have never used any type of compiler before. It will take awhile just to learn how to compile the source code you have input via an editor and possibly to assemble and/or link other modules to arrive at an executable program. Unlike compilers, RUN/C allows you to "begin learning" immediately. The turn-around time between program conception and actually attempting a run should be cut by a factor of 10, at least. This means that you can do 10 times more learning with RUN/C than you can with many compilers while spending the same amount of time behind the keyboard.

If you make a syntax error, so what? That is what learning is all about. With RUN/C you can quickly make a change and, just as quickly, run the program again. You can run a program 10 times and make 10 corrections in the same amount of time it would take you to run a program once under a compiler.

Do not misunderstand, I am not knocking C compilers. But for the beginner, RUN/C is an easier environment in which to work. Later, a compiler will be manda-tory if you want to write serious applications that execute at reasonable speeds. How-ever, RUN/C will still continue to be an invaluable tool for testing, debugging, and so on. For the more experienced C programmer, RUN/C will augment the program-ming environment provided by the C compiler.

RUN/C is available from

> Lifeboat Associates
> 55 South Broadway
> Tarrytown, NY 10591
>
> (914) 332-1875

CHAPTER SEVENTEEN

CBREEZE

The CBREEZE BASIC-to-C tutorial translator is an exciting addition to learning tools now available to budding C programmers. It is aptly named in that it tends to make the usually difficult assignment of learning C language a relative breeze. CBREEZE was written to "think" like an experienced C language programmer whose duty is to translate Microsoft BASIC programs into C source code. Its output code is very close to that which would be rendered by a human programmer. One amazing thing about the source code CBREEZE outputs is its *beauty*. The code strictly adheres to the format and style presented in *The C Programming Language* by Brian Kernighan and Dennis Ritchie (Englewood Cliffs, N.J.: Prentice-Hall, 1978), still the bible for C programmers. It does not just display C source code equivalents of BASIC programs but displays this code in blocks (the way a programmer would) and with special attention to providing the proper indentations, spacing, and so on, which quickly identifies a good programming style.

For example,

```
10  FOR X%=1 TO 400
20  PRINT X%
30  NEXT X%
```

is translated as

```
main()
{

    int x;
```

179

```
                    for (x = 1; x <= 400; ++x)
                        printf("%d\n", x);

        }
```

This is exactly the way it would be expressed according to Kernighan and Ritchie, including indentations, line spacing, and white spaces on the same line.

CBREEZE sticks to this critical adherence to style regardless of BASIC program complexity. It is surprising in that it will accurately translate quite complex BASIC structures without a complaint. The translator was designed specifically for tutorial purposes, but this does not mean that the code cannot be compiled or used by an interpreter. All output code is fully usable by any system that can run C programs.

More examples and a fuller technical discussion are presented later in this chapter, but after many, many hours of simply playing with CBREEZE, it would seem that it does all that is claimed for it.

CBREEZE is a product of Robert J. Traister & Associates in Front Royal, Virginia. The author, in addition to creating CBREEZE, is also the author of more than 50 books, many on computer subjects. Up until the CBREEZE project, Traister & Associates wrote technical books for several large publishers. More recently, a software division has been created which concentrates mainly on C language products.

CBREEZE was a direct result of the extreme difficulty that I experienced while learning C. I started learning C in 1982, and, as a BASIC-only programmer, it was an experience I shall never forget. It has to have been one of the most difficult things I ever attempted. The only reference source available was the Kernighan and Ritchie book, which is not a tutorial. Most of what I found in this text was completely incomprehensible to me. I started with a very nonstandard compiler, which did not help matters one bit. It took me over a month to compile my first program because the first version of this compiler did not work at all. It was several weeks before I finally figured out that the problem was in the compiler and not with me. Anyway, by simply experimenting for about three months, I finally gained a smattering of understanding. I even wrote a book about these early experiences, providing a few simple C programs and a lot of storytelling about where I had gone wrong. Although this book would be rated as quite inadequate today, mail from readers was encouraging. Apparently, they were having the same problems I had had and this simple text was enough to get them over a few humps.

At this stage, I simply gave up on going further into C and concentrated on writing books in other subject areas. However, in 1983 Lifeboat Associates sent me a copy of their Lattice C compiler, based on a request for research materials that I had made some months before.

When the Lattice C compiler arrived, I almost returned it immediately, since I had no further interest in learning what seemed to me to be a difficult, nearly useless language. Instead, I simply tossed it in a drawer with the idea that I might play with it sometime in the future when I was feeling especially masochistic. A month or so later, I had just completed a book and did not feel like starting on

CBREEZE   Chap. Seventeen   **181**

another, so I pulled out the compiler with the idea of "fooling around" a bit. This was a major turning point in my programming direction. The Lattice compiler was a complete C compiler. It did not limit me to integer math as the prior one did, and it followed the Kernighan and Ritchie standard for C language. Also, it compiled most programs in a minute or so, whereas the other one took five minutes or more. I began to have fun with this new language. Bit by bit, I began to gain a better understanding of what C was all about. This was a laborious process which entailed writing thousands of C programs, three-quarters of which did not run correctly on the first three attempts. Sometimes I would spend days or even weeks trying to work out a very simple problem. The Lifeboat Associates people were quite helpful in all of this, although their technical support department was geared toward helping users with implementation problems and not to teach them to program. After months of study, I wrote another book on C programming and still another. These were popular books that are still in print and selling well.

I was after the completion of one of these books that I took a closer look at the needs of the BASIC programmer who wants to learn C. All of my books on the subject had drawn on personal experiences, but I realized that other BASIC programmers might not identify with all of these. I surmised that if there were some way to tailor a tutorial to the student's personal needs, the process would be far less painful. The method of accomplishing this, however, eluded me.

I had been deep in thought for about an hour and was toying with the idea of writing a book on learning C that would include five coupons which could be filled in by the reader to include a BASIC program example that he/she wished translated into C. The reader would mail in this coupon and I would mail back a C language equivalent as an aid in getting over a particular hump that my book did not fully explain. However, figuring an average first-year sales of 5000 books, I realized that I simply could not handle up to 25,000 personal requests. Then it dawned on me that a program which would perform this conversion would be the practical answer to the problem! I immediately sat down at my IBM PC and began writing a translation program I called "CGEN," for "C generator." As it turned out, CGEN was not the actual start of CBREEZE. It would be nearly two years before CBREEZE was begun and a year after that before it was completed.

I wrote CGEN in Microsoft BASIC. This language was chosen because there were a lot of machines running it and far fewer for which C compilers were available. Then, too, it would be a fairly easy task to rewrite the finished program in Applesoft BASIC, as the Apple II machines were very popular at the time. This would make CGEN quite portable and available to a lot more interested programmers. I worked about 12 hours a day for three months and arrived at a very primitive translator. The program was insufferably long, restricted, and slow, even when run under a BASIC compiler. I realized at this point that what I was seeking just could not be written in BASIC. Because of the unstructured nature of this language, I began to lose track of where I was and what I had done previously. The restrictions on the BASIC input code that CGEN would accept moved it into a completely different category from that of a versatile C language translator. It would have taken a 300-

page text just to inform the user about the format the BASIC input code must take. By this time, I was terribly behind in fulfilling several book contracts, so I gave up on the idea completely.

Over the next eighteen months, I thought little of a BASIC-to-C translator. I did note that one or two of these translators were being advertised by other companies. I checked on them and discovered that they offered no tutorial advantage, in that they used special, hidden functions to emulate BASIC statements and functions. They were designed solely to allow BASIC programs to be compiled under C for the faster execution times. A look at the C source code output of these translators quickly revealed a highly unorthodox coding that depended heavily on the translator's specialized library functions that were not readable. The translators did allow many BASIC programs to be compiled under C, but offered absolutely no means of teaching C.

However, my experiences with CGEN had provided me with something that turned out to be invaluable. I had gained a very intimate understanding of the relationships between BASIC and C. I also knew where there were no clear-cut relationships that would be of a good tutorial nature.

I had just received a letter from a gentleman who had read one of my books. He was not looking for additional help but just wrote to say that this book had done more to help him through his troubles with C than 12 other books he had read on the same subject. He also told me that he had just been hired as a junior-level C language programmer by a midwestern software firm. In the same mail was a copy of a review of this book in a popular computer magazine. The reviewer stated that I had not yet learned that C could *not* be taught in a framework of BASIC. He went on to aver that the BASIC programmer must start from scratch and unlearn all the bad habits BASIC had taught. He further stated that a person who knew no language at all could learn C faster than one who already knew BASIC. I usually do not feel personally attacked when a reviewer pans one of my books, especially since a previous bad review addressed a book of mine that a short time later led the computer best-seller list for over a month and was in the top 10 for over four months. Some 150,000 readers disagreed with this reviewer, as did a major computer manufacturer, which endorsed the book during its second printing.

I considered the reviewer's remarks to be prejudiced against BASIC programmers in general. There is an old adage that equates programmers who know only BASIC with the word "dumb." At this point, I again sat down in front of my IBM PC and began writing CBREEZE in Lattice C. I worked on nothing else until CBREEZE was complete.

CBREEZE came about because of my earlier experiences with CGEN, but nothing could be drawn from the first attempt other than the inherent relationship between the two languages that CGEN demonstrated in my mind. Whereas CGEN was a shot in the dark, CBREEZE was written with a specific set of goals in mind. These goals were well thought out and aimed directly at accuracy, style, and versatility.

To be truly effective, CBREEZE had to be very versatile in what it would accept. If a programmer is accustomed to providing a white space between the PRINT statement in BASIC and the double quotes that follow, so be it. If he/she places

CBREEZE   Chap. Seventeen   **183**

the double quotes immediately after PRINT, that's fine, too. This required that, up front, CBREEZE reformat the BASIC input code. CBREEZE had to output its C source code in a style that followed Kernighan and Ritchie. I wanted all indentations to be correct. I also wanted to achieve line spacing between certain program blocks. CBREEZE had to *teach* C programming, not simply convert BASIC programs to be run under C. Any BASIC statement, function, or operation that was not tutorially relevant to C would not be supported. In other words, CBREEZE would be designed in a manner that did not reinforce bad programming habits while in a C environment. It is for this reason that CBREEZE does not support GOSUBs, for instance. True, a GOSUB in BASIC is similar to a C function call and most of the BASIC-to-C compiling converters support this statement by declaring all variables externally. However, no C programmer is going to do this in everyday programming applications. Supporting GOSUB would, in my estimation, reinforce bad C programming habits. Therefore, it is simply not supported. Examples of C function calls are provided, however, whenever such functions as LEFT$, RIGHT$, and MID$ are used in the BASIC input code. Filekeeping in C uses a different set of tools than does the same operation in BASIC. I labored for a day or so over the idea of supporting simple filekeeping but decided not to, in order to stay within the requirement of not supporting BASIC operations that offer no tutorial advantage in C. Finally, I changed my mind again. CBREEZE does support very elementary filekeeping routines, and a future version may delve more deeply into this area of programming. However, I feel strongly that filekeeping is best learned after a good base has been laid in other C operations. It is then easier to see the relationship between the screen function *printf* and the equivalent file function *fprintf*. Both work in an identical manner save for the different directions of their outputs.

Most important, CBREEZE must *force* the user to know what types of variables and/or constants are required as arguments for various functions and operations. This means that floating-point variables cannot be used to name array positions or as arguments to statements or functions that should require integers. The translator will accept such inaccuracies, but the output code will not be correct. When you try to compile or run such code, an error message will be received. These errors are documented in an accompanying manual, telling the user what he/she did wrong. I could easily have handled this by changing the inappropriate argument types using cast operators, but this would reinforce bad C programming, even though you can get away with it in BASIC. I wanted the BASIC programmer to be thinking in terms of C even while inputting BASIC source code. All of these requirements had to be met fully before I would consider CBREEZE to be complete.

It was nearly a year and 3000 programming hours later that I judged CBREEZE complete. The testing procedure involved the use of early versions of CBREEZE by BASIC programmers who were trying to learn C. Their experiences helped to shape CBREEZE into a very versatile program translator.

I was surprised at the lack of criticism received after the first testing of CBREEZE by these BASIC programmers. It soon became apparent that many of them were enthralled by the "magic" of a program that would accurately translate their BASIC renderings into textbook C. So I told them to "tear it apart" to "crash" it, so to speak. They were limited to BASIC statements and functions supported by CBREEZE and all BASIC programs had to be executable. My hope was to discover combinations that threw the translator for a loop. I was rewarded in this search. Many unusual combinations showed up and all of these were addressed. This is not to say that you cannot confuse the translator, but it is hard to do while staying within the realm of generally acceptable programming practices.

CBREEZE was the most intense effort of my life to this point. Most days, I wrote from 10 in the morning until 3 or 4 in the morning. Writing it was difficult, owing mainly to the massive number of situations that I had to anticipate, but there was never a time when I thought it would not be finished. After the first two days, I was rewarded with actually seeing the results of my efforts in the output code that was produced. Supporting the BASIC PRINT statement was the most difficult single aspect of this project. I would estimate that three solid weeks were spent on this single statement. The INPUT statement did not take as long to support, because of the time spent on PRINT. Many of the translation algorithms for PRINT also applied to INPUT.

Once CBREEZE had been debugged and was translating properly, there was still one more problem to be dealt with. It was quite slow! This was the only complaint that had not been dealt with and the single stumbling block to calling the program complete. I knew that I was running into an undesirable situation three-quarters of the way through the program. What had started out as a very fast translator was now laboring under a couple of thousand tests that had to be run on every program line with each translation. My intentions were to optimize the code once the initial user test had been completed. Fortunately, CBREEZE calls about 75 special, internal functions to translate BASIC source code into C, and this is where it is easiest to optimize. I went through each and every function, making execution-speed improvements. These increased overall speed by about 20 percent, but this was not enough. It still required about a minute and a half to properly translate 15 lines of code. The problem lay in the fact that CBREEZE was constantly reading, writing, and updating the final output disk file. Although it was a single-pass translator, most of its time was spent in filekeeping. I spent another two weeks writing virtual filekeeping functions that would directly replace the disk file functions which are standard in C. My goal was to access the disk drive only twice: once to read the BASIC input file and again to write the output C source code. All other previous disk file operations would be carried out in memory. After a lot of testing, I finally arrived at the right combination. This cured the speed problem. With these improvements, a program that required two and a half minutes to translate now took only 23 seconds. Version 1.0 of CBREEZE was finally complete!

Code optimization allowed me to compile CBREEZE using the small-memory model of the Lattice C compiler (Version 2.15). This makes for the most compact executable code and faster execution time. It also means that CBREEZE does not require a lot of RAM memory. It will run just fine on an IBM PC with 256K RAM. It is fast, accurate, and again, outputs beautiful C source code. Additionally, it is not terribly concerned about the format of the BASIC input code. It ignores most white spacing, as does the MS-BASIC interpreter.

As to the future of CBREEZE, I don't think that you will see it change drastically from what it is now. Certainly, as more and more persons use CBREEZE, certain anomalies will crop up which will be addressed. I do not see this going to 10 different versions as is the case with most software these days. Fortunately, it is written to be infinitely expandable. It has a built-in "open end" which can deliver its output to yet another processing stage. If I choose to support other types of BASIC operations, all I have to do is write a program that will process the present output from CBREEZE before writing the final C code to disk. For this reason, we may offer options to be used with CBREEZE such as one that would support special graphics packages designed to be called from C. The only thing that could bring about a significant change in CBREEZE would be the adoption of a universal C standard, which I understand is being considered. This might mean the addition of new functions that would be relevant to a tutorial translator and the deletion of some others. However, the point is that CBREEZE does what it was designed to do and that is to teach C language by drawing direct examples from user input Microsoft BASIC programs. To my way of thinking, that was its major goal and it meets that goal well. I think it will be a boon to most BASIC programmers who want to learn C when coupled with a full-function interpreter or compiler.

As of this writing, CBREEZE is a brand new product. It was judged to be fully complete less than one month prior to this writing. Robert J. Traister & Associates is presently the sole marketer of this product. This may or may not change. The company is now geared toward the marketing of software. The few commercial software products that I have written in the past are marketed by one of my publishers, but CBREEZE lies outside their effective target areas. I approached several C-language-oriented software companies shortly before CBREEZE was completed. Although one offered a contract, most were not even interested in discussing the translator. In almost every case, their remarks centered around the fact that the buyers of their C compilers were made up mostly of professional software developers and not BASIC programmers. Their main interest seemed to lie in products that would qualify as adjunct tools for their compilers. However, this attitude may be changing before too long. Hopefully, many major suppliers of C products will realize that there is a vast untapped market of potential C programmers presently programming in BASIC. I feel that if more advertising emphasis were placed on telling why it is advantageous to learn C, many BASIC programmers would make the switch.

I realize now that CBREEZE can be marketed successfully only by a company that has an understanding of the needs of the BASIC programmer who is trying to learn C. This means technical support from persons who have been there themselves. Through small ads, a few reviews, and word of mouth, we have already sold a substantial number of packages. Technical support is provided by me and me alone. Fortunately, the time required for such support is minimal, because problems have been few. However, I see a time when it will be necessary to train a small technical staff if sales continue to increase. I think CBREEZE will eventually be distributed nation-

186   CBREEZE   Chap. Seventeen

ally, but it will be necessary to keep the price down to near its current $119.95. If it goes considerably higher, it may be out of the practical range for many of its potential users. My goal is to sell 2500 copies within the next year. This is certainly small potatoes, but all profits are put back into advertising CBREEZE. Admittedly, CBREEZE was a sideline for me, since the company's major income source was book royalties. But this sideline has developed into a separate division of the original company. I feel our support for CBREEZE and concern for the customer is more personal than that offered by any other software company in the world. It is my goal to preserve this support and to make it a requirement of any other company that may be marketing CBREEZE in the future.

USING CBREEZE

CBREEZE is extremely simple to use. All that is necessary is to write a BASIC program, make sure it runs correctly under BASIC, and then save it as an ASCII file. *Note*: It is preferable to write the BASIC program using BASIC's editor as opposed to another line editor. CBREEZE expects all BASIC statements and variables to be in uppercase. The BASIC editor will do this for you automatically. If you use another editor, make sure that uppercase is used for all but quoted phrases.

Let's assume that a BASIC program has been saved as *TST.BAS*. You may now return to the operating system that contains the CBREEZE program generically called CB.EXE. Specialized versions of CBREEZE for various compilers and interpreters may be named differently. For example, the RUN/C version is named RUNCB.EXE. For this discussion, we will use the generic name CB.EXE. Invoking CBREEZE is accomplished under the following format:

CB FILENAME.BAS FILENAME.C OPTION

where FILENAME.BAS is the name of the BASIC file to be translated; FILE-NAME.C is the name of the new file to hold the translated C source code and OPTION is equal to either 0 or 1. The zero option value is specified when the source code is not going to be executed. In this mode, the source code for special functions that emulate BASIC functions such as MID\$, RIGHT\$, and LEFT\$ is not included as a part of the C file. If you intend to run your translated program under a C compiler or interpreter, use an option value of 1. This will trigger the translater to include the source code for any specialized functions, and the program should be fully executable.

When you hit <return>, the CBREEZE logo will appear on the screen and a prompt tells you which BASIC program is being translated and the name of the holding file. If you would prefer to have the translated code displayed on the monitor, simply specify SCREEN for FILENAME.C. This file may also be directed to the parallel printer by specifying PRINTER. If you specify a nonexistent or inappropriate

Using CBREEZE   187

file, or if you do not include enough arguments when invoking CBREEZE, an error message will appear and execution is halted.

CBREEZE gives the BASIC programmer a great deal of flexibility in the types of programs that may be translated into C source code. However, its purpose is to teach C language, not to support or reinforce bad programming habits by correcting mistakes automatically. The user must be aware of the types of arguments that certain C functions expect to receive as well as the types of values they return. The documentation with CBREEZE thoroughly instructs the user regarding this fact and suggests methods to stay within the scope of what CBREEZE will accept and translate into executable C source code. For example, arguments to functions such as LOG, SQR, and SIN must always be double-precision floating-point values. This means that all variables must be of double-precision type [i.e., the variable must be followed by the *octothorpe* (#)]. If a constant is used for an argument, it must contain a decimal point, as in 14.3 or 6.0. CBREEZE will not balk if you provide an inappropriate argument. It will translate it without a single complaint. However, the C source code will not execute properly because the equivalent functions in C require double-precision arguments. CBREEZE will simply carry your error into the C program. Messages generated by your compiler or interpreter will target such errors.

Although the transference of errors may seem to be a disadvantage of CBREEZE, it is not. To the contrary, it provides a very strong tutorial advantage. It is not an error to provide a function such as LOG in BASIC with an argument that is not a double-precision value. However, this is an error in C and *log*() will not return a correct value. As explained previously, it would have been a very simple task to have allowed any type of argument to work with such functions by causing CBREEZE to automatically include the cast operator (*double*) at the start of the argument to *log*(). But this would have enforced a practice that causes BASIC programmers tremendous headaches when making the switch to C. The purpose of CBREEZE is to teach C language, not simply to translate *any* BASIC program to C source code. The actual beginning of this tutorial starts in the BASIC environment by instructing users as to the types of arguments that should be used with functions that have direct C equivalencies.

To explain CBREEZE further, it is necessary to go through several program translations. The following pages will show actual BASIC programs and their C source code as translated by CBREEZE. In all cases the BASIC source code is shown exactly as it was input to CBREEZE and the C source code is exactly as it was output.

The first translation involves a simple FOR-NEXT loop that counts from 1 to 100 in steps of one (default). On each pass of the loop the value of the loop variable is displayed on the monitor screen:

```
10  FOR X%=1 TO 100
20  PRINT X%
30  NEXT X%
```

This program requires no explanation other than to note that integer variable X%
is used for the loop variable as opposed to floating-point variable X. The reasons
for this usage lie in the fact that the loop variable need only represent integer values,
so this is the most efficient way of writing the program.

Assuming that this program was saved to disk file as TST.BAS, the following
CBREEZE invocation will translate this program and store the C version in disk
file TST.C:

CB TST.BAS TST.C 1

An option value of 1 is used in this example, although a 0 would have sufficed as
well since there are no special functions (i.e., MID$, RIGHT$, etc.).

The following listing is the exact translation of the preceding BASIC program
by CBREEZE:

```
main()
{

        int x;

        for (x = 1; x <= 100; ++x)
                printf(" %d \n", x);

}
```

If this looks like standard "textbook" C source code, that is because it is. Seasoned
C programmers may have noticed a peculiarity in the *printf* line. Most C programmers
would have omitted the spaces before and after the *%d* conversion specification.
However, CBREEZE translates quite literally and in BASIC the instruction

PRINT X%

will cause the value of X% to be displayed with a preceding and trailing space.
Therefore, this translated C source version is an actual equivalent of the BASIC
program. Now, suppose that the BASIC source code had used a single-precision
floating-point loop variable, as in

```
10  FOR X=1 TO 100
20  PRINT X
30  NEXT X
```

This program would be translated by CBREEZE as

```
main()
{

        float x;
```

Using CBREEZE   189

```
for (x = 1; x <= 100; ++x)
    printf(" %f \n", x);

}
```

This program is perfectly correct; however, the results displayed when run under C will not be the same as those of the BASIC program. The latter BASIC example will display the values of 1 through 100 as integers. In BASIC, floating-point values that have no fractional portion (other than 0) are displayed as integers. Therefore, both BASIC program examples will display the same thing, although the integer version will run faster.

In C, the situation is different. The C translation of the first BASIC example will output the same information to the screen as the BASIC program did. The translation of the second BASIC example, however, will result in a screen display of

```
1.000000
2.000000
3.000000
4.000000
5.000000
etc.
```

Notice that the *printf* function in the second C translation uses a conversion specifier of *%f*. This tells *printf* to expect a floating-point argument and to display it in standard float format. Both the BASIC program and the C translation do exactly the same thing. They count floating-point variable X (x) from 1.000000 to 100.0000. The differences lie only in the way the values of this variable are displayed. BASIC does it one way and C, another.

Although these program examples have been quite simple, they do address the user friendliness of CBREEZE. The FOR-NEXT statement in the BASIC programs did not contain a STEP specification. In BASIC, the omission of STEP simply brings about a default which tells BASIC that STEP is equal to 1. CBREEZE makes the same assumption and outputs a *for* loop with a step value of 1. In other words, CBREEZE defaults in the same manner as BASIC. The following BASIC program is a modification of the first two examples and uses a STEP value of 2. Also, a mathematical operation is performed on the loop variable before its value is written to the monitor:

```
10  FOR X%=1 TO 100 STEP 2
20  PRINT X%*4
30  NEXT X%
```

This loop counts in increments of two for a sequence of 1, 3, 5, 7, ... On each pass of the loop the value of X% is multiplied by 4 before it is written to the screen.

When run through CBREEZE, the program above is translated as

190   CBREEZE   Chap. Seventeen

```
main()
{

    int x;

    for (x = 1; x <= 100; x += 2)
        printf(" %d \n", x * 4);


}
```

Again, this is a literal translation and this C version will run exactly like the BASIC program it translated. The step value is represented in compressed form as x +=2. This is the exact equivalent of $x = x + 2$. The mathematical operation is carried out within the *printf* function and, again, is presented in standard textbook C format.

Now let's see how CBREEZE handles nested loops by asking it to translate the following BASIC program:

```
10  FOR Y%=1 TO 10
20  FOR X%=1 TO 100 STEP 2
30  PRINT X%*4
40  NEXT
50  NEXT
```

As can plainly be seen, this example takes the previous BASIC program and nests it within another FOR-NEXT loop. Each time the outer loop cycles, the inner loop is run in its entirety. The outer loop cycles 10 times, so the inner loop counts from 1 to 100 ten different times.

The C translation of this program is as follows:

```
main()
{

    int y, x;

    for (y = 1; y <= 10; ++y)
        for (x = 1; x <= 100; x += 2)
            printf(" %d \n", x * 4);


}
```

This example points to one of the supreme niceties of CBREEZE and relates directly to the formatting of the source code. Notice that CBREEZE observes the "whitespace" C source code convention. Each line of code is indented the proper five spaces within each individual block. This is the way Kernighan and Ritchie would have written it.

Many textbooks devoted to teaching C language do not adhere as closely to these source code formatting conventions as does CBREEZE. You will also notice that mathematical and conditional operators are separated from their left and right

Using CBREEZE   **191**

mer in quickly understanding what has already been written. This is part of the "portability" that C is famous for. Although the term *portability* is really intended to indicate that C source code can be quickly brought up to run on different computers, following the proper source code formatting conventions can also allow for a certain portability of understanding. Another point is made for CBREEZE in the area of user friendliness, which is demonstrated by this translation. Notice that the BASIC program ended each loop with a NEXT statement that was not followed by the name of the loop variable. In Microsoft BASIC, it is not necessary to include the loop variable with NEXT. MS-BASIC can figure out which loop is controlled by untitled NEXT statements. From the C translation, it can be seen that CBREEZE can do likewise.

Now let's see how CBREEZE handles braces by translating the following BASIC program:

```
10  FOR Y%=1 TO 10
20  PRINT"Start of run #";Y%;"in nested loop"
30  FOR X%=1 TO 100 STEP 2
40  PRINT X%*4
50  NEXT
60  NEXT
```

This program is not significantly different from the preceding example. An extra PRINT statement has been added at line 20 and displays a prompt at the beginning of each entry into the nested loop, stating the outer loop cycle count.

The CBREEZE translation of this program is

```
main()
{

    int y, x;

    for (y = 1; y <= 10; ++y) {
        printf("%s %d %s\n","Start of run #", y, "in nested loop");

        for (x = 1; x <= 100; x += 2)
            printf(" %d \n", x * 4);
    }


}
```

This translation is certainly correct and shows that CBREEZE knows when and where to include braces as well as when and where not to. The outer loop contains two statements, *printf* and *for*, the latter being the start of the nested loop. When multiple statements are used within a loop, these must be enclosed by braces. However, when only one statement is found within a loop, braces are not necessary. In this example the outer loop has multiple statements and these are enclosed by braces. However, the inner loop contains only a single statement, so braces are not included. This program closely follows the unwritten rules of C source code formatting,

192   CBREEZE   Chap. Seventeen

although some programmers would not have included an empty line between *printf*
and *for*. Generally, CBREEZE will precede any loop with an empty line. This applies
whether or not a loop is nested. CBREEZE invokes quite an elaborate routine in
order to display the C source code in textbook style. This occurs near the end of
the translation; prior to this point, the C code lines effectively begin at the left-
hand margin. The formatting routine looks for indications of programming blocks,
assignment operators, and a host of other C code factors. It then decides how much
whitespace is required at each line to present a properly formatted display.

As a final test in this series of loop translations, the following BASIC program
should put CBREEZE through its paces in figuring out the brace placement for
the various nested loops. Note that this program has three levels of nesting. The
outer FOR-NEXT loop contains an inner FOR-NEXT loop, which in itself contains
an inner WHILE-WEND loop:

```
 10  FOR Y%=1 TO 10
 20  FOR X%=1 TO 100 STEP 2
 30  PRINT X%*4
 40  D%=0
 50  WHILE D%<=100
 60  D%=D%+10
 70  PRINT D%
 80  WEND
 90  NEXT X%
100  NEXT Y%
```

This can be considered a nonsense program as written, but such constructs are not
uncommon in BASIC. However, one generally sees the WHILE-WEND loop far
less often than the FOR-NEXT variety.

The translation of this program as output by CBREEZE is as follows:

```
main( )
{

    int y, x, d;

    for (y = 1; y <= 10; ++y) {
        for (x = 1; x <= 100; x += 2) {
            printf(" %d \n", x * 4);
            d = 0;

            while (d <= 100) {
                d = d + 10;
                printf(" %d \n", d);
            }

        }

    }

}
```

Using CBREEZE

193

Again, there were no problems with this translation. Notice that CBREEZE inserts a full line of spacing prior to the outer *for* loop and the nested *while* loop. However, the nested *for* loop does not contain this same spacing. CBREEZE will insert a line of whitespace prior to the start of all loops, nested or otherwise, unless the line prior to this loop contains another loop statement. This is the case with the nested *for* loop because the outer loop immediately precedes it. However, the nested *while* loop was not preceded by any type of loop statement, so a full line of whitespace was provided.

It is time to move on to other types of programs and see how CBREEZE translates these aspects of the BASIC language into C source code counterparts. The following BASIC program uses the MID$ function to extract a portion of a string value:

```
10  CLS
20  A$="CBREEZE TRANSLATOR"
30  B$=MID$(A$,1,7)
40  PRINT B$
```

This program extracts the first seven characters in A$ and assigns this value to B$. The value of B$ is then displayed on the monitor screen. C language contains no equivalent of the MID$ function, so this is a situation where CBREEZE must supply its own function to cover the mechanics of MID$. Fortunately, any special functions such as this one cause CBREEZE to access certain built-in source files which are displayed as part of the translated C source code. The following translation demonstrates this:

```
main( )
{

    char a$[80], b$[80];

    cls();
    strcpy(a$, "CBREEZE TRANSLATOR");
    mid$(b$, 1, 7);

    printf("%s\n", b$);

}

mid$(a, b, x, y)
char *a, *b;
int x, y;
{

    --x;
    y += x;
```

194   CBREEZE   Chap. Seventeen

```
while (x < y && x <= strlen(b))
    *a++ = *(b + x++);

*a = '\0';


}
```

This is the first translated example that involves string variables. Notice that they are declared CHAR arrays at the beginning of the program. Each array can hold up to 80 characters, which breaks down to a maximum of 79 standard characters plus the terminating null character. This is not an exact translation of the BASIC program example, although one would never know it by viewing the program run results. In MS-BASIC, each string variable can hold up to 255 characters. In C, this would mean CHAR arrays dimensioned to 256 characters (255 standard and 1 null character). I chose to dimension the translated arrays to 80 characters since this represents more storage space than most programmers will ever need for a single string variable. If each array were sized to 256 bytes, there could be a problem with storage space when a program that contained many string variables was run. Some interpreters and compilers might not be able to allocate the needed memory space. With most compilers, the stack space could be enlarged, but this could lead to confusion among beginning programmers.

When programming in C, character arrays are dimensioned with a knowledge of the size of the strings they will be used to hold. CBREEZE has no knowledge of what the programmer intends in this area, so a value of 80 was chosen, which should be large enough (or even overly large) for most applications and still small enough to at least attempt to conserve stack space. If there is a problem, you can always edit the translated program and increase the size of the arrays.

This program is translated by the RUN/C version of CBREEZE. Note that the CLS statement in BASIC has been converted to *cls*() in C. No source code is provided for this C function, because it is a part of the RUN/C function set. Other versions of CBREEZE devoted to other interpreters and compilers may substitute another function for CLS which is integral to that particular environment. If no CLS equivalent is contained in the function set of a compiler or interpreter, source code for such a function is generated by CBREEZE. Naturally, this source code is both machine- and compiler-dependent.

The *strcpy*() function is used to copy the string constant to array a$. At this point, *mid*$() is called. This is a built-in CBREEZE function that is displayed properly at the bottom of the executable portion of the C program. In other words, CBREEZE has generated the code to emulate BASIC's MID$ function in C. This is a portable function and should work with any C compiler or interpreter that follows the Kernighan and Ritchie standard.

This generated function accepts four arguments. The first is the CHAR array that will contain the extracted portion of the second argument, which is also a CHAR array. The next two arguments are integers that specify the starting character position

Using CBREEZE   195

and the number of characters to be extracted. The source code of the function is
fairly straightforward and uses CHAR pointers to assign the desired contents of *b*
to *a*. Notice that at the end of the function the null character (\0) is tacked on to
the end of *a*. This signals the end of a character string.

The final line of the portion of the program executed under *main*( ) calls *printf*
to display the value of b$. Both the BASIC and the C program clear the screen
and then display the first seven characters of A$(a$) on the monitor screen.

The next BASIC example dimensions a string array and fills it within the body
of a FOR-NEXT loop with the constant "HELLO". Another loop is entered and
the assigned contents of the array are written to the screen in sequential order:

```
10  DIM A$(10)
20  FOR X%=0 TO 10
30  A$(X%)="HELLO"
40  NEXT X%
50  FOR X%=0 TO 10
60  PRINT A$(X%)
70  NEXT
```

CBREEZE translates BASIC string arrays as arrays of character pointers in
C. Multidimensional character arrays can also be used to represent the equivalent
of BASIC string arrays, but in CBREEZE I chose to use arrays of pointers to provide
the user with some experience in handling these. The translation follows:

```
main( )
{

    char *malloc( );
    int x;
    char *a$[11];

    for (x = 0; x <= 10; ++x)
        strcpy(a$[x] = malloc(80), "HELLO");

    for (x = 0; x <= 10; ++x)
        printf("%s\n", a$[x]);

}
```

This translation was performed by the generic version of CBREEZE and differs from
the RUN/C version only in that the *malloc* function is declared a CHAR pointer.
In the present version of RUN/C, built-in functions are not declared, although this
is a departure from the way most C interpreters and compilers expect the format
of their source code. If you remove the *malloc* declaration from the top of the program,
the source code will run without a hitch under RUN/C.

The *malloc* function is a standard UNIX memory allocation function which

196   CBREEZE   Chap. Seventeen

causes $a\$[x]$ to point to an allocated area of memory which is of adequate size to hold an 80-character string. The Kernighan and Ritchie standard calls for *malloc* to be declared a CHAR pointer or, more appropriately, a function that returns a CHAR pointer before it is used in a program. The argument to *malloc* is 80, and this sets aside 80 sequential bytes in memory to hold any assignments to this array pointer. This assures that a free area of memory is provided for the storage and that important areas of memory are not overwritten.

On each pass of the loop, the *strcpy* function is called and copies the string "HELLO" into the memory location pointed to by $a\$[x]$. Notice that x has been declared an *int*. If the BASIC program had used a loop variable of X instead of $X\%$, the translated C code would have declared this variable a float. A floating-point variable cannot be used to name an array position in C. Therefore, an error message would have been displayed when the program was run or compiled.

When the first *for* loop is exited, another one is entered and the content of the array of pointers is displayed in sequential order. The program then terminates normally, after displaying each array value on the screen.

As pointed out in the CBREEZE documentation, memory allocated by *malloc* or other memory functions should be freed when those locations are no longer needed. This can present problems with CBREEZE translations that are actually executed should a great deal of memory allocation take place. CBREEZE does not provide the code for freeing allocated memory, because it has no way of knowing when a particular pointer is no longer required. There is no problem in the sample program, because allocated memory is freed upon program exit. However, if the program were expanded to include other arrays of pointers, it is conceivable that you could run out of memory storage space if you did not free up allocations to pointers that were no longer to be used.

The next program example puts CBREEZE through some paces in translating BASIC mathematical operations and functions into C source code. This program uses double-precision, single-precision, and integer variables together with the BASIC LOG and raise-to functions:

```
10   REM TEST OF MATH FUNCTIONS
20   X#=13.23
30   Y#=1.25
40   D%=LOG(X#)
50   A=X#^Y#
60   S#=LOG(X#^2.1^A.5^Y#)
70   PRINT D%;A;S#
```

In line 40, integer variable D% is assigned the value of LOG(X#). Since LOG returns a double-precision value, only the integer portion of this return will be represented by D%. In line 50, single-precision variable A is assigned the double-precision value of X# raised to the Y# power. Finally, in line 60, double-precision variable S# is assigned the return of the LOG of X# raised to various powers. Here two

Using CBREEZE   197

functions are involved with raise-to returning a value to LOG, which returns a value
to S#.

CBREEZE translated the foregoing program in the following manner:

```
/* TEST OF MATH FUNCTIONS */

main()
{

        double x, y, log(), s, pow();
        float a;
        int d;

        x = 13.23;
        y = 1.25;
        d = log(x);
        a = pow(x, y);
        s = log(pow(pow(pow(x, 2.1), 1.5), y));

        printf(" %d %f %lf \n", d, a, s);

}
```

Again, this translation was made by a generic version of CBREEZE. The
RUN/C version would not have declared *log*() or *pow*() as doubles. This is required
by most C environments, but RUN/C is an exception to this, at least the version
used for researching this book was.

This translation is picture perfect as far as textbook C programs are concerned.
Notice too that the various blocks of the C program are separated by a full line of
whitespace. The declaration block is separated from the assignment block, which in
turn is separated from the screen display block. Block definition will not always be
so well defined by CBREEZE, but in every case the CBREEZE translations are
quite easy to read and understand.

At this stage it is appropriate to show an example of how CBREEZE can
translate a program literally and correctly and still end up with C source code that
will not give you the results you expected. This can be especially true when complex
mathematical operations are involved. The following program is simple and CBREEZE
has no trouble translating it, but due to the literal translation it will not run under
C.

```
10 X%=14;PRINT LOG(X%)
```

Note that this program contains two statements on the single line and this is
fine with CBREEZE. It has no trouble in deciphering the various statement elements,
so the use of the colon separator (:) is perfectly legal with CBREEZE as it is with
MS-BASIC. The translated version of this program is as follows:

```
main( )
{

    double log( );
    int x;

    s = 14;

    printf(" %lf \n", log(x));

}
```

At first glance, this program would appear to be correct, but the problem lies with the argument that is passed to *log*(). In C, the *log*() function requires a double-precision argument. Here variable *x* has been declared an *int* and this will not work with *log*(). On some compilers, the executable code will be produced without an error message. On others, an error message will appear, stating that another type of argument was expected. Regardless of whether or not an error message is generated, the *log*() function will return an erroneous value because of the improper argument. The program can be made to run correctly by changing *log*(*x*) in the *printf* line to *log*((*double*) *x*). Using the double *cast* operator coerces integer *x* to a double-precision value. It is exactly the same as CDBL (X%) in BASIC.

Remember, CBREEZE is designed to teach *proper* C language programming technique by using BASIC programming examples provided by the student to arrive at C language equivalencies. For the most part, CBREEZE effects a literal translation. This requires the student actually to be thinking in C while programming in BASIC.

In C, it is practical to treat individual characters as separate data types, different from strings and numbers. In BASIC, there are only two general data types, string and numerical. There is no direct equivalent to CHAR in C. If we wish to represent alphabetic characters, we have to use a string variable. However, CBREEZE has the ability, in some program translations, to make use of C's ability to display individual characters. The following BASIC program demonstrates this capability when translated into C:

10 PRINT CHR$(65);CHR$(66)

Here the CHR$ function is used to return a string composed of the characters represented by ASCII 65 and 66. In C, single characters do not need to be displayed as a string. They stand on their own and can be represented as the character itself (contained in single quotes) or as the ASCII character code. CBREEZE translated the example above in the following manner:

```
main( )
{

    printf("%c%c\n", 65, 66);

}
```

Using CBREEZE   **199**

The *printf* function in this program uses two *%c* conversion specifications to display the character equivalent of the integers that serve as arguments to *printf*. All references to CHR$ have been deleted. Only the arguments to CHR$ have been retained, and these values displayed as characters by *printf*. This can carry over to other BASIC functions as well. The following program will demonstrate:

10 PRINT CHR$(65),HEX$(48),OCT$(127)

This program displays the character represented by ASCII 65, the hexadecimal value of decimal 48, and the octal equivalent of decimal 127. Notice also that the functions are separated from each other by commas instead of semicolons. In BASIC, comma separators bring about a special formatting of arguments to PRINT in that a field of 14 spaces is set aside for each argument. This program will display

A   30   177

CBREEZE translates this example in literal form as

```
main()
{

        printf("%-14c%-14x%o\n", 65, 48, 127);

}
```

This C equivalent has done away with the specialized BASIC functions that will display decimal values as strings containing hexadecimal and octal equivalents of decimal numbers. Again, the CHR$ function has been deleted as well. These functions are deleted because they are not necessary in C, at least not for the displaying of these various types of information. Notice that the first two conversion specifications are preceded by −14. This value indicates that 14 spaces are to be set aside for the display of the argument that this specification represents. This allows the literal translation of a BASIC PRINT statement line that uses comma separators. In addition to the *%c* conversion specification, you will also see *%x* and *%o*. The latter two convert integer values to hexadecimal and octal format, respectively. These are still integer values, but are displayed in a form that uses a base other than 10. These are not string values as they would be in BASIC. Such conversions speak to the versatility of C language as well as to the capability of CBREEZE to make accurate literal translations of BASIC programs when desirable. This versatility expands when a literal translation is not desirable, as in the example above. This could reinforce misconceptions of those learning C. Instead, CBREEZE throws away unnecessary BASIC functions and strikes out in true C style when such conversion is desirable. The example above is not a literal translation. Rather, it is an interpretation of a BASIC program, much like one that would be made by an experienced C language programmer. Either way, the C language version creates the same screen display as the BASIC program does.

200   CBREEZE   Chap. Seventeen

To move further into the ability of CBREEZE to handle string conversions, the following BASIC program assigns two string variables the constants "COMPUTER" and " GRAPHICS", respectively. Next C$ is assigned the value of the first two strings added together. The result is then displayed on the monitor screen:

```
10  A$="COMPUTER"
20  B$=" GRAPHICS"
30  C$=A$+B$
40  PRINT C$
```

This program will display the phrase "COMPUTER GRAPHICS".

The CBREEZE translation is

```
main()
{

    char a$[80], b$[80], c$[80];

    strcpy(a$, "COMPUTER");
    strcpy(b$, " GRAPHICS");
    sprintf(c$, "%s%s", a$, b$);
    printf("%s\n", c$);

}
```

The logical choice to represent the adding of BASIC string values in C is the *sprintf* function, which works just like *printf*, except that the output is not written to the screen but to a *char* array. One must make certain that the array size (80) is adequate to contain the concatenated string values. For instance, if a$ contained 45 characters and b$ contained 40, the total added length would be 85 characters. This would be larger than the dimensioned size of c$, since CBREEZE dimensions all *char* arrays to 80 elements. When two or more very large strings are added, it may be necessary to edit the C source code in order to enlarge the size of the array that receives these strings to a value capable of containing the new length.

The following BASIC program increases the complexity of a string add operation:

```
10  A$="HEX VALUE OF DECIMAL 100 IS"
20  B$="OCTAL VALUE OF DECIMAL 100 IS"
30  C$="A$+" "+HEX$(100)+"  "+B$+" "+OCT$(100)
40  PRINT C$
```

When this program is executed, the screen will display

HEX VALUE OF DECIMAL 100 IS 64 OCTAL VALUE OF DECIMAL 100 IS 144

This program adds seven separate string values (including string constants). C$ is equal to the entire phrase which is finally displayed. Notice that HEX$ and OCT$

Using CBREEZE   **201**

are called to supply the proper values to match the quoted strings. CBREEZE translates this program as

```
main()
{

    char a$[80], b$[80], c$[80];

    strcpy(a$, "HEX VALUE OF DECIMAL 100 IS");
    strcpy(b$, "OCTAL VALUE OF DECIMAL 100 IS");
    sprintf(c$, "%s%s%x%s%s%s%o", a$, " ", 100, " ", b$, " ", 100);
    printf("%s\n", c$);

}
```

This is a correct and literal translation of the BASIC program, except for the deletion of HEX$ and OCT$. The program is executable, but not with the RUN/C interpreter. The complexity of the *sprintf* line is too much for the interpreter (Version 1.32), but the Lattice C compiler had no difficulty whatsoever. However, this is another nonsense program designed to test CBREEZE. The desired results of such a program can better be obtained without resorting to string add operations.

This brings us to another matter. *Do not try to be overly complex with your BASIC programs.* Chances are that CBREEZE can translate them, but highly complex constructs or combinations of functions and statements can sharply detract from the decided tutorial advantage that CBREEZE offers. C is a simple language which can be used to construct highly complex routines, but such construction involves the combination of many simple routines.

The following BASIC program is an exercise in the ridiculous:

```
10  DIM Q$(1)
20  Q$(0)="3"
30  Q$(1)="1"
40  A$="1234567"
50  C#=2.23
60  X#=C#^(LOG(VAL(MID$(A$,FIX(VAL(Q$(0))),FIX(VAL(Q$(1)))))))
70  PRINT X#
```

This is the difficult way of writing

10 PRINT 2.23^LOG(3.0)

The ridiculous construct in line 60 is necessary to extract the numeric values from the string variable and string array that result in a value of 3.000000. The final result is the display of

2.413526058197022

202 CBREEZE Chap. Seventeen

CBREEZE is fully capable of handling such a translation, as the following source code demonstrates:

```
main()
{

    char *malloc(), *pmid$();
    double c, x, log(), atof(), pow();
    char a$[80], *q$[2];

    strcpy(q$[0] = malloc(80), "3");
    strcpy(q$[1] = malloc(80), "1");
    strcpy(a$, "1234567");

    c = 2.23;
    x = pow(c, (log(atof(pmid$(a$, (int) (atof(q$[0])), (int) (atof
(q$[1])))))));

    printf(" %lf \n", x);

}
mid$(a, b, x, y)
char *a, *b;
int x, y;
{

    --x;
    y += x;

    while (x < y && x <= strlen(b))
        *a++ = *(b + x++);

    *a = '\0';

}
char *pmid$(a, x, y)
char *a;
int x, y;
{

    char *ptr, *malloc();

    if ((ptr = malloc(y + 1)) == 0) {
        puts("Insufficient Memory");
        printf("%c", 7);
        exit(0);
    }

    mid$(ptr, a, x, y);

    return(ptr);

}
```

Using CBREEZE   **203**

Perhaps you can gain some tutorial advantage from this, but chances are that you
cannot. This program is too complex for RUN/C but does work with the Lattice
C compiler. However, a ridiculous program in BASIC is equally ridiculous in C, if
not more so. If you just want to play around with programs that will cause CBREEZE
to spit out all kinds of outlandish code constructs, this example is a good place to
start. But if you are serious about learning to program efficiently and knowledgably
in C within a short period of time, a simpler and more serious approach is necessary.

   Although I never intended to support filekeeping translations, I changed my
mind near the end of the project. CBREEZE will support extremely simple, sequential
filekeeping routines such as those presented by the following BASIC program:

```
10  OPEN "TST.FIL" FOR OUTPUT AS #1
20  PRINT #1, "Testing elementary filekeeping"
30  CLOSE #1
40  OPEN "TST.FIL" FOR INPUT AS #1
50  IF EOF(1) THEN CLOSE #1:END
60  INPUT #1,A$
70  PRINT A$
80  GOTO 50
```

This program is typical of many written by BASIC programmers who are simply
dabbling in the areas of computer filekeeping. The C translation is

```
#include <stdio.h>
main()
{

    char a$[80];
    FILE *fp1, *fopen();

    if ((fp1 = fopen("TST.FIL", "w")) == NULL) {
        printf("File Open Error\n");
        exit (0);
    }

    fprintf(fp1, "Testing elementary filekeeping\n");

    fclose(fp1);

    if ((fp1 = fopen("TST.FIL", "r")) == NULL) {
        printf("Cannot open file\n");
        exit(0);
    }

BR50:

    if (feof(fp1)) {
        fclose(fp1);
        exit(0);
    }
```

204   CBREEZE   Chap. Seventeen

```
fgets(a$, 79, fp1);

printf("%s\n", a$);

goto BR50;

}
```

This program is certainly compilable and/or executable, but it really is not the way most C programmers would write a routine to accomplish the same purpose. One cannot expect to gain a great deal of tutorial information in the area of filekeeping from CBREEZE. The differences between the programming of filekeeping routines in BASIC and those in C are too great to draw many tutorial parallels. This example also points out the fact that CBREEZE fully supports the oft-abused GOTO statement.

If you write a C program that contains a *goto* statement, 99 percent of the time this program could have been better written without it. Branch statements corrupt structure and make the program difficult to decipher in many instances. In BASIC, GOTO is necessary, but this statement is used far too often as a result of "programmer laziness." There is nothing worse than trying to decipher a program that someone else has written when it contains many GOTO statements. Even if you have written the program yourself, GOTOs can cause you to lose track of what you have done when a program requires several sittings to complete.

I originally planned not to support GOTO at all, but comments from persons testing the early versions of CBREEZE caused me to change my mind. I compromised by supporting GOTO (as well as ON GOTO) and cautioning against its use in the CBREEZE documentation. ON GOTO was supported more for a tutorial advantage than to allow multiple branch statements. CBREEZE uses *switch* statements to arrive at an ON GOTO translation, the only area of translation where such statements are incorporated. The following BASIC program uses ON GOTO:

```
10  INPUT A%
20  ON A% GOTO 40,50,60,70
30  END
40  PRINT"BRANCH TO 40":END
50  PRINT"BRANCH TO 50":END
60  PRINT"BRANCH TO 60":END
70  PRINT"BRANCH TO 70"
```

This is a simple demonstration program that displays the number of the branch line whenever a value is input at the keyboard. The CBREEZE translation uses *swtich* and *case* to effect the same operations in C:

```
main()
{

    int a;

    scanf("%d", &a);
```

Using CBREEZE

205

```
switch((int) a) {
        case 1:
                goto BR40;
        case 2:
                goto BR50;
        case 3:
                goto BR60;
        case 4:
                goto BR70;
}

        exit(0);
BR40:

        printf("BRANCH TO 40\n");

        exit(0);
BR50:

        printf("BRANCH TO 50\n");

        exit(0);
BR60:

        printf("BRANCH TO 60\n");

        exit(0);
BR70:

        printf("BRANCH TO 70\n");

}
```

It can be seen from this translation that *scanf* is used to retrieve information from the keyboard. *Scanf* is the input equivalent of *printf*. It scans the keyboard for information and reads it into memory. Notice that the control string specifies an integer and that the argument is the memory location of variable *a*. The memory location is specified by the ampersand (&). The switch statement contains a cast operator which coerces any other type of numeric variable to type *int*. This statement requires an integer argument. The use of the cast operator is a safety feature that CBREEZE builds into its translation. The value of *a* determines which *case* statement takes control, and in turn, which *goto* statement performs the branch. In most switches, a *break* statement is included at the end of the *case* statement set. This causes the switch to be exited after the statements under the active case have been executed. However, *break* is not required in this application, because the *goto* branch automatically exits the switch.

The following BASIC program reads three different values from the keyboard and displays them on the screen:

206   CBREEZE   Chap. Seventeen

```
10  INPUT"Input a string, a double, an integer";A$,X#,Y%
20  PRINT A$;X#;Y%
```

The input statement writes a prompt to the screen, telling the user to input three different types of variables. Each argument is typed in via the keyboard, followed by a comma to separate it from the one that follows. The second program line displays the three inputs. CBREEZE translates the foregoing program using *scanf* to get the keyboard input:

```
main()
{

        double x;
        int y;
        char a$[80];
        puts("Input a string, a double, an integer");
        scanf("%s %lf %d", a$, &x, &y);

}
```

This is not an exact translation of the BASIC program. To do so would require a special function that would call *scanf* after trapping for the comma separator. This program will operate like the BASIC example, except that the different inputs must be separated by spaces. Note that there is a space between each of the conversion specifications in *scanf*. We can use commas to separate inputs to *scanf* as long as no strings are involved. If they are, the comma is made a part of that string. Commas in strings are illegal in BASIC. The C program line

```
scanf("%d,%f,%lf", &a, &b, &c);
```

accepts three different data constants from the keyboard, and each may be separated by a comma. For example, you could input

```
14,228.51,14.3
```

and each value would be assigned to its respective variable. But you could also type

```
14 ,228.51 ,14.3
```

or

```
14t,228.51r,14.3
```

and the same assignments would be made. *Scanf* reads the input until a specific break or separator character is encountered (such as a comma in an example above) *or* until a character is input which does not correspond to the conversion specification. If *scanf* is expecting a number, a letter or space signifies the end of that portion of

Using CBREEZE

207

the scan. When *scanf* expects a character string, it will continue to read and assign all input until a space is encountered. This breaks the scan and the next field is read. *Scanf* is not the same as *gets* when it is reading a character string. *Scanf* can accept only a single word (so to speak). For example, it cannot assign a string equal to "computer graphics." The space between the two words will cause the read to break after "computer." On the other hand, *gets* reads input until a carriage return is detected.

The CBREEZE translation of the BASIC program is different in two ways. First, the space bar must be hit to move on to the next programmed keyboard scan. Second, the character string must contain no spaces; therefore, the input is limited to a single word or string.

CBREEZE will use *scanf* any time that a BASIC input statement has more than one variable argument. Any prompt line included with INPUT is translated as a separate *puts* function. *Printf* could also have been used, but CBREEZE tries to provide as much diversity as possible and shows that different functions (such as *puts* and *printf*) can share many of the same responsibilities, just as they do in BASIC.

These translations could go on forever, but the previous pages have demonstrated the ability of CBREEZE to translate BASIC programs into C language equivalents that present excellent tutorial examples for persons learning C. CBREEZE is available in a generic version which sticks to the original C language, but there are also dedicated versions designed specifically for various commercial C environments, including the Lattice C compiler and RUN/C. CBREEZE is also available as a package that offers a full-function C compiler in addition to the translator.

For BASIC programmers who want to delve seriously into C programming, CBREEZE is a tool that should be extremely valuable. It will reduce the comprehension time by a very large factor. With CBREEZE, there should be far less confusion on the part of BASIC programmers, and their journey to a working, practical knowledge of C language should be a speedy one.

CBREEZE is available from

> Robert J. Traister & Associates, Inc.
> 513 Manassas Avenue; Suite 2114
> Front Royal, VA 22630
>
> (703) 635–8562

Note: As this text was going to press, Traister & Associates was completing final negotiations with Lifeboat Associates on a distribution agreement.

CHAPTER EIGHTEEN

Learn C in Two Weeks

In this final chapter we present an overview of a study program for the serious student who wants to "work" at learning C. This project will take concentration, effort, and a stick-to-it attitude. The recommended learning aids are the RUN/C interpreter, priced at around $100; the CBREEZE translator, also $100; and any C language texts you can acquire. Kernighan and Ritchie's *The C Programming Language* (Englewood Cliffs, N.J.: Prentice-Hall, 1978) is a must, as it will serve as a reference source after the basics have been learned and you are familiar with the terminology. Total cost for these learning aids should be between $255 and $300, assuming that you already own or have access to an IBM Personal Computer or MS-DOS compatible capable of running the software. The cost can be cut significantly if your library offers an abundant selection of C language tutorials. Also, the software may be available at significant savings from mail-order discount houses.

If you currently own a computer that is not MS-DOS compatible, some changes will have to be made. As of this writing, RUN/C is available only for the MS-DOS machines. The same is true of CBREEZE. However, by the time you read these words, it should be available for the Apple Macintosh and other popular machines which can be programmed in MS-BASIC and for which a C compiler or interpreter is available. Fortunately, C compilers are generally made available for the most popular makes of microcomputers, so you should have no problem obtaining a proper C language environment.

For this discussion it will be assumed that you have a standard MS-DOS machine and the software listed in the first paragraph. The tutorial portion of this book will be adequate to start you on your journey to C, but the K&R text will be a necessary reference source. Also, try to obtain as many C language texts aimed at the BASIC

208

Learn C in Two Weeks   Chap. Eighteen   **209**

programmer as you can. Check your local library before you start paying for these texts.

For most people, the best way to learn a new computer language is through one continuous effort. Ideally, this would mean six to eight hours a day of study, five or six days a week. However, most persons will not be able to budget this amount of time. The next best way is to set aside a minimum of three continuous hours a day to study. This schedule will take longer to get you to the level of proficiency desired, but the period will be much shorter than if your study hours are a hit-or-miss proposition. Preferably, all study activities will take place in front of the computer. This will allow you to input programs immediately and run them under RUN/C.

Start with extremely simple programs such as the K&R standard:

```
main( )
{

    printf("hello, world\n");

}
```

You may also wish to start with any of the programs listed in this text. The point is to choose a program that is simple and one that you can comprehend. Once the program is entered, run it to make sure that you have made no input errors. When you are sure that the program executes correctly, you can then make changes and note the results during the next run.

For example, you might wish to modify the program above to

```
main( )
{

    printf("hello,\nworld\n");

}
```

See what the result is when this program is run. You can probably spend an hour or more making modifications to the original program and noting the results. When your experimentation is complete, you should be extremely familiar with *printf()*. Repeat this process with the other C functions.

This method sounds simple, but it is one that few persons practice when studying on their own. You *must* be completely familiar with one function or element of C before moving on to another. The *printf* function is a good one to start with because you will use it over and over in most of your experimentations to display program results on the screen. These results will be your only indication of what you have accomplished through your programming efforts. If you do not fully understand the nuances of *printf* before you move on to something else, you may suspect problems

210   Learn C in Two Weeks   Chap. Eighteen

in other areas of future programs, when, in fact, you have made some simple mistake with *printf*.

I have observed many instances where a student spends hours trying to figure out a mistake that he/she has made in a new area of programming, only to discover that the mistake resulted from a previously unsuspected error involving a function whose full use was thought to be known. If you feel that you know a particular function, this should mean that you have "played" with it for a good while. You know how it can be used and, more important, how it cannot or should not be used. Some functions will require more "play" than others.

Don't experiment unnecessarily! When learning a new language, it is only natural that many students become pleased and even intrigued with the fact that they have learned certain experessions, functions, and/or statements so rapidly. In such situations, productive experimentation can turn into useless repetition. Often, this is an indication of hesitancy on the part of the student, who is not looking forward to tackling a new phase of the language which he/she may be especially wary of due to some imagined difficulty. Instead, a known part of the language is used over and over, just for the thrill of being able to program something (anything at all) in C. Remember, the focus here is to learn C in a short period of time. Useless experimentation has no place in such a program.

Instead, move on to a new area of programming. Try to merge this new study area with the statements, functions, and operations that you have already learned. This is the building-block learning method, where some of what has already been learned is applied directly to the new study area.

You are encouraged to stay within a particular programming area until it has been learned to the extent that you can move on to something else. The tutorial sections of this book are an attempt to follow this concept. Programming sections are presented in logical order, with each new section building from the preceding ones.

Use CBREEZE to convert simple BASIC programs that address the things you want to learn in C. Once the translation has been made, run the program under RUN/C or any other C language environment you may have chosen. Now, experiment again by changing the program slightly. See what will work and what will not. Then refer to your study materials for an explanation of why certain combinations or expressions result in error messages. If you are using RUN/C, its error detection routines will prompt as to what the problem may be.

Don't study too long in one sitting! Learning C language in two weeks will take a concentrated effort. But if you study for too long at a time, your effort will no longer be concentrated, because you will not be able to concentrate. Only you can determine the productive length of a single study period. The same goes for the time required between sessions. Certainly, both of these periods will be affected by other factors and will not hold true for all occasions. In any event, when you feel yourself getting fatigued, choose an appropriate place in your studies and simply quit for a while. Get completely away from the computer and the area in which you are studying. When you feel refreshed, immediately pick up where you left off.

When You Get Stuck   **211**

Don't wait too long between study periods! I have seen students put in many
hours or even days of intensive study, only to take a week's leave to do something
else. In many cases, much had been forgotten when study was resumed. This will
lead to many extra hours of review. Even experienced programmers suffer certain
mental lapses when they do not program for moderate periods of time. Your study
program should include a set amount of time each day and every day until the
entire program is finished. Something you know well one day may be quite fuzzy
the next, especially when learning something brand new. It takes months for this
type of knowledge to become second nature. For now, it rests at the top of the
mind and can easily be occluded by inattention.

Map out a complete study plan for each day! This can be more easily accomplished
after the first day of study, as you will have an idea of how you are progressing
and how fast you can comfortably proceed. For instance, you might decide that
you will learn to comfortably use five new functions during a study period. Or learn
how to use all of the input or output functions. Again, take a clue from the chapters
in the tutorial section of this book and proceed in a similar, orderly fashion.

Try to stay away from other languages! During your study program, try not
to do any extensive programming in another language (BASIC in this case). You
will have to write simple BASIC programs to be translated by CBREEZE, but this
should be the full extent of any programming activities in languages other than C.
The idea here is to eat, drink, and breathe C during this two-week study period.

Review, review, review! The first hour of each day's study should be devoted
to reviewing what you learned (or thought you learned) the day before. It is simply
amazing how much you can forget overnight. Refresh your memory by writing programs similar to the ones that were written the day before.

WHEN YOU GET STUCK

You will undoubtedly reach several plateaus in your quest for proficiency in C language. There can be many reasons for this, including study fatigue. However, the
most common cause of what seem to be insurmountable problems lies in misunderstanding what you *thought* you knew before. We human beings tend to give full
concentration to a problem or area of a langauge which interests us but gloss over
those areas which we consider to be boring or inconsequential. Do not do this while
learning C.

When you cannot seem to understand a facet of the language, and hours of
experimentation on the computer prove futile, take a break for at least one hour.
Try not to even think about the problem. Occupy yourself with something totally
unrelated to computer programming. Better yet, take a nap. When you feel completely
refreshed, come back to the problem and try again. Be sure to peruse your study
manuals, in hopes of finding a sample program that will closely match what you
are trying to do.

Another method involves simply moving on to another area of C language,

212 Learn C in Two Weeks Chap. Eighteen

assuming that the problem area is not crucial to further understanding. By working with a brand new area, you may pick up clues that will solve your "insurmountable" problem.

Don't give up! There is no problem that *you* cannot solve, assuming that you are equipped with the proper tools listed at the beginning of this chapter. Today, many microcomputer programmers use C. Perhaps you know or can locate one who might help you by telephone. There are thousands of sources of C programming information available to you. Your job is to track them down. A local computer club or one in a neighboring town or city is a good place to start. Or try one of the thousands of bulletin boards available by telephone.

TESTING YOUR PROFICIENCY

At the end of every study session, program something in C without the help of CBREEZE or any study materials. Just imagine an operation in your head and program it. Sometimes, the more superfluous the operation, the better. For instance, write a C program that will accept a string input from the keyboard and then display it with the characters arranged in reverse order. Write a program that will print the values of a loop variable on the screen unless the variable is evenly divisible by 2.5. Write a function that returns the binary value of an integer as a string of 1's and 0's. Write anything you like as long as it requires you to use what you learned during the most recent study session.

Later, list some of your favorite BASIC programs and rewrite them in C. After you have arrived at a successful run, use CBREEZE to see how the programs compare. Do not select a program idea based on what you know. Rather, choose an idea, and see if you have the knowledge to commit it to a C language program.

SUMMARY

If you are presently an accomplished BASIC programmer, there is no reason why you cannot be as accomplished in C within a short period. With study sessions lasting six hours daily, six days a week, you should be able to reach or closely approach your goal within a two-week period. If you cannot devote this much time to studying C, it may take a month or more. Either way, you will learn C far more quickly than many of us did a few years ago, thanks to the excellent study aids now available.

If you are *not* an accomplished BASIC programmer at present, there is no reason why you cannot learn C as rapidly as you do BASIC. You may wish to study both languages simultaneously. One day might be devoted to BASIC, while the next would involve the same types of operations in C. C can teach you more about BASIC than you might learn from BASIC-only materials.

Remember, C is not nearly as difficult to learn as a lot of people would have you believe. It may have been difficult for them, but it does not have to be for you

Summary   **213**

with the aid of RUN/C, CBREEZE, and a host of new study materials. Perseverance is required together with dedicated effort. The rewards are worthy of this effort. When you program in C, you are using one of the most powerful languages available today. If you are interested in a computer programming career, C is one of the languages you will probably need to be successful. By knowing C, you will be better prepared to learn other languages, such as PASCAL, Assembler, and some new ones yet to be invented.

Now, ask yourself the following questions:

- Am I satisfied to program only in BASIC?
- Do I really want to have better command of my computer?
- Do I want to be proficient in the leading applications development language?
- Do I want to be prepared for a possible career in computer programming?

If you answered "yes" to two or more of the above, ask yourself one more question:

- Am I willing to put in the hours, the effort, and the concentration required to reap these rewards?

If the answer to the last question is also "yes," obtain the necessary tools, set aside the required time, begin your journey into the ranks of the professional programmer, and *learn C in two weeks*!

APPENDIX A

BASIC-to-C Equivalencies

The following tables contains a list of C functions that are equivalent or roughly equivalent to BASIC statements and/or functions. Features common to RUN/C only are so marked. C statements and functions are those commonly found in C environments for microcomputers.

BASIC	C[a]
ABS	abs()
ASC	NR
ATN	atan()
AUTO	AUTO (RUN/C only)
BEEP	NR
BLOAD	None
BSAVE	None
CALL	None
CDBL	(double)
CHAIN	fork()
CHR$	NR
CINT	(int)
CLEAR	None
CLOSE	close() or fclose()
CLS	MD
COLOR	MD
COM	None
COMMON	fork()
CONT	None
COS	cos()

214

BASIC-to-C Equivalencies   Appendix A   215

BASIC	C[a]
CSNG	(float)
CSRLIN	locate() (RUN/C only)
CIV-S-D	NR
DATA	NR
DATE$	dosdate() (RUN/C)
DEF FN	#define
DEF SEG	None
DEF type	NR
DEF USR	NR
DELETE	DELETE (RUN/C)
DIM	NR
EDIT	EDIT (RUN/C)
END	exit()
EOF	feof()
ERASE	None
ERR ERL	None
ERROR	None
EXP	exp()
FIELD	None
FILES	FILES (RUN/C)
FIX	(int)
FOR-NEXT	for
FRE	sizmem()
GET	fgets()
GOSUB-RETURN	function calls
GOTO	goto
HEX$	NR
IF	if
INKEY$	getch(), kbhit()
INP	inp()
INPUT	scanf,gets, getchar,getch
INPUT#	fgets()
INPUT$	fgets()
INSTR	index
INT	(int)
KEY	None
KILL	unlink()
LEFT$	None
LEN	strlen()
LET	NR
LINE INPUT	gets()
LINE INPUT#	fgets()
LIST	LIST (RUN/C)
LLIST	None
LOAD	LOAD (RUN/C)
LOC	ftell()
LOCATE	locate() (RUN/C)
LOF	NR

BASIC-to-C Equivalencies   Appendix A

BASIC	C[a]
LOG	log()
LPOS	MD
LPRINT	lprintf() (RUN/C)
LSET RSET	NR
MERGE	NA
MID$	None
MKI$ -S$ -D$	None
NAME	None
NEW	NEW (RUN/C)
OCT$	NR
ON COM	None
ON ERROR	None
ON GOSUB	None
ON GOTO	None
OPEN	open(), fopen()
OPTION BASE	always 0
OUT	outp()
PEEK	peek()
POS	locate() (RUN/C)
PRINT	printf, puts, putchar, putch
PRINT#	fputs, fprintf
READ	None
REM	/* remarks */
RENUM	None
RESET	rbrk()
RESTORE	None
RESUME	None
RETURN	return
RIGHT$	None
RND	drand()
RUN	RUN (RUN/C)
SAVE	SAVE (RUN/C)
SCREEN	MD
SGN	None (usually)
SIN	sin()
SOUND	MD
SPACE$	None
SPC	None
SQR	sqrt()
STOP	exit()
STR$	sprintf()
STRING$	None
SWAP	None
SYSTEM	SYSTEM (RUN/C)
TAB	TAB (RUN/C)
TAN	atan()
TIME$	dostime() (RUN/C)
TRON TROFF	TRON TROFF (RUN/C)
USR	fork()
VAL	atoi(), atof()

BASIC-to-C Equivalencies   Appendix A   **217**

BASIC (cont.)	C[a] (cont.)
VARPTR	pointer
VARPTR$	pointer
WAIT	None
WHILE WEND	while, do-while
WIDTH	MD
WRITE	printf()
WRITE#	fprintf()

[a] NA, not applicable; NR, not required; MD, machine-dependent.

APPENDIX B

BASIC Statements and Functions Supported by CBREEZE

ABS	IF-THEN
ASC	INKEY$
ATN	INP
BEEP	INPUT
BLOAD	INPUT #
BSAVE	INPUT$
CDBL	INSTR
CHR$	INT
CINT	KILL
CLOSE	LEFT$
CLS	LEN
COLOR	LINE INPUT
COS	LOCATE
CSNG	LOG
CSRLIN	LPRINT
DATA	MID$(fun)
DATE$	MID$(stat)
DEF FN	OCT$
DEF SEG	ON GOTO
DIM	OPEN
END	OUT
EOF	PEEK
EXP	POINT
FIX	POKE
FOR/NEXT	POS
GOTO	PRINT
HEX$	PSET

218

BASIC Statements and Functions Supported by CBREEZE   Appendix B   **219**

RANDOMIZE	SQR
READ	STOP
REM	STR$
RIGHT$	SWAP
RND	TAN
SCREEN	TIME$
SGN	VAL
SHELL	WHILE/WEND
SIN	WIDTH

Index

A

Age of Reason Company, 4, 163
Ampersand used with *scanf*, 31, 33, 34, 154
AND (&) bitwise operator, 49, 51, 52
AND (&&) logical connective operator, 49, 52
Argument to the function, 134
Arrays, 82–87
  char, 17, 18, 28, 82, 84–87, 97, 194
  integer position argument in, 9
  multidimensional, 83–84, 113
  numeric, 86
Assignment line, 21, 144, 152
Assignment operator (=), 49, 52, 153

B

BASIC language:
  ASC, 77
  CHR$, 17, 78
  CLS, 159
  CSNG, 10, 43

DEF FN, 35
DEF SEG, 105, 107
DIM statement, 82
EXP, 12
FIX, 10
FOR-NEXT loops, 2, 61, 62, 65, 70, 195
GOSUB, 2, 132
GOTO, 2, 61, 74, 75
HEX$, 79
IF-THEN-ELSE, 55
INPUT, 30, 31, 125
LEFT$, 18, 141
LEN, 90
LOCATE, 159
LOG, 12
MID$, 18, 101, 141, 193, 194
nested loops, 65, 69, 70
OCT$, 79
OPTION BASE, 82
PRINT, 30, 31
raise-to function, 12, 47
RIGHT$, 18, 141
SIN, 12
SQR, 12, 44
statements and functions supported by
  CBREEZE, 218–19

221

222   Index

BASIC language (*cont.*)
  STR$, 126
  TAN, 12
  WHILE loop, 67, 69
  WHILE-WEND statement, 2, 17, 61, 67, 70
BASIC-to-C equivalencies, 214–17
Bitwise operators, 49, 51, 52
Block move, 115
Braces, 21, 53, 54, 148, 191
  do-while loop, 73
  for loop, 62, 63, 66, 67, 151–52
  if-else sequence, 55
  while loop, 68, 70
break statement, 57, 58, 74, 205

C

Calling program, 133, 134, 136
calloc( ) function, 112, 115
case statements, 57, 58, 204, 205
Cast operator, 43, 104
CBREEZE, 4, 5, 6, 7, 34, 44, 113, 141, 142, 173, 179–213, 218–19
Character, 14–19, 28
  arrays, 17, 18, 28, 82, 84–87, 97, 194
  conversion, 76–81
  pointers, 82, 96, 97, 99, 100, 113
  strings, 16–19, 28, 97–98
  variables, 76, 77
Closing braces, 21, 148
  do-while loop, 73
  for loop, 62, 63, 66, 67
  if statement, 53, 54
  while statement, 68
cls( ) function, 115
COBOL, 6
Commas:
  used to separate multiple arguments, 21
  used with *scanf*, 32
Concatenation of strings, 91–92, 200
Conditional expressions, 58–59
Connective operators, 49, 50
continue statement, 75
Control string, 21, 26, 27

Conversion specifications, 22, 25, 27, 155, 156
  %c, characters, 77
  %d, integers, 22, 25, 27, 63, 105
  %f, floats, 25
  %ld, longs, 25
  %lf, doubles, 25
  %o, octal, 80
  %x, hexadecimal, 79
  for loop, 63
  quoted phrase, 27
  scanf, 33, 34
  vertical printing format, 26

D

Data types, 13
Declaration:
  of arrays, 82, 86, 87
  of variables, 13–14, 21, 44, 144, 147, 149
default statement, 57, 58
Double-precision floating-point values, 12, 24
  pow( ) function, 47
  sqrt( ) function, 44, 45, 46
doubles, 13, 15, 24
do-while loop, 61, 72–73

E

Equality operator (==), 49, 50, 52
Equals sign (=), 49, 153
exit( ) function, 52, 54, 55
exp( ) function, 43, 140

F

fclose( ) function, 129
fgets( ) function, 129
Filekeeping, 126–31, 203, 204
Floating-point division, 41, 42, 43

Index   **223**

Floating-point values, 8, 9, 12, 23, 39, 150
    double-precision, 12, 24, 44, 45, 46, 47
    single-precision, 8, 10, 12, 23, 24, 39
Floating-point variables, 9, 10, 11, 12–14, 42
    and mathematical operations, 39
floats, 13, 15, 23, 24
fopen( ) function, 126, 127, 129
for loop, 61–68, 106, 108, 113, 133, 146, 147,
    151–52, 189
    nested within a *while* loop, 71
Formatting conventions, 29, 144, 145, 192
fprintf, 125, 131
fputs( ) function, 129
free( ) function, 117
fscanf( ) function, 125, 131
Functions, 21
    writing, 132–43

GH

getch( ) function, 36–37, 123
getchar( ) function, 35–36, 79, 123, 124, 125
gets( ) function, 35, 99, 113, 114, 123, 124,
    142
goto statement, 61, 72, 205
    label name following, 72
Hexadecimal conversion specification, 79, 80

I

if-else construct, 55, 58, 59
if/else-if/else construct, 57
if statement, 49, 55, 73, 127, 146
    relational and logical connective operators
        used with, 52, 53, 54
Increment operator (++), 100
Inequality operator (!=), 50
Initial value of variables, 14, 19, 68, 152
Input/output operations, 30–37, 123–31
int, 13, 15, 16, 23, 24
Integer division, 41, 42
Integer values, 8, 9, 12, 39
    of functions, 140

Integer variables, 9, 10, 11, 12, 23
    assigned a floating-point value, 40

KL

Keyboard operations, 30–37
Left shift (<<) bitwise operator, 51
Less than (<), 49
Less than or equal to (<=), 49, 51, 153
Lifeboat Associates, 4, 159, 178
log( ) function, 12, 43, 140, 198
Logical connective operators, 49, 50, 54
long int, 13, 15, 24
Loops, 61–75, 147, 148
    see also Nested loops
Lowercase characters, 14, 147

M

macros, 35
main( ), 20, 21, 144
malloc( ) function, 112, 113, 114, 115, 116,
    195, 196
Mathematical operations, 28, 38–47, 136–37,
    190, 196, 197
Members, 119, 120
Memory access, 96–118, 138
Mistakes in programming, 144–58
More than (>), 49
More than or equal to (>=), 49, 51
movmem( ) function, 116
Multidimensional arrays, 83–84, 113

N

Negative stepping loop, 62, 68
Nested loops, 67, 70, 71, 148, 190, 192, 193
Newline character (\n), 22, 154
    for loop, 63, 64
    quoted phrase, 27
    string values, 35
    vertical format, 26

224 Index

Not equal to (<>), 49
Null byte (0), 88, 89, 90, 115
NULL character (\O), character strings, 17, 28, 35, 84, 85, 97, 113, 124
Numeric arrays, 86
Numeric variables, 8, 23–25, 38
   scanf function, 35

O

Octal conversion specification, 80
One's complement (unary) (^) bitwise operator, 51
open( ) function, 126
Opening braces, 21, 144, 148, 150
   do while loop, 73
   for loop, 62, 63, 66, 67
   if statement, 53, 54
   while statement, 68
OR (^) bitwise exclusive operator, 51
OR (:) bitwise inclusive operator, 49, 51
OR (::) logical connective operator, 49
Output. *See* Input/output

P

Peek operations, 104, 105, 106, 107, 108, 111, 170, 171
Pointers, 17, 31, 33, 96–118, 138
Poke operations, 104, 107, 108, 170, 171
Positive stepping loop, 62
pow( ) function, 12, 47
printf function, 21, 34, 36, 124, 125, 130, 142, 205
   displaying a character string, 28–29, 98, 100, 103
   displaying a string constant, 26
   mathematical operations, 28
   multiargument example of using, 25
   newline character used with, 22
Programming mistakes, 144–58
putchar, 78, 79, 124, 125
puts( ) function, 123, 124, 142, 143

QR

Quoted string, printing, 27
Reading files, 123–31
Relational operators, 49, 51, 54
return statement, 136
Right shift (>>) bitwise operator, 51
RUN/C interpreter, 4, 5, 7, 12, 44, 104, 107, 108, 111, 114, 159–78

S

scanf function, 31–35, 52, 55, 79, 80, 123, 124, 125, 130, 135, 151, 154, 205, 206
Semicolon, 146
   in assignment line, 21
   in declaration line, 21
   trailing which converts a function into a program statement, 22
SET TRUST ON, 107, 170, 171
short int, 13, 15, 24
sin( ) function, 12
sizeof( ) function, 115
sprintf( ) function, 92–93, 126, 200, 201
sqrt( ) function, 12, 43, 44, 45, 46, 140
Statements, 48–59
strcat( ) function, 91–92
strcmp( ) function, 93–94
strcpy( ) function, 18, 28, 85, 88–90, 98, 103, 112, 194, 196
String comparison, 93–94
String concatenation, 91–92, 200
String functions, 88–95, 137
String variables, 8, 14–19
   and *scanf* function, 33, 34
   and *gets* function, 35
strlen( ) function, 90
structs, 119–22
Structures, 119
Structure tag, 119, 121
switch statement, 56–58, 204, 205

T

tan( ) function, 12
Terminating character, character string, 17

Index   **225**

Ternary operator, 59
Time-delay loop, 132–33
Traister and Associates, 4, 180

U

Unary operator (*), 97
    used with a pointer, 100
Unassigned variables, 14, 19
unions, 119–22
UNIX math functions, 43–47
UNIX memory allocation functions, 111

unsigned integer, 13, 15, 24
Uppercase characters, 14, 147

VW

Vertical format, 26
while loop, 70, 72, 101, 152
    nesting a *for* loop within, 71
while statement, 61, 102, 146, 147
Writing:
    files, 123–31
    functions, 132–43